"An amazing story of valor and commitment, and the best read I've had all year! *Blue Yonder* is an admiring tale, passionately revealed in truth and steeped in historic, military accuracy. Susan Gemmill's writing follows the accounts and struggles of a real-life young aviator coming of age through unimaginably intense and gritty wartime settings. This story demands to be read and brilliantly delivers a genuine patriotic rush!"

—Stephen Brust, LCDR USN helicopter pilot

"What a lovely book. As an Air Force brat, I love stories about the men and women who fought so bravely in the air. Indeed, *Blue Yonder* partially parallels my own family story, as my mom and dad were newlyweds stationed in Pearl Harbor when it was bombed. Susan Gemmill's narrative resonates with me because I've heard many similar stories ... and never tire of them.

"*Blue Yonder* is an enthralling tale. It's partly memoir, partly a daughter's love for her father, partly an adventure story, and partly oral history. It's a universal story of persistence, commitment, and hard-earned success. Although the events actually happened, it reads like a novel. If you love a good story, you'll love this book."

—Travis White, PhD, traviswhitecommunications.com

"Susan Gemmill's biography of her military father, Bill Gemmill, reads like a novel; it is a loving and inspiring tribute.

"The varied settings of Bill Gemmill's story are made tangible because of bold details, as of the stifling heat on a train carrying the young military recruits through the flat plains of Arkansas, of the beauty and chaos of a Marrakesh bazaar, and of the thick layers of clothing that the Chetnik people of Yugoslavia wore in winter, making them waddle 'like windup dolls.' Even the subtle expressions of crewmates are noted, whether they are relaxing on land or navigating storms and missiles in the air.

"*Blue Yonder* is a historical biography that captures the coming-of-age of a young soldier against the backdrop of World War II."

—*Foreword* Clarion Reviews

"*Blue Yonder* is not just another book about WWII; this one takes a personal and pointed look at the bombardiers, who had a very particular role to play in what is now called 'the good war.' We see it all through the humanity, heart, and bravery of this larger-than-life young protagonist.

"The author has a gift for painting a picture, drawing the reader into each scene, fully igniting all of our senses. She makes us feel as if we are side-by-side with the characters, experiencing it all from their exclusive vantage point. The book discloses what shaped these distinctive military men as they navigate the treacherous terrain of war, yet also reveals a personal side to these soldiers, who were connected not only by their mission but also through their passion, patriotism, and heart.

"While this book is a true tale of the unique and pointed role of these WWII bombardiers, it reads like a page-turning novel; at once engrossing, heart-wrenching, evocative, and touching. A beautiful and moving read."

—Paula Friedland, Corporate Trainer, Counselor,
Executive/Life Coach

"It may be difficult for young people today to understand why anyone would eagerly volunteer to risk his or her life in a brutal war that rages across the ocean on another continent. In her book, *Blue Yonder*, Susan Gemmill helps us understand the pervasive spirit that swept across America in the early 1940s, a spirit that compelled her father to join the fight knowing he might not come home.

"Like Susan Gemmill, I was raised in an Air Force family, and like her, I remember seeing my father wearing his 'dress blues' to special occasions. Only later in life did I fully understand why he felt it important to distinguish himself in that way. Gemmill's book, *Blue Yonder*, accurately captures the volunteer spirit that swept across America prior to our involvement in World War II and the incredible sacrifices made by our men and women in uniform."

—Phillip R. Bellury, President and Founder, The Storyline Group

"Susan L. Gemmill's father, Bill Gemmill, was a bombardier on more than 50 WWII missions who took pride in his multitude of medals and decorations. But it wasn't until his daughter's son, an aviation buff like his grandfather, turned 20 that Bill opened up to Gemmill about his service. The resulting biography is more about 'coming of age,' she writes, 'than the art of war.'

"Indeed, the 'art'—and destruction—of war is here, but Gemmill goes deeper, showing her father wrestling with the world he'd been thrown into, one far from his native Chicago. There are light moments: Stationed near L.A., he got to pal around with Dorothy Lamour and June Allyson. And somber moments: When he visits the Vienna Parliament Building 15 years after the war, he tears up observing the damage his bombs had done.

"Gemmill consulted with surviving members of her father's crew to confirm the stories and reconstructed dialogue. Both contain the absolute ring of authenticity. She has done an excellent job here, delivering an engaging military biography, told lovingly, with vivid writing and great thought."

—BlueInk Review

"*Blue Yonder* is part biography and part a coming-of-age story about the points of connection between a girl and her father. It captures the backstory of one of the young men from what became known as our greatest generation. I've read so much about these young guys who wanted to enlist after the bombing of Pearl Harbor; these young airmen became comrades and family as they flew sorties over Europe.

"As a student at Tuskegee Institute in the early sixties, I was enrolled in the Air Force ROTC and all of my instructors were Tuskegee Airmen. They were proud of their service, escorting bombers behind enemy lines and never losing one. This book highlights their role, and for that reason, has special meaning for me."

—James Lawson, retired mechanical engineer

"A ton, by weight, of books have been written about the WWII Mediterranean Theater. Far fewer have articulated the nuts and bolts of procedure, endurance, bravery, and shared terror of the young airmen flying bombers over FLAK blossoming territories. In *Blue Yonder*, Susan Gemmill skillfully elucidates these themes. Her father, at the youthful age of eighteen, signed up to become an aviator in what was then called the United States Army Air Force. He was a fun-loving young man in the vein of the actor Jimmy Stewart, enamored over the arranged meetings with the Hollywood icons Dorothy Lamour and June Allyson. Later, as the bombing raids increase over the breadth of the continent, the youngster rapidly matures into a hardened veteran. Finally, he is shot down. He and members of his crew are rescued by Yugoslav partisans and, after a hard slog, reach Italy.

"Susan Gemmill has done an excellent job of evocatively telling her father's story. From romances to tears, to the camaraderie and affection for his fellow crewmen, it is a soliloquy on wartime in the skies. There are no side comments on strategies and tactics. She rightly sticks to the subject: the life of a bombardier and his mates during a hellish time. This book is eminently worth reading."

—Nicolas Van Gelder, former associate editor of
CASCADES magazine, former chairman and CEO of
International Communications Management,
author of peer-reviewed journal articles

"In short, engaging chapters, this book takes readers from light-hearted, humorous anecdotes about music and food to deathly serious tales of dramatic events, such as a plane crash that left Bill temporarily stranded in Yugoslavia. Gemmill's sanguine writing style reveals her to be a skilled storyteller who shows great pride in her father's accomplishments. ... the book is immensely readable ...

"An often engaging story of a war veteran that's optimistic and harrowing, by turns."

—Kirkus Reviews

Blue
YONDER

Blue YONDER

SUSAN L. GEMMILL

MERRY DISSONANCE PRESS   CASTLE ROCK, COLORADO

Blue Yonder

Published by Merry Dissonance Press, LLC
Castle Rock, CO

FIRST EDITION
2021

Publisher's Cataloging-in-Publication data

Names: Gemmill, Susan, author.
Title: Blue yonder. / by Susan L. Gemmill.
Description: First trade paperback original edition. | Castle Rock [Colorado] : Merry Dissonance Press, 2021. | Also published as an ebook.
Identifiers: ISBN 978-1-939919-63-2
Subjects: LCSH: World War, 1939-1945. | Military biography.
BISAC: BIOGRAPHY & AUTOBIOGRAPHY / Military. | HISTORY / Military / World War II.
Classification: LCC D802.A2 | DDC 940.544–dc22

ISBN 978-1-939919-63-2

Book Design and Cover Design © 2021
Cover Design and Book Design by
Victoria Wolf, wolfdesignandmarketing.com
Editing by Donna Mazzitelli, writingwithdonna.com

In loving memory of Lt. Colonel William B. Gemmill Jr.
And appreciation for the bomb crews of the
United States 15th Army Air Corps.

"When the legend becomes fact, print the legend."

~Rance Stoddard,
The Man Who Shot Liberty Valence

CONTENTS

Yonder

REUNION OF THE VULGAR VULTURES

Susan L. Gemmill

The men remind one another they had all been
thinner then, young and eager to serve.
The laughter in their throats barely contains
the memory alive in their eyes.

They trained in khakis in the brave
Texas sun.
Bill jokes about
the endless drills in the sepia desert.
Joe recalls mesquite trees, barbs-in-waiting
impaling an unwitting cadet who climbed
for a view of anything
but the surrounding bleakness.

Faces tighten as officers talk their way back
to Cadet graduation
silver wings and
deep brown leather flight jackets.
Faint echoes of raids on Ploesti,
Vienna, Trieste, Innsbruck
ride on the crews' voices.

Fear stalks;
tension leans in then
Bravery shuffles through the waist,
takes a spin in the nose,
brushes past Ritt in the tail.
Mike rescues the bombardier
low on air, out on the catwalk.
Losing oil, Wes feathers number one,
Murph coaxes the remaining engines over the Alps then
home.

Ordering another whiskey, they softly remind themselves of
those early days
when it was easy to be eager.

SILENT PARTNER
A Prologue

IT WAS AN EVENING RITUAL. I would sit on my parents' bed as my father methodically prepared his military uniform for the next day. A kind of reverence was at play in the way he brushed the slightest bit of lint from the jacket, his fingers skimming the pleat of the pant. Dad had the keenest vision: a hawk's eyes.

There were nights the ritual was brief: a simple inspection and brushing were all that was necessary. Then there were the nights the uniform was fresh from the cleaners. Spread out before me on the bed, the jacket became an artist's canvas, laid bare awaiting paint and inspiration—only the picture never changed.

Dad arranged the wings and ribbons over the left breast of the jacket. He had executed this so many times before, I believe he could have done it blindfolded. Each ribbon bar represented a medal. The Distinguished Flying Cross (DFC) was the one he was most proud of having been awarded, with its bands of blue, red, and white signifying singular heroism and voluntary actions in the face of danger while in aerial combat. Next was the Air Medal, with its broad band of ultramarine bounded on each side by stripes of golden orange—the original colors of the Army Air Corps. Sitting atop the ribbon were one silver and two bronze oak leaves. The colorful European–African–Middle Eastern Campaign Medal (EAME) with one silver and two bronze oak leaves on the epaulets. At the center of the ribbon, a broad stripe of green was flanked by pinstripes of green, white, black, and red. As he pierced the gabardine with the ribbon's prongs, Dad explained that the green, white, and red were the colors of Italy, where he had been based during World War II, and the black-white-black pinstripes represented Germany. The ribbon served as a reminder of the Axis powers of Europe he helped defeat.

I relished the mystery, the symbolism, the routine. Dad nestled the DFC into place after the Legion of Merit and before the Airman's Medal. The EAME ribbon took its spot before the WWII Victory Medal. When the adornment was complete, Dad hung his Air Force "Blues" on a wooden valet, trousers folded over a bar. The hanger filled out the shoulders so that it looked as though a body was in there somewhere.

I remember being in awe of my father at the time and never tiring of my role as a silent participant. Yet as I grew, so did my curiosity. I was a competitive swimmer and I had earned medals too. Those oak leaf clusters intrigued me. One evening, my question broke the quiet. "What are all those acorns and leaves for?"

Dad had described what each medal stood for, but what about the extra accoutrement? He explained how the oak leaves multiplied the medal: the silver leaves represented having been awarded the same medal six times, and the bronze ones a subsequent one or more times. The ribbons were colorful, but the medals were works of art. All of them were cast in bronze and carefully stored away in the top drawer of Dad's dresser. The DFC has narrow-at-the-center arms that flare in a curve, providing a base for angled rays upon which a four-bladed propeller sits. The Air Medal is a rose with an eagle in the forefront, its wings extended, carrying two lightning bolts in its talons. The scene etched into the EAME medal was designed to portray elements of the US Army, Navy, and Army Air Corps: troops amassed on a Landing Ship, Tank (LST) landing craft and an aircraft. If he wore all the medals at once, he teased, he wouldn't be able to stand up straight. I laughed as he mimed being bent over from the bulk of all the brass. Dad was always clowning around.

The weight of the bravery, and the recognition of that bravery, was held in those medals. Years later, when he at last began to tell me his stories, Dad focused mostly on the fun parts and left out the tales of terror and responsibility he felt for the men in his crew and the job he had joined up to do. It was as if the more dramatic memories were still too painful to resurrect. If I asked anything he wasn't comfortable answering, his face would darken, he'd knit his brows, and I would retract my inquiry before he shut me down completely. He just wasn't ready to go to some places in his memories.

Dad grew up an only child in a Midwestern upper-middle-class family. He was very close to his parents. When World War II began for the United States, Dad was seventeen and a senior in high school. Living in Chicago, he was exposed to all the news stories, banners, and posters calling for young men to join the war after the Japanese attack on Pearl Harbor in Hawaii. What did he know of hardship and death? Neither had come to him yet. Still, now eighteen years old, he made a big choice and followed his heart into battle. He wanted his team to win, and he figured he was just the guy to do it.

Ours was that quintessential fifties-sixties family, fully engaged in the television or stereo, with one manmade sound or another prevalent. Calm moments were rare, and time alone with my larger-than-life father was rarer still, yet Dad didn't mind my watchful presence. I liked his quiet, implicit acceptance. And I preferred the silence. It spoke of an importance I could know little about. His participation and his courage were wrapped in the hush. Was he riding some memory from World War II, thinking of his earlier days as a bombardier, reliving tense moments in the air with his crew, his buddies, or remembering the day he received his first Air Medal?

The more aware I became of the fight as a whole, about the war and its outcome, the more my curiosity infused the silent space between us. What, I wanted to know, was he thinking? What was he feeling? Dad didn't offer many details. Yet, seeing those medals and ribbons and bars and clusters and finding out what each of them meant, it wasn't hard to conclude that my father had done something meaningful years before I was born, and I have held that belief all the days and years that have followed.

In the shadows late at night, the uniformed valet soldier stood at attention. Once, deep in the belly of the night, I slipped into my parents' room seeking comfort from a haunting dream. My mother sensed me kneeling by her side and woke to listen to my imaginings. Like conspirators, we spoke in whispers so as not to wake my father. The jacket, with its accoutrement placed just so, seemed to lean in to catch the conversation.

Beneath the aroma of my mother's lotions, potions, and Tabu perfume, beneath the bold essence of my father's Old Spice, the bedroom carried the scent of history. Mystery was woven into the threads of that uniform that smelled of dry-cleaning solution, or Dad, or both.

Time pushed us on; the gaps in our evenings together grew for a variety of reasons, which made those nights I could be on hand for the decorating of the "Blues" even more a treasure. It was on one of those last evenings in the house on Whippoorwill Lane, when I was eighteen—before my parents' divorce, before my father's retirement, before life carried us in opposite directions—when I began to ask all my deepest questions. And here, on the following pages, are the tales my father shared with me. The tales of my father's coming of age coinciding with my own.

*Off
We Go*

One

EAGER TO SERVE

*Chicago, Illinois,
Spring of 1942*

FIRST BELL RANG at Chicago's Harvard School for Boys. Students in white shirts, navy blue blazers, and striped school ties poured out of every room of learning and down every hallway, streaming toward classes in Latin, Greek, and Ancient History. The details of fifty separate conversations bounced off the buff-colored walls of the hallways, melding into one unintelligible uproar. After stashing his blazer and brown canvas book bag, Bill Gemmill slammed shut the door to his locker, the sound of metal on metal resounding down the hall as if to announce his urgency. He then dodged and darted through the crowd as he beelined toward the quad—the appointed meeting spot—where his best friend, Norrie Swindle, waited.

"Try to keep up, Norrie. We don't have a lot of time to catch that EL train," Bill called over his shoulder.

"You know darned well I don't run as fast as you, Gemmill," Norrie shot back as he did his best to keep up with Bill.

Together, they ran to catch the Ellis Avenue EL, shirttails coming untucked with every stride, their blue-and-gold striped repp ties flying behind them like shoulder-height kites. As a member of the school track team, Bill had an advantage: he was long and lean and ran hurdles every day during track season. And those efforts in track complemented his position as placekicker on the school's football team. Norrie played tight end and was built more solidly; he struggled to keep up, yet keep up he did. The two high school seniors caught the EL with little time to spare and headed downtown to join the Queue of the Determined, as Bill was fond of calling the ever-growing ribbon of men and boys itching to enlist. He felt as if he had been swept up in a great wave, gaining volume and speed, with every click of the EL's steel wheels on the rails.

Norrie took one look at Bill and said as he caught his breath, "If I look as sweaty and disheveled as you do, neither one of us is going to make a very good impression."

Taking the hint, Bill began running his fingers through his now-damp chestnut brown hair. He tucked in his shirttails, straightened his tie, and asked, "How do you like me now?"

"Yes! Much more presentable. How about me?" Norrie answered.

"You're as shipshape as can be, Norrie. Why didn't we think to bring a comb?" Bill said, indicating Norrie's wild, nearly untamable mane of blond curls.

∞

The Queue of the Determined waiting to enter the US Army Air Force recruitment offices snaked around three corners of the building on South State Street, downtown Chicago. Fresh-faced teenage boys—straight out of class from the hundreds of high schools across the city—mingled with collegiate types in letter sweaters, businessmen in their suits, and laborers in blue jeans eager for the chance to strike back at the Japanese and German militaries.

As they walked from the EL to the recruiting station, Bill noticed the early blooming crocuses adorning the city's planters, heralding spring. He had always liked how cheerful his mother's window boxes made him feel as he approached the house after a long day of school and athletics. But today, what stood out more than planters were the men and women passing by, causing him to wonder how many of them had lost fathers, brothers, cousins, uncles, aunts, and sisters in the war so far.

For months now, Bill had heard his parents talk about friends, or friends of friends, who had perished in the attack on Pearl. Mere days after the Japanese Air Force struck Hawaii, he and Norrie had devised a plan to cut school during finals week—Bill liked to call it "final finals" since they were high school seniors—and head downtown to enlist in the Aviation Cadet Program.

When he and Norrie cooked up this scheme, Bill had regaled his friend with the stories his father had shared with him when he was a kid: stories of the Gemmill family's long military history in North America dating back to their first arrival in 1745, their participation in the French and Indian Wars and, ten years later, as patriots in the American Revolution.

"Wow," said Norrie, "your family history goes way back."

"And it continued. Dad has tales of his time in France during World War I, driving for the Ambulance Corps. He also has stories about floating above the killing fields as a balloon observer. He relayed intelligence to officers in the dirigible above the balloon and in trenches dug into the ground below."

Bill had cut his teeth on the power of those stories; stories of his ancestors' determination and sacrifice and his father's discipline and commitment. He was aware of the profound effect they had had on him. Now, he felt motivated by a sense of destiny.

"I'm pretty sure neither of my parents knew anyone over on Oahu," Norrie said. "My heritage is dental, not military, but everyone in my family is outraged about the attack on Pearl. My dad is disappointed he is too old to enlist; my uncle is too. But I can!" He, too, felt violated by Japan's bold attack and felt compelled to join up and fight back.

Theatrical newsreels from *Pathé News* and *News Parade* and promotional films courtesy of Hollywood, like *Earning Your Wings* narrated by the actor Jimmy Stewart, a bomber pilot fighting the US air war, inspired hundreds of potential recruits. For the first few months after Pearl, cinemas around the country presented at least one short recruitment film prior to the feature. The brief films attracted boys like Bill and Norrie, who were already huge movie buffs. Sometimes they'd return to watch a favorite release again and again just so they could re-watch the newsreel. Eddie Rickenbacker, the American fighter ace from WWI, ruled the day and fueled a sense of heritage and duty. It was his voice on many a newsreel, extolling the daring-do of fighter pilots in a new era of aviation.

"Eddie Rickenbacker is a hero," Bill enthused, his voice rising an octave or two. "And, besides flying, he also drove an ambulance in WWI, just like my dad."

"He really is one of the best pilots we've ever had, isn't he?" Norrie agreed.

At long last, five months after the attack, and unbeknownst to Bill's parents, the boys were putting their plan in motion to become aviation cadets, motivated by a combination of family history, recent events, and subsequent newsreels. Just like Eddie, they were going to wage war from the sky.

∞

Progress in the line was agonizingly slow. To harness their excitement and pass the time, Bill and Norrie replayed the scenario they had imagined in detail for months.

"This is how it's going to go, Norrie. Today is just step one in a whole lot of steps," Bill announced.

"What do you mean, Gemmill?" Norrie asked.

"Today is step one, signing up. Then, we pass the physicals and get through basic training, that's steps two and three," Bill began to enumerate their plan.

"Then, the Aviation Cadet Program," Norrie offered.

"Well, we'll need to pass the college equivalency first to even stand a chance at getting into the cadet program. Remember, only officers can be pilots," Bill reminded his pal.

"Right! Then, it'll be on to the Pacific where we'll help shoot down as many Imperial Air Service Zeros as we can. I will personally see to it that Isoroku Yamamoto is destroyed," Norrie puffed up his chest and boasted, referring to the marshal admiral and commander-in-chief of the Imperial Combined Fleet.

"Is that what you're going to tell the recruiter? What if we end up in Europe?" Bill asked Norrie, referring to the European Theater of Operations. "I plan to tell him that being sent to Europe will be our chance to destroy the Nazi regime; Hitler himself if we're lucky enough.

US Army Air Force High Command will be happy to see we are highly decorated; after all, we'll be air aces like Rickenbacker and Doolittle!" Bill said. "We'll show the enemy … you don't mess with America. Yeah, we'll show 'em."

"You have a point there, Gemmill. We could be shipped anywhere," Norrie agreed. "I don't care where I end up, Europe or the Pacific."

"I have to confess, Norrie, I'm pretty nervous. I've never done something as important as this without talking it over with my parents."

"I can see that, Bill. Your parents might be disappointed you didn't consult them. No doubt they'll wonder how you could turn down football scholarships at two universities. But you three respect each other so much, they'll come around," Norrie said, trying to ease Bill's concern.

The boys continued to shuffle along in line, designing their triumphant, post-war return stateside, until they reached the doors and entered the recruitment office, applications at the ready.

Norrie was the first of the two to be summoned to a desk. "Go get 'em, Norrie!" Bill called to his friend as he walked away. When he heard "Next!" Bill approached the recruiting sergeant who gestured for Bill to come forward. The sergeant wore a crisp khaki Army Air Corps uniform, its creases pressed to a knife edge. Battle medals and bars adorned his jacket, which he shed and draped across the back of an uncomfortable-looking metal chair. Bill was a full six foot, three inches of moxie and physical grace. In front of the sergeant, he stood as straight as he ever had and gathered all the composure he could muster for the presentation he was about to make. He had to convince the man that he, Bill Gemmill, belonged in aviation cadets.

The sergeant leaned back in his chair and listened respectfully to the boy's dreams of becoming a fighter pilot: picking off enemy Zeros, ME-109s, and Fokkers. "I don't care where I end up," Bill heard himself saying.

The sergeant met his eyes for a moment. Bill was certain the recruiter was sizing him up the way a man can do. After all, this is how the recruiter had been spending hours a day, every day: carefully determining a person's worthiness to fight.

Noticing the sergeant's demeanor, Bill continued his reasons for wanting in. "I'm in great shape and have lots of stamina. I'm ready for anything you can throw at me to get me over there."

As he delivered his impassioned speech, Bill noticed the sergeant looking back over his application papers. Those documents revealed much about the eager candidate standing before him, including the fact that he was his parents' only child. When his monologue came to an end, the recruiter looked up and asked, "What do your parents think of your decision?"

Bill answered honestly as he felt his stance waver. "Well, they don't exactly know I'm here. They want me to continue on to college. We graduate next week."

"That your school uniform?" the sergeant asked.

"Yes, Sir, well … most of it. I left my blazer in my locker. It's warm today," Bill involuntarily knit his eyebrows together, wondering what his school uniform had to do with the enlistment procedure.

"Is your father serving?" The sergeant righted his chair and leaned forward, genuinely interested in Bill's answer.

"Yes, Sir. He's in North Africa with the Judge Advocate Corps. He's watching over POWs out there."

"And, you're an only child?" the sergeant pressed on, watching Bill's face intently.

"Yes, Sir," Bill replied. He had his hands crossed behind his back. They were sweating.

The sergeant moved on to his next concern. "I see by the letters you've included in your packet here that you've been accepted to both

Michigan and DePauw with full football scholarships," he said. "What position do you play?"

"Placekicker, Sir, and I've been known to play quarterback some too," Bill answered. He had found his stance again, tall, straight, and snapped-to, very much like a military man.

The recruiter took a deep breath and said, "Son, I'm accepting you into the Aviation Cadet Program ..."

Bill had stopped listening after hearing the word "accepting." He was instantly over the moon; his thoughts triumphant as they raced ahead to his near future. He grinned as he interrupted the sergeant, shouting, "Hot dog!"

"... *and*," the sergeant continued loudly to bring Bill back to earth, "I'm giving you a student deferment. Make your parents proud and get that college degree." Then he signed and stamped Bill's papers, placed them in a pile of applications in a box labeled "DEFERRED," and called out "Next!" as he gestured to the next man in line to step forward.

❧

His dream deferred—something he never expected to happen. Stunned, Bill stood, collected his papers, and high-tailed it toward the door, desperate to get away from the hubbub of recruitment. He didn't think he could bear the weight in his heart. Waiting for him at the entrance was Norrie, bursting with enthusiasm.

"We're going! We're going!" shouted Norrie. He threw his arm around Bill's shoulder as they headed out the door and down the stairs of the building.

"*You're* going," Bill said as he kicked at nothing on the sidewalk, his head hung low. "My recruiter read all my records, the letter of recommendation from Senator Brooks ..." His voice rose in pitch and exasperation as he continued, "… the college letters from Michigan and DePauw. He let me tell him our whole story, yours and my plans, then he gave me a deferment! Wants me to go to college, 'make your parents proud,' he said." It was too much to bear, telling Norrie.

"Well, why did you accept it?" asked Norrie.

"I have no idea," Bill answered. "When he started telling me I was accepted into the program, I thought 'This is it! I'm in!' That I'd be going straight into training with you after graduation next week. I got excited, and I guess I interrupted him. It was over so fast."

"My recruiter tried the same crap on me after he went through my papers, and I told him I'd get my education behind the stick of a P-47 Thunderbolt!" said Norrie. Norrie hadn't been offered any football or academic scholarships. He was clear to go.

"I don't think anything would have budged my recruiter after he saw those scholarship offers …" Bill's voice trailed off.

"Well, how do you like that?" Norrie's jaw dropped and his shoulders slumped at what Bill's news meant for him. All the joy he had been feeling moments before evaporated. "What am I supposed to do now, Gemmill? Go on without you? How can I do that? You're my best friend. We had plans!" He chucked Bill on the shoulder, trying to break the tension between them. Nothing doing. Bill was way, way down in the dumps—physically folded in on himself.

Gone was Bill's naturally erect stance and confident stride. He couldn't speak, he couldn't find the words, and he couldn't stop the pain he was feeling—his heart actually hurt. Norrie had never seen him clench his jaw so fiercely—not even when they had lost the state football tournament. They walked the rest of the way back to the EL station in silence.

Taking his seat for the ride back to Hyde Park, Bill's thoughts sifted through his conversation with the recruiter over and over. The movement of the train helped him sort them out. Could he have been more adamant like Norrie? Could he have shown more determination? He had aimed for a balanced approach as he painted that vision for the recruiter, something between too gung-ho and just the right amount of bravado. Why Norrie and not him? Was it a numbers game for the recruiters, some quota set by the Army Air Force? By the time the EL pulled into their station, Bill knew one thing for certain: somehow, he was going to fight in this war. He was going to fight as an officer because only officers could become pilots. He was going to become a pilot, like his hero, Eddie Rickenbacker. The when and the how would reveal themselves, and when they did, he would be ready with all the right answers. He turned to Norrie as they walked down the stairs from the EL and reached the street.

"When do you report?" Bill asked his friend, his voice soft yet sincere.

"One month after graduation," Norrie answered. "Are you going to be OK?"

"Yes. I'm going to be OK, Norrie Swindle, Aviation Cadet!" Bill was laughing again as he slapped Norrie's back. He was going to miss his friend and all the dangerous adventures they most likely would have had together. He was going to miss getting into the war according to schedule. He'd just have to find out what he's made of at DePauw because, he thought, *As of this moment, I am going to accept their generous offer of placing me as a varsity punter. I'll be the only freshman on the varsity team and that can't be all bad.*

And so it was that Bill Gemmill, aspiring World War II ace, graduated Chicago's Harvard School for Boys, accepted a football scholarship at DePauw University in Indiana, and detoured to his destiny.

Two

CALL TO WAR

*DePauw University, Greencastle,
Indiana, September 1942*

AFTER ACCEPTING the recruiter's decision, at least as far as his heart
was able, Bill spent the summer getting ready for college life. The week
after accepting DePauw University's scholarship offer, he drove Norrie
to Union Station and wished him luck at basic training—even though it
was painful to see Norrie go without him. Back at home, he helped his
mother with chores. To Bill's mind, his was a summer of the mundane,
seeing to the everyday details of living rather than being miles away,
training for war.

∞

The Sunday morning mist swirling around the Deke fraternity house cushioned the din of a big bomber's engines; a muffled drone like an oncoming winged swarm announced her rugged approach. The unusual sound brought Bill to the edge of waking and nudged at his attention. Instead of the familiar orchestral rumble from the frequent military aircraft ferrying missions crossing the campus, Bill heard a disturbing screech and whine from the heavy machinery. He soon realized the steady rumble was outside, not inside his head, which ached from too much fun the night before. The sound grew larger and filled the dorm room, and at this, Bill snapped into full alert: a bomber's engines all right, and from the noise they were making, something was distinctly wrong. Bill fumbled on a new cardigan—his mother had knit it for him in DePauw's school colors of black and gold—over his pajamas and grabbed his new field glasses. He had traded his last sugar ration card for the binoculars, certain he would need them for spotting details on the aircraft flying overhead. He slipped his feet into a pair of Converse trainers and bolted out of the room.

Sprinting through the still-slumbering Deke house and bounding down the stairs, Bill let the front door slam with a bang behind him as he floated over the wide porch. He easily cleared a hip-height boxwood hedge and landed in the front yard, where he tore into a dead run toward the backyard of the house. The aircraft was cloaked in fog. Bill's ears had become a finely tuned radar system of their own. He homed in on the plane's location and trained his field glasses in the direction of the vibration. Finding it impossible to run and use the binoculars at the same time, he stopped in his tracks and aimed the glasses toward the source of the sound.

It was almost above him; the reverberation of the engines shivered through him. All his newsreel watching and trips to the aviation section of the Chicago Public Library informed his gift of aircraft recognition; half his school reports involved aviation in some form or another. He could just make out a shadowy figure through the mist and recognized the engines' rumble: it was a twin-engine, high speed Martin B-26 with a thundering, off-key Pratt and Whitney R-2800-23 hum. Then he spotted the bomber through the vapor—she was riding low. Bill let the glasses drop and watched bare-eyed. As she emerged from the mist, he was enveloped in the viscid black smoke pouring from a stuttering left engine. *She looks clumsy,* he thought. *She's lurching and tugging against whatever the pilot is trying to coax out of her. And she's too damn low.*

As he wiped the smoke's oily residue from around his eyes, Bill imagined the pilot: a fresh, young lieutenant on a ferrying mission, sweating out a joyride gone sour, terrified at being so close to the ground with a new plane all atilt. Or, perhaps, one of the many lady pilots of the Women's Air Force Service Pilots known as much for their bravery as for their competence and efficiency ferrying bombers and other aircraft from manufacturing plants—often converted automobile plants—to Army Air Force bases around the country. Most likely, whoever was flying the plane, he or she was flying solo. At the most, he hoped, there were only a few airmen on board—a skeleton crew. Whether from the bomb squadron stationed at Baer Field in Fort Wayne or a plant in Michigan, this newly minted bomber was now headed for the fields of Grafton Longden Farm situated behind the Deke house. Bill stopped to calculate the plane's trajectory, then headed to where he was certain it would go down, all the while watching the aircraft lose what little altitude the pilot had left.

The bomber moved into a suspended nosedive, then dipped its left wing deeply, as if to scoop up the earth. The tail swept upward, the nose drove down, and the plane met the earth in a fiery crash. A curtain of hot death reached out from the hold, rapidly engulfing the aircraft and any who might have been on board. The rumbling din had shaken the rest of the Deke house awake, and dozens of sleepy young frat boys began spilling out of the house and onto the back lawn. They gathered in their pajamas and robes, faces frozen in shock and disbelief, watching as Bill raced toward the field. Instinctively, he glanced behind him. Dozens of other students were following. Members of the faculty joined the throng, adding to the size of the crowd. Helpless, they ran as they watched the bomber burn belly up in the fertile Indiana farmland, an inverted beauty sprawled like a helpless beast on its back.

The heat was too intense for rescue, and it was unlikely anyone on board had survived the relentless blaze. Bill stood at the edge of the scene, bearing witness. Dense black smoke billowed from the wreckage, painting an unctuous slick across his eyes and cheekbones. With the bomber grounded, the burning fuel oil coated everything it landed on: the grass, the soil, his hair. He wiped his face with a pajama-top sleeve, careful not to ruin his new sweater with burnt aviation fuel, but he only made the smear worse. The heat intensified and forced him to back away, but he continued to stare numbly at the debris through the smudged air.

Perhaps it was the keening of the flames, yet Bill believed he could hear the souls of the downed crew calling to him: "Fight our fight. Take our place. Do your part." He struggled to collect his sense of the events—his body was shaking, tears coated his eyes, and his stomach wrenched. The taste of seared fuel clung to his tongue, and the scent of burning rubber assaulted his nose. "This sort of thing isn't supposed to happen over here," he whispered into the air. "I can't believe I watched it happen and couldn't save even one member of the crew."

In an instant, it seemed that all of Greencastle had gathered at the crash site, drawn by the smoke and flames. Churches emptied. Late sleepers abandoned their beds. Coffeepots were left to percolate. The sudden tragedy lured townies and collegians alike to the edge of the disaster. Anxious for signs of life, they strained to hear above the roar of the fire and exploding magnesium flares. A curtain of fume and vapor descended on the morning, still warm around the edges and bright with the gradual rising light of Indian summer.

∞

It was the plane crash that brought Bill Gemmill to war. Turning his back on the burning, twisted metal, Bill looked down Anderson Avenue toward the fraternity and sorority houses of DePauw University and contemplated the past few months. *What had I been thinking when I first arrived home after being put on deferment? I allowed myself to be distracted from my commitment to join the fight, that's what I did. What can fraternity parties and football games possibly offer me now?* Gone in an instant was his desire for parties or sports. The crash moved Bill to consider the possibility that he had been biding his time all along, waiting for that one opportunity that would clear the way to his activation. *I do believe the answer to that question is a resounding 'This moment,'* he thought.

In his two months of university life, Bill had continued to study newsreels from the war like he should have been studying his prelaw courses; he was forever eager to see the latest Pathé offerings. *Take a Letter Darling*, the most recent film he had seen, opened with a clip that followed the progress of a new bomber from Ford's Willow Run plant near Ypsilanti, Michigan. The segment showed the bomber rolling out of a massive manufacturing building and concluded with it being ferried to an airfield in Kansas.

Bill and his college buddies with a similar passion for all things airborne liked to boast that they knew more about the military machinery being produced than most journalists knew. They devoured the evening paper in search of obscure facts and delighted in critiquing short news reports. And along with swing bands, Edward R. Murrow's reports from the front were required radio listening among Bill's crowd. Censored letters to friends and family from soldiers and airmen in various theaters of war added another dimension to their arsenal of information. Throughout the summer before leaving for college, Bill had continued to frequent the cinema with pals who had also delayed signing up for the military and who contributed to his study of war news, paying particular attention to the air war.

He made it a point to check in with friends and neighbors who had family already fighting overseas. No detail was too small for him. His good friend and soon-to-be fraternity brother, Weir Cook Jr., had to postpone his application to the cadet program because his father, Colonel Weir Cook, had recently been shot down over the Pacific. The army had deemed his body irretrievable, compounding the family's grief. Weir didn't have the heart to leave his mother so soon after the tragedy and chose to remain in Chicago to console his mother and sister while also helping with funeral arrangements. Now Bill recalled the stories his buddy Weir had told him of his father's prestigious air war record: how Weir Sr. had flown in a squadron under the command of none other than Eddie Rickenbacker in World War I. As they chatted quietly over the phone, Weir revealed that, in his last letter home, his father had joyfully reported how he and his former commander had reunited on some undisclosed island in the South Pacific. Bill also kept in touch, albeit sporadically, with Illinois Senator Wayland Brooks, a friend of the family. The senator already had a son in training, not that that had helped to convince the sergeant at the recruiting station.

After that morning's events, there could be no more living the war through newsreels and radio, thousands of miles away from the challenges men young and old were facing in the Pacific, Burma, Africa, and Europe. Lingering at the crash site, Bill decided he was done struggling with his freshmen studies. He wouldn't dream of piloting a fighter, chasing ME-109s away from a squadron of Allied bombers—he'd get out there and do it. The war was no longer an abstraction; it had come to the Midwest. *Lives are about to change*, Bill thought.

∞

MPs quickly cordoned off Stilesville Road to traffic. Bill began walking, haltingly at first. With each step, his body shed another bit of the burden he'd been carrying around for months: the burden of choosing college for everyone else's reasons. *What about my reasons for wanting to delay higher education?*

As he considered that question, Bill contemplated the legacy that preceded him. His father, William Billings Gemmill Sr., was a tall-dark-and-handsome man with sharp features, piercing blue eyes, and a strong sense of patriotism. Before World War I ramped up, he drove an ambulance in France for the American Field Service (AFS). For his service to the country, he received the highest French honor, Le Croix de Guerre, and family lore has him encountering Ernest Hemingway— also a member of the AFS—during his adventure. It makes for a good story, especially when there is no evidence to the contrary.

William Sr. made certain his son was well aware of his military heritage. His five-times-great grandfather, also named William, and his wife, Jeanette, sailed from Irvine, Scotland, to the New World in 1745. William served as a lieutenant with the British forces during the French and Indian Wars and later, having embraced the vision of American patriots, was made a major in the York County Pennsylvania Militia during the Revolutionary War. William and Jeanette's eldest son, John, the first Gemmill to be born in America, served as a lieutenant in the same militia. His son, Robert, also served the rebels. Military service was in Bill's blood.

The surprise attack on Pearl Harbor had stirred something deep and inherent in Bill that—like a burr under a saddle—never quite eased up. For him, there was never any question that one day he would answer the call. The recruiting sergeant's insistence that he defer caused a mere pause in his inevitable journey toward a military career. Now, in light of what had just happened, he could no longer postpone the inevitable.

He crossed Jackson in a cloud of emotion and somber thought. By the time he reached Berry Street, his spine had straightened; he was standing tall, shoulders back, head high. Determination quickened his pace as he turned the corner at College Avenue. He was clear in his mission, sure in what he had always intended to do. He had been kidding himself all along.

The door of the recruiting office was ajar. A finger of late morning sun reached inside, beckoning Bill to enter. A disheveled, soon-to-be-middle-aged gentleman hovered over the single desk in the room, gripping a handful of papers as if to squeeze his grief back into pulp. His grim face was smeared with remnants of oily black smoke, and his untucked uniform was striped with more of the greasy residue. Bill recognized him as the campus Army Air Corps recruiting officer, and it was obvious where the man had just been. The officer was too absorbed in his anguish to notice the frat boy peering in the doorway, his face similarly streaked black from the fuel that had caught fire and poured from the crashed bomber. He hadn't yet noticed the boy, poised and determined to launch a great shift in his life. It was time to cash in his student deferment. Bill stepped over the threshold, the distressed engines of a B-26 still bellowing in his ears.

Three

FRANCES

Union Station, Chicago,
Illinois, February 1943

THE WINTER OF 1943 had its usual icy grip on the Windy City. Frances felt the brittle February air split and crackle as the throng at Chicago's Union Station dipped and heaved like an ocean swell, spilling through the massive metal doors on Jackson Street, down the sweeping staircase, and into the Grand Concourse. The momentum carried Frances and her son, Bill, along with the flow. She hooked her mahogany leather handbag over an elbow and drew the collar of her beaver fur coat up around her face, thinking, *This is the coldest winter I can remember.*

Bill worked through the crush of people as if on the football field, one arm draped protectively around his mother's waist while, at the same time, keeping a tight grip on his well-packed government-is-sued duffel bag. With the duffel slung over his shoulder, he resisted the random shove or block from an occasional outstretched hand. A right sweat was building up from the effort. Spotting a lull in the rush, he steered his mother to a pillar and stopped to remove his sheepskin jacket—the one his father had given him last Christmas—opened his duffel, and stuffed in the tawny mass of warmth.

Frances made a mental note: he was wearing the latest argyle sweater she had knitted him, the one with the brown, blue, and white pattern. Being a master knitter, she saw to it her son never wanted for a good-looking sweater to wear. Frances smiled as she watched him gather his gear, admiring her handiwork and the boy in it, memorizing the moment. With his jacket secure, mother and son dove back into the melee of People on a Mission.

Inside the station's Great Hall, a weak sun tried vainly to penetrate the paint-blackened windows of a domed skylight that rose ninety feet into the chill sky. By order of President Roosevelt, the glass had been made opaque for the duration of the war. Chicago endured many a blackout in these times, and that skylight was a perfect beacon for any enemy intent on destruction. Frances observed the young men around her, boys really, some walking with others, some moving along alone. They, too, wore their best civilian clothes, and their waterproof canvas bags looked as full as Bill's. She smiled kindly at a father who wore his Marine uniform and medals from the First World War. She supposed the gesture was to honor his son's commitment. The man stood tall and proudly carried his son's bag as if it were a trophy. She watched the faces of the men and women, young and old, walking toward her: the ones who probably had just said goodbye to their sons. Some faces wore tears; others wore a mask to get them through the station without falling apart in public. Some wore no expression at all.

The multitude shuffled across a floor of pink Tennessee marble toward a set of stairs leading down to iron tracks where train engines idled in anticipation of an enthusiastic crowd. The click of high heels, the stomp of hobnailed boots, and the squeak of rubber soles reverberated off the natural stone and mixed with the coughs, calls, and low-voiced conversations circulating through the air. Travelers mingled with well-wishers in the station's immense waiting room, everyone anxious to be on their way. Frances had read in *The Tribune* how 100,000 people—mostly military or recruits—passed through this station every day now. She found the scene surreal.

"All my years coming to this station ... I have never seen so many people all at once. It takes my breath away, it truly does!" Frances exclaimed, her eyes growing wider as she took in the scene. She was struggling with his imminent departure. When she saw Bill watching her, she knew he saw the struggle. As a diversion, she removed her fur hat, the one that matched her coat, and peeled off her brown kid gloves. If she had had a place to put them, she would have removed her winter boots too.

The steady pulse of the station's charged atmosphere concerned Frances but seemed to energize Bill. "Yes! Isn't it swell? So many people!" he exclaimed, as he guided her along, glancing up at the gigantic posters lining the walls of the Grand Concourse.

Frances followed his gaze toward the artwork commissioned by the War Department to stir patriotism, sell war bonds, and instill confidence in a sure victory. The plea from those posters for men and boys was heard all too loudly by mothers like Frances, who had but a single son to offer.

∞

After the attack on Pearl Harbor, the pace of Frances's life had tripled. She and Bill had seen Bill's father off from this historic location only a few short months after the surprise assault by the Japanese Empire. At the request of the United States Army Reserve, William Senior had taken a leave of absence from his law practice to join the army's Judge Advocate General's Corps and was currently in North Africa coordinating the incarceration of Italian and German prisoners of war. It wasn't his first war experience. Yet that war had ended over twenty-five years ago. He was a husband and a father now, with responsibilities. With Senior gone, it fell to Frances to pick up his duties on top of her own, which included the promoting and selling of war bonds.

Just a few months ago she had—all on her own—sent Bill off to college. She alone had made all the arrangements and seen to it that their son was safely tucked away at DePauw University studying prelaw. She took pride in having accomplished so much with William Sr. gone and took comfort in the fact that her son was a mere one state away from her.

Even after he activated his deferment, Frances advised her son to remain in school until he received his orders to report because, honestly, who knew how long that would take? She knew he was itching to get his training over and jump into the air war. Since high school graduation, less than a year ago, she had heard him express his greatest desire of becoming a fighter pilot. Ad nauseam. The notion had unsettled her, knowing the dangers he'd face, and also caused her heart to lift a bit in pride at his enthusiasm.

Frances appreciated Bill's letter describing the plane crash and how it had motivated him to activate his deferment, and she wrote him back with letters of encouragement. She knew her son needed to hear her thoughts about how important it was for him to remain in school, at least until it was time to report for duty. His father wrote from North Africa, adding to the moral support Bill needed to last the long pause between activation and reporting for duty.

As it happened, Bill wasn't called up for five months. And, as hard as it must have been for him to heed his parents' advice, Frances was proud of how Bill bided his time at DePauw. He continued his studies, even though his heart wasn't in either his required or prelaw courses. And he continued to find time to write home. Over those 152 days—Francis had been counting—her son's letters managed to mention the sports he had been playing and the movies he had been watching, but nothing about his academics. He wrote privately to her, admitting that his heart wasn't in his studies and never had been since his arrival at DePauw. It was apparent to Frances that her son's focus remained on the Aviation Cadet Program. He'd remained determined to get there. And now, well, here they were.

As soon as Bill received his orders, he called Frances. "I've suspended all my classes," he informed her. "When the dean heard my reason, he shook my hand and told me my place would be waiting for me after the war." Bill packed up his belongings and returned by train to Chicago; he had only three days to prepare. Fortunately for her, Bill had warned Frances about the quick turnover, so she went right to work. By the time he arrived home, she had washed and pressed all the clothes he hadn't taken to college, since she didn't know what he would need or want to take with him. She saw that he packed extra pairs of his favorite socks—white, mid-calf, athletic—and made certain he'd leave with a full complement of clean underwear. Frances had waited out those five months too, and now, her wait, *their* wait, was over.

∞

"Don't forget about the scrapbook, Mom," Bill reminded Frances as he steered her toward the trains and his imminent departure. "I'll send you all the bits I think will make it interesting, all the moments I won't want to forget."

She had been amenable to the idea, even encouraged it. She thought keeping a scrapbook might even be a way she could continue to feel close to him. Pasting in letters, photographs, and other mementos would keep her occupied and aware of his thoughts and concerns.

Outwardly, she was the epitome of brave. Yet, with Bill joining the fight, she found herself clinging to that impossible shard of hope that someone might appear to tell them there had been a mistake, that Bill's deferment had not been activated, that he should return to Indiana and DePauw. Of course, she wasn't about to show her concern to her son. Especially not here at the station where anyone could see. Frances saw herself as a model military wife and mother, bearing her fears and concerns in silence.

It wasn't that she doubted her son's strength and commitment. Those summers spent working in the steel mills of Gary, Indiana, and the years of school sports had served him well, both mentally and physically. At eighteen years of age, he had grown into a capable leader. She didn't question that, after weeks and months of training, her son would graduate as a first lieutenant in the United States Army Air Force. She knew he was hungry for a commission, and whenever she saw Bill with that amount of resolve, he always achieved his goal. He would graduate and he would enter the war, leaving her twice concerned. She'd double-down her membership in "women on the home front," joining the ranks of preoccupied women on home fronts everywhere. Frances gathered the collar of her ankle-length fur coat around her face as if the strength of those pelts could hold her escalating sadness. The coat muffled her words: "Mmmmfff ... long trip ... feed you ..."

Bill bent down to hear her better. "Say what, Bobs?" Frances teared up at the pet name. All three of them, their little family, called each other "Bobs" as a not-so-secret code word of endearment. They'd had several fond names for one another through Bill's childhood, and not one of them could remember how those names came about. Frances pulled her chin out of her coat collar to reply, "I said, certainly they will feed you on the train. It's a long ride to Texas!"

"I don't know, Mom, my Notice to Report wasn't exactly full of details about menus, just the when, where, time of departure, and destination," Bill replied.

Passing a display of the national flags of the Allies, Frances and Bill reached a set of stairs where they descended deeper into the station. She was lost in a moment, and he was in the here and now, eager to arrive on time as ordered. They merged with a large crowd of recruits, trainmen, porters, and well-wishers. Bill mumbled, rambling expectations about Texas and how he was going to manage all the required college courses, where he'd go afterward for flight training, and any other requirements he'd have to meet if he was going to become an officer.

"Imagine," Frances interrupted his flow with a tease, "they let *you* into the program." She needed the laughter, needed some bucking up. So she played upon his sense of self. He was good-looking and talented and knew it. Yet the tease in her breath hung like a cloud, as chilled and immobile as she felt. In fact, she could still see a little puff of white when she spoke, as if the whole world had gone frigid.

"Heck Bobs, I'm just happy I've made it this far!" Bill sounded over the moon with his activation. A dream deferred and all. "Can you believe I'll be going to classes seven days a week? Me?" he said.

Frances pictured Bill's words hanging in a visible cloud of breath, mingling with hers, draping themselves over the arctic-like atmosphere of the unheated station. "You know I was teasing, right Darling? You'll make a fine officer and leader. Much like your father, I suspect," she said. "And maybe," she continued, "the war will be over and your father home by the time you've earned.that commission." Well, it was possible. There was no telling when this war would end. Frances had revealed her true feelings after all.

Bill didn't respond to his mother's last sentence. It hung suspended in the frosty air. Like mother, like son. He steered her around a larger-than-life sign advertising war bonds: a pretty woman dressed in a khaki mechanic's jumpsuit was holding a bond saying, "This Is My Fight Too!" Everyone was urged to invest in the war, to feel they had a part in it.

Frances needed no reminding that qualifying for the cadet program was priority number one with Bill. She knew he could not, would not, allow anything else to matter. She knew his eyes were on the ultimate prize: earning his pilot's wings. She knew, too, that if the war was still raging when he had those wings, he would put all that training to great use. Reading her son's face, guessing his thoughts, Frances said loudly, "You'll have to stay focused on your studies, Bobs. You want this too much to goof off."

"I'll be top of my class, Mom, you'll see!" Bill said, trying to reassure her.

They arrived at platform No. 10, the platform designated on Bill's transport papers. Down here by the rails, the acrid smell of grease and steel, combined with the hot-tar scent of burned anthracite, assaulted the nostrils and seemed to thicken the air. Young men jostled their way toward the awaiting cars as Frances and Bill took in the scene. Frances glanced around, trying to avoid Bill's gaze. Reaching into her handbag, she retrieved one of her signature embroidered hankies and dabbed, not at all discreetly now, at the corners of her eyes. Her resolve to be strong at this goodbye had all but melted away.

"All aboard!" called the train conductor. The crowd on the platform swung into action. Sweethearts began their tearful partings, fathers too old or too wounded from battle or years of physical labor working steel clapped the backs of their sons. Mothers, like Frances, at last let go the tears they had been so painfully holding back. Would they ever see their sons again? When they did come home alive, how changed would they truly be?

"Alllll aboooooard!" came the second call from the conductor. At that, Bill scooped Frances up in a playful bear hug, lifted her off her feet, and plopped her back down on the platform. He kissed one cheek, then the other, and then he kissed her forehead. "For your smarts!" he called out as he moved toward the train car. The conductor blew his whistle as a last warning to board or be left behind. Frances was still catching her breath when Bill turned and tossed his duffel bag to a waiting porter, then she watched as Bill leapt onto the steps of the car.

Steam billowed from beneath the engine, the train lurched in turn, and its wheels began their slow strain against the rails. Grabbing his duffel from the porter, and with a salute and an air kiss to Frances, Bill disappeared inside the train. He stashed his belongings and squeezed his way through a mass of recruits, wedging himself into an open platform side window. He wasn't the only boy jousting for one last look at his family. Using his football scrimmage skills, he held firm. Frances was standing exactly where he had left her when he boarded the train. Her sky-blue eyes swept over the train car windows, seeking him out. When their eyes met, Frances held onto her son's gaze, knowing she would remember this moment forever. The train lurched as the cars linked up to the engine and began to pull away.

∞

Frances had no idea how long she stood on that platform, willing the red lantern on the caboose to remain in view. Her world had just tilted, and she waited for it to right itself before venturing back up the stairs and into a cold only lake effect can produce. She was proud of her son, of his determination to join "the Good Fight," as the papers and politicians were now calling this war. The last one was tagged "The War to End All Wars," and Frances could sure see the irony in that. Still, she decided she couldn't dwell on anything negative. She'd already comforted a few friends who had received the War Department's letter of regret, those whose sons were not coming home alive. No, she would not put her focus there. Her son was on his way to meet his destiny, whatever shape or form that took. She would keep him safe in her heart and design him home alive and well. She had been tasked with keeping his scrapbook up to date. She'd make Bill's favorite fruitcake, write him letters, and send him care packages. Anything to remind him of home.

She backed away from the platform and retraced her steps past the posters, through the main concourse, and up the grand staircase. She paused at the heavy metal doors to don her gloves and tuck her chin-length hair under her beaver fur hat. By the time she stepped out into the biting cold, Frances was unaware of the jostling crowd. She had a goal, a task, and it made all the difference.

Four

COWBOY LINGO

Chicago, Illinois, to Wichita Falls, Texas, February 1943

AS THE TRAIN BEGAN its slow pull away from the station, Bill stood in the vestibule between cars. He waved to his mother and to all the other mothers until their faces melded together, the engine drawing them ever further apart. He remained on the metal plank, impervious to the arctic air, memorizing the scene. He realized in that moment that he wouldn't be seeing Chicago or Frances for a long time. The look on his mother's face lingered in his mind's eye; an unlikely mix of pride and sorrow crinkling her brow. He couldn't help but notice his mother caving at the end and appreciated how difficult it must be for her to watch her son and only child leaving to train for war. Bill's heart tugged every which way, and he was certain he would remember this moment forever.

He had single-handedly assumed the role of jester in the family, the one who always managed to lighten a dark moment. He reflected on his last attempt to distract her.

"You can send me care packages, Mom. Even your famous fruit-cake! I'll be the envy of every boy in Texas," he had teased, eager to ease his mother's worries and concerns. Frances had merely smiled at that last remark and nodded her agreement.

The metal floor of the vestibule conducted the chill up his boots. Like one of the fox terriers he grew up with, the cold insisted on biting at Bill's ankles until he felt he had no choice but to respond. He was glad he had thought to pull out his jacket before tossing his duffel up to the conductor. With his belongings in mind, he turned to face a jam-packed compartment and stepped further into the train car.

∞

The warmth of all the body heat in the car, coupled with the train's heating system, enveloped him like a blanket. Bill pushed himself through the crowd of excited young men milling about the front of the compartment, making eye contact or exchanging a smile with several of them as he progressed through the congestion. He didn't recognize any of them. Spotting an open window seat, he nodded to the kid already seated on the aisle, as if to say, "Save that seat for me, will you?" The kid's face reminded Bill of Alfalfa from the *Our Gang* films he had loved while growing up in the '30s: he had a noticeable cowlick on the crown of his head, dark bangs slicked down with hair oil, and his suit jacket was a few inches too short in the sleeves. The Cowlick Kid responded to Bill's signal by placing his winter parka by the window. Bill wedged himself through a cluster of boys standing just in front of the seat, blocking it from easy access, and plopped down. He now felt overly warm and removed his sheepskin jacket as he engaged his seatmate.

"Thanks," he said to the kid with the aisle seat. "I appreciate you saving this for me."

"You're welcome," the kid answered, keeping his response brief. Bill figured he was overwhelmed. Heck, he admitted to himself, the whole experience of boarding the train and leaving Chicago had been overwhelming for him too. And exciting.

"Where are you from?" Bill asked the kid, hoping to strike up a conversation to pass some time and get to know one of his fellow aviation student hopefuls.

"South Side," the kid responded, then crossed his arms, closed his eyes, and leaned into the seat.

Bill was from the South Side too, but he got the hint: the kid just wanted to be quiet. Bill turned to look out the window. Frost had gathered at the edges of the glass, creating a delicate frame. He cracked the window open to allow in some fresh air, and the acrid scent of steel and coal, so distinct to open-air train platforms, mingled with the indoor warmth. Then Bill heard the wheezy release of the train's brakes and felt the slight lurch beneath him as the car responded to the pull of the car ahead of them. The jolt got all the boys' attention and, after a bit of a scramble, each one found a place to rest their excited, fired-up selves.

The engine picked up speed, the train's steel wheels squealing as it carried the boys south through the outskirts of the Windy City. Sliding the window shut against the freezing air, Bill turned to survey the recruits in the jammed Pullman. He still didn't see anyone he knew. Bill had never been on a train this crowded before. Dozens of intersecting conversations streamed through his ears. He recognized the distinct accents from neighborhoods around the city: South Shore,

Woodlawn, Oak Park, Hyde Park, Forest Glen, The Loop. *A train car full of home*, he thought.

Across the aisle, he heard five boisterous young men from Lincoln Park, judging from their dialect, excited to be striking out on an adventure together.

"We'll get those sneak-attack cowards," a medium-height, stocky boy with coal-black wavy hair said for everyone to hear.

"Yeah! We took the fight to them and I'm gonna be there until we win," another kid in a plaid jacket boasted. The group of five cheered and roared with enthusiasm.

Toward the back of the car, Calumet Heights was represented by a handful of intimidating toughs sporting leather jackets and glossy Brylcreemed hair, greased back to perfection. They were speaking in low murmurs and looked intimidating. Watching them, Bill wondered how they'd take to uniforms and close-clipped haircuts.

Up and down the compartment, he saw athletic collegiate types mixing with steelworkers; teens exchanging their anticipation with young men in their twenties. Some sophisticated recruits listened thoughtfully to the experiences of the well-traveled. The less extroverted kept to themselves or tentatively made new acquaintances. Bill found himself identifying with most of them. His life experience already reached beyond that of high school and college. Those summer jobs at Indiana steel mills—where he worked with career laborers—had taught him a thing or two about the hard life. He realized just how fortunate he had been to have met people from every neighborhood, from upscale to the bluest of collars. He felt everyone in the mix now shared a singular purpose: to join the war in whatever capacity they could, but mostly to fulfill their dreams. As he looked around, Bill surmised that all the young men in his compartment were eager to participate in thwarting the enemy before it tore the world apart.

The train was bound for Sheppard Field in Wichita Falls, Texas. Twenty-one days of basic to toughen up. Bill chuckled to himself at the thought as he scanned the rest of the kids in his car. Not that he thought of himself as soft or in need of toughening up. He was already pretty strong and ready for anything the army could throw at him. Nothing he had heard about the marching and pushups, measuring and weighing, or the eye charts and dental exams seemed daunting to him. He didn't know what anyone had to complain about, but if someone did, they must not have had football coaches to yell at them when they weren't performing to their highest potential. Like many of his peers, Bill had heard stories from friends and family already in training that he would be under the watchful eyes of drill sergeants and junior officers, where he'd be evaluated and sorted into categories meant to identify a potential cadet's greatest strengths. He wasn't worried. He was born disciplined.

From Sheppard Field, where he'd learn military discipline and receive basic training, he'd head over to Texas Tech in Lubbock, where he'd take a "crash" college equivalency course at the aviation student program. He needed those lieutenant bars if he was going to be a pilot, and Bill was determined to fly. At Tech, he'd have a few short months to cram two years of college into his head. Between course studies, military drills, and training, he'd have zero free time ... and he couldn't wait to get started.

∞

The energy on the car relaxed as the train gained speed and distance. Bill grew curious about where everyone was going to sleep, and since his seatmate had made it clear he was not up for conversation, Bill left his window view, climbed over the Cowlick Kid, and braved the crowd once again. Standing in the aisle, he saw a train attendant approaching. The man was weaving his way through the boys still standing in the aisle, as if he was on the open seas. Bill noticed the man clearly had the legs for the job. He decided to ask the attendant a question that had been forming in his mind.

"Where are we all supposed to sleep?" he asked politely.

"Oh, we have berths in the back," the attendant replied, nudging his head toward the rear of the train, "and there's always the seat," he said, glancing at the closest set of seats. Bill imagined himself trying to catch decent shuteye on the seat of a train and wasn't troubled—he could sleep anywhere.

Just then, the train lurched in an off-balance way, sending Bill into the back of a tall, bushy-haired kid who looked to be about his own age.

"Sorry about that," Bill said to the kid's back. Bill felt embarrassed and wanted to smooth any ruffled feathers. "I bet you weren't expecting to be tackled on the train!"

"That was some jolt!" the kid replied over his shoulder as he turned to face Bill. He was smiling and seemed genuinely happy.

"Did you expect this kind of crowd when we boarded?" the kid asked Bill, who was still smiling good-naturedly.

"No, not exactly," Bill said, "but you saw the same crowd at the station as I did."

"Guess we both missed the clues," the kid answered.

Ready for introductions, Bill extended his hand.

"Say, I'm Bill," he said and initiated the handshake.

The skinny kid with reddish-blond hair and a face loaded with freckles reached for Bill's hand and pumped it wildly—they stood about eye to eye.

"Jimmy!" the kid said with gusto. "The name's James Leroy Thurston, The Third, but everyone calls me Jimmy."

For a moment, Bill thought he could make out a map somewhere in the design of those freckles. *If only he'd stand still*, he thought. Tearing his gaze away, he looked past Jimmy's shoulder and noticed the train attendant again, his arms now loaded down with a stack of blankets. Bill wondered if he might be heading for the sleeping berths. He motioned for Jimmy to follow, and they shadowed the attendant to the sleeping car, where they paused to examine the situation. Immediately, Bill was struck with an idea that could even the odds of gaining the best possible sleeping arrangements. He felt clever.

He looked into the car behind him and at the space above the windows. A bronze rack extended along the ceiling above the seats on both sides. Every square inch of rack space was crammed with duffel bags. He figured his bag was in the jumble somewhere, hopefully on top for easy access, since he had been one of the last to toss his bag to the attendant. It wasn't a stretch to realize the berths would present a similar conundrum to store so many bags filled to the brim with personal essentials.

In every football huddle, Bill was one to quickly size up the situation, and it was no different here: there were obviously more guys on the train than there were berths. Certainly, that was the case in his car, at least. Bill decided to share his idea with Jimmy.

"Wouldn't it be easier to share the lower bunks? That way, everyone can lie down. Head to feet maybe, like stacks of firewood. And if someone on the lower bunk rolls over too far the wrong way, well, the floor is a mere ten inches down; he won't have far to fall!"

"OK," said Jimmy, his brows furrowing while he figured out the concept. "How are we going to decide who sleeps up top? Who has to double up?" He seemed game.

"How about we draw straws for the upper bunks?" Bill explained, his vision growing details as fast as he spoke. "Short straw is the lower berth and a long straw gets the top. Whoever gets lucky can have the top bunk all to himself. What do you say?"

"Why does the top bunk get to sleep alone?" Jimmy pressed on.

"Because it's a much longer fall from the top!" Bill explained as he imagined that happening, visualizing the possible injuries that would ensue after such a drastic drop.

The train attendant was standing within earshot of Bill and Jimmy and moved quickly, in sync with Bill's idea. His dark blue uniform disappeared between a stack of duffel bags blocking a tall, narrow door. The man was no spring chicken, yet he was surprisingly spry, lifting fully stuffed duffel bags with ease. When he reappeared, he was holding a coal-dust-encrusted broom. The old trainman grinned as he handed the broom head up to Bill. *My guess is*, Bill mused, *this isn't our railroad man's first rodeo since Pearl.*

When Jimmy saw the broom, he said, "Excellent idea, buddy. Let's see how it works. You go first." Bill never did like being called "buddy," but he let this one slide.

With a wink and a nod of approval to the attendant, Bill pulled a "straw" from the blackened brush, then handed it to Jimmy who drew his own straw before passing it on. Bill drew short, as did Jimmy. The two boys grimaced at one another, and Bill shrugged his broad shoulders. It was too late to revise his plan now. The idea caught on quickly with the rest of the boys in their immediate vicinity, each of them yanking out a piece of straw before passing it along with an explanation to the next boy. The broom made its way down the aisle. Even the toughs from Calumet Heights joined in while also mocking the idea of having to share a bunk with anyone. Everyone understood he had an equal shot at drawing a long straw and a chance to sleep in single splendor, and the broom passed from hand to hand with much camaraderie.

Bill and Jimmy stood next to a lower bunk, pondering their dilemma.

"Do you really think we can do this?" Jimmy asked as he mentally measured Bill. Both of them were tall—well over six feet.

"Do we have a choice?" Bill answered as he wiped the soot from his hands with a clean handkerchief. An image of Jimmy's bare feet in his face floated into his thoughts. He couldn't push that picture out of his head fast enough.

"Heck, I only just got married. I'm still learning how to sleep with my wife in the bed, much less head to toe with you!" A deep crimson was rising in Jimmy's cheeks as he confessed his innocence to Bill.

"Well, it was my big idea," Bill sighed. He considered his near future: three nights to Sheppard Field, Texas. *They're going to be long nights*, he thought.

Late that evening, during his first experiment in close-quarter bunking, Bill awoke to Jimmy's arm draped across his chest. He lay awake, unable to sleep as the train chugged on through the night. Alternatives crowded his thinking. Maybe he and Jimmy could take turns sleeping in the berth, maybe he'd kick Jimmy out altogether, but most certainly, they'd have to come up with some other sleeping arrangement.

In keeping with his idea of quick-witted fun, Bill assigned a nickname to his bunkmate: Jimmy the Bridegroom. He couldn't help himself from nicknaming people; it was pure entertainment. He never knew what would trigger his imagination, yet something about a person, some quirk, tic, look, or status begged for embellishment. Most people, to his way of thinking, just needed a moniker. He didn't have to think hard; the inspiration came easily, and he tagged people all the time.

∞

On their second day of travel by train, and after a brown-bag break-fast of cold toast, a boiled egg, and one lonely cold link of sausage, the recruits and cadet-hopefuls settled into a loose routine of dozing, chatting, and card games. Bill, still hungry after the measly repast and tired from not having slept a wink all night, decided to remain in the seat he had skillfully commandeered from a friendly recruit from Peoria he met in the aisle. From his vantage point, Bill managed to survey his domain: Jimmy was busy writing, probably to his new wife. Bill imagined it was a letter that began "My Dearest Darling," because that is what all the letters in the romance movies opened with. Besides, Jimmy the Bridegroom kept glancing guardedly around the car as if he was hoping no one was reading over his shoulder.

Cigarettes were passed around; experienced smokers instructed some of the guys learning to smoke for the first time. They relaxed on the bench seats, watching the slender spiral of smoke wend its way to a crack in the window and out into the open air, their thoughts flying with them. Bill decided to pass on the smokes, his inner athlete reminding him not to start what could become a habit.

Others sat staring out at the passing scenery, lost in their own compelling imaginings. The landscape sliding past them was a testa-ment to winter: snow lined the tracks and clung to bare tree branches, bales of hay, and low-slung roofs. Milky drifts ended their gallivanting at fence lines, piling up one atop another like a dogpile on a football field. The sky was snow-gray, more of the white stuff building for its next crescendo.

The conductor came through and announced they were moving through the southern lowlands of Arkansas and soon would be cross-ing into east Texas. Watching out the window, Bill noticed the land in southern Arkansas was as flat as the Illinois plains, not much to see but the river they were crossing. Snow had followed them the entire trip. It lay across rocks at the river's edge and in the nooks and crannies of the bridge supports. Bill drew a mental picture from the snow-flocked trees and fences of Indiana, the snow-covered railway station and platform in Missouri, the chalky smoke billowing from the engine's stack that seemed to stamp itself onto the sky. It hung suspended in the air, slow to dissipate as smoke behaves in a frigid atmosphere.

On the evening of their second day of travel, school fight songs broke out from the collegiate section; "the swells" preferred crooning love ballads. Most of the lower-bunk guys simply slept while they had the chance, oblivious to sound. Bill's eyelids grew heavy at last, and he slept so hard he missed dinner.

Bill's eyes slitted open the next morning, allowing the first hints of a new day to register in his brain. He felt the velvet brush of the rising sun intensify on his cheek. He had fallen asleep in the window seat, and by the looks of his immediate surroundings, several other lower-bunk sleepers had decided to do the same. Just as he did in a duck blind when hunting with his father, Bill didn't stir. The difference with this daybreak was that instead of waiting for wild fowl to appear, he watched the dawning light reveal more of the map of his ever-expanding world. The sun slowly danced away from the horizon. It was not yet high enough to throw morning's long shadows over the land. Overhead, a tapestry of lavender, pink, and orange drifted across a sky of possibilities. *Daylight already?* The thought bounded unbidden into his stream of consciousness. He longed to remain amongst the cobwebs of sleep, yet the sunrise was insisting it be gazed upon. *Another first to remember*, he thought as he leaned against the window pane. *Dawn over the prairie.*

The boys had been riding this train for three days running and were advancing on Wichita Falls on schedule. Bill had found a deep sleep in his window seat. Any way he sliced it, sitting up all night sure beat sharing a berth with Jimmy. Plus, he could escape the ripe scent of body odor wafting through the stale atmosphere of the car by cracking the window occasionally. Fresh air was at a minimum on the jammed train, and to add to the mélange, they were moving through the dry South, pulsing with heat waves that defied the weather he had left behind two days ago in Kansas.

"Did you see that?" said Leather Jacket, Bill's nickname for the tough guy with the slick-backed hair who never removed his black studded motorcycle jacket.

"Wha?" So much for firsts and sunrises. Having fallen asleep again, Bill was now fully awake.

"Cowboys," one of the collegians chimed in, describing, "Real honest-to-goodness cowboys! You know, Zane Grey, *Riders of the Purple Sage* cowpokes?" Riders on horseback, sporting chaps over their blue jeans, came into view.

Sure enough, out on the prairie some of the scruffiest cowboys Bill had ever imagined were steering their horses toward the train. Of course, the only cowboys Bill had seen were from Hollywood. *This must be what real working ranch hands looked like: cattlemen.* They were close enough for Bill to easily see some the tools of their trade: coiled ropes attached to saddles, a rifle poking out beneath a blanket, a rope coiled around a saddle horn, a battered canteen. The train slowed, easing on through the cattlemen's territory in no great hurry. *Even the cattle are moving faster than this,* thought Bill. He cracked the window and was surprised by the warmth rushing in. He opened it wider. The sound of soft leather chaps on hard leather saddles drifted into the Pullman car as the cattlemen approached. Bill heard a weathered and worn creak harmonize with the shrill metal-on-metal sound of steel wheels on iron rails. The lowing of cattle clustered not too far away came, adding gentle undertones to the mix. It was dry out here; every step of man or beast kicked up billows of dust. The waterless air frizzled; it carried the scent of grass and hay and animal sweat into the Pullman. The pace was nice for observation, but he sure could use the breeze of a faster-moving train. *We all could*, he thought. The sun was pouring its heat into the glass windows; more boys were waking. They stretched and adjusted their positions.

Bill remembered a Wild West show his parents had taken him to when he was little. This was the real deal. Here were the tall, broad-brimmed hats, well-worn boots, and braided lariats of ranchmen in action. And, just like in the movies, a thin ribbon of smoke trailed up and out of a pipe in the roof of a ranch house in the distance. *Breakfast*, Bill thought hungrily.

The doggie-wrangling, most likely weary horsemen drew up by the rails and watched the troop train as it lurched slowly past. Their charge, a sizeable group of cattle, too many in number for Bill to count, stopped their munching as they, too, watched the train cars pass, their heads moving in unison as they followed the movement. Beyond the big house, and after a small watering hole, the range was showing the first signs of an early spring—patches of green dotted the open grasslands as far as Bill could see.

"Who the hell is Zane Grey?" asked someone with an accent from The Loop.

"The cowboy writer," answered one of the toughs, surprising Bill. He dubbed the guy Novel Joe to remind himself not everyone was who he thought they might be. He hadn't figured a greaser to be a fan of Western novels.

The banter began. "Say, Pahdnah, you gonna use that bedroll tonight?" said an older man who, by the looks of his arms, had to be a former steelworker. They were the only men Bill knew who could develop biceps like that. Bill admired how the guy had stripped to his undershirt. He wasn't the only one feeling the compartment had grown toasty.

"Git along little Doggie, git along outta my bedroll!" replied one of the collegiate boys, who still looked crisp and sharp in defiance of how hot the inside of the Pullman was growing.

"I'd lose the accents, fellas; you ain't going to no Hollywood!" responded someone from the direction of the Lincoln Park quintet.

"Wonder why those guys aren't overseas fighting?" A challenger stood up from his seat and opened his window. He wore his shirtsleeves rolled up over muscly, tattooed arms, a pack of Lucky Strikes neatly tucked in at the bicep bulge. Because he was sitting with the group from Calumet, Bill pegged him for a tough and dubbed him Des Moines Dan. Bill liked the name even if the guy's real name wasn't Dan—he liked all the names he found to identify people.

He considered Dan's question. There were physical and student deferments, Uncle Sam wouldn't allow ex-cons to fight, and he had heard there were men who refused to fight on conscientious grounds. There would always be guys too afraid to fight. He imagined his mother's response; Frances always thought the best of people. Bill heard her saying something like, "It's likely that at least one grown man in that group fought early on and is back on the family ranch safe, sound, and thankful for it."

Instead, he said, "Who knows? Someone's got to stick around to work the ranch. Someone has to feed us and the entire G.D. army!" Bill was on a roll. He surveyed the crowd and saw many heads nodding in agreement. Bill wasn't so sure of what he'd started by his comment.

"Hang on … he's got a point. I mean what if they're yellow?" Jimmy the Bridegroom declared. "I would never turn my back on our country or my crew." This got the boys to shouting and cheering, puffing up with their own sense of confidence and valor.

Bill felt he had to regain his position of support for the working men at home. He firmly believed they were part of the war effort too. He had seen farmers and ranchers in the newsreels. He knew the sacrifice they were making to feed the men in training as well as the men overseas fighting. Yet, he thought it wise to restrain himself from adding any as-yet-unearned bravado, preferring to be entertained by the others' show. *First*, he mused, *we have to separate the men from the boys.*

More images from the many newsreels he had seen ran together in a montage through Bill's mind: recruits marching, recruits studying, practicing bailouts, and training to duck and cover when they hit the ground.

Stretching out his legs, Bill yawned and reached for the ceiling. The move appeared to lengthen him another inch or two. Closing his eyes, he pondered his immediate future. How many of the boys on this train were traveling to Texas with the intention of qualifying for cadets? How many just wanted to participate regardless of rank or status? Bill knew the only way to achieve his dream was to excel as an aviation student, move on to cadets, and graduate as a second lieutenant, where he would receive pilot training and achieve his first lieutenant bars at final graduation. Would he be one of the chosen hundreds who crisscrosses the country from base to base, honing his skills so he could do what he was trained to do and come home alive?

The train picked up speed as it crossed the open country and moved into the desert again, the rhythm rocking Bill back to some interrupted, half-forgotten dream. He was saying goodbye to a woman at a train station; she was taking snapshots with a Brownie camera. No one else was in sight, yet he could hear a great crush of voices, feel the press of bodies as they pushed past. Or was that Jimmy the Bridegroom gone all cuddly again?

∞

Flat, barren, and bleak. Bill's first impression of Sheppard Field was nothing but disappointment, but he had precious little time to stew about it. When the train pulled into the depot, a staff sergeant boarded the car and instructed them to follow him out. Bill barely had enough time to identify his gear from the pile and replace his toiletry kit inside his duffel. He threw on his sheepskin jacket and placed his writing paper and pencil in a deep, outside pocket. Once on the platform, they were instructed to toss their bags into the back of a four-by-four truck and line up. He exchanged silent, wide-eyed glances with Dan and Jimmy as all three of them did their best to form a decent row according to the sergeant's command. They telegraphed their confusion with eye rolls and squints, with Jimmy managing a few smirks behind the sergeant's back.

Once the sergeant had the group collected and squared up to his liking, he marched his new charges to Sheppard Field, not more than two miles distance. They entered the base and continued marching until they reached a group of whitewashed wooden barracks. Bill was grateful for the opportunity to observe the layout of the base, and he took mental note of the few signs that served as markers. A young first lieutenant was waiting for them out front, clipboard in hand. The junior officer handed each young man instructions indicating their barracks assignments before informing them they had one hour to stow their belongings and regroup back in front of their buildings. The young men broke ranks, grabbed their duffel bags off the truck, and rushed into their designated barracks, looking for their ideal spots in rows of army-issue cots.

"I don't much care where I end up," Jimmy announced to anyone willing to listen. "I'm just glad to see the bunks are side by side rather than one on top of the other!"

"Well, I do care, Jimmy," Bill called out to his new friend, "and I'm liking this cot at the end. Look, it's right next to a desk with a lamp and a window!"

"You're always writing, Bill. Who're you writing to? You got a girl back home?" Jimmy's congenial smile hid the tease.

More like, girls, plural, Bill thought before he answered. "My mom, mostly. My dad. Sometimes I write to them both in the same letter. My grandmother out in California. Friends already training. I expect once I have a known address, I'll have more letters to write to friends and family."

"Come on, Gemmill, I know you're writing to all your pretty girl-friends," Jimmy teased Bill.

"I seem to recall you wrote letters the entire ride down here your-self," Bill reminded Jimmy.

"Yeah, but I just got married! I don't want my wife to think I've forgotten her already," Jimmy explained, holding his head in his hands in mock distress.

"Hahahaha! You think you two are going to have time to write letters, Gemmill?" Des Moines Dan had walked up to check out Bill's area of the barracks, laughing all the way. "I took the cot closest to the door so I can be the first to line up for roll call!"

By the door had been Bill's second choice, should someone have aced him out of the cot by the desk. But when he looked around the room, he was convinced he had chosen well. Whoever else sat at that desk—because Bill had every intention of utilizing it for long stretches of time—would be quiet. And if they had the lamp turned on, well, he could sleep through most anything. He looked at Dan and faked a frown.

"Instructor's pet," he teased.

And so, it began. The basic training, the forming of friendships—some fleeting and others destined to last a lifetime.

Five

SPIDER WOMAN MAGIC

Sheppard Field to Santa Ana Army Air Force Base, June 1943

HIS MONTHS OF TRAINING in Texas felt like an eternity to Bill as his excitement at a new adventure wore off, yet the days passed like time-lapse photography—sped up and hurried. The weeks spent at Sheppard Field and then Texas Tech in Lubbock melded together in a blur. He learned to march, to line up in a tidy row, and to take orders. He completed all the required advanced college courses for cadets going on to officer training, and now he was on to preflight school where he would earn his classification.

All that learning and knowledge had been compressed into a matter of hours. *What good is learning ancient history when all I want to do is fly a fighter?* Bill wondered. *How is knowing that the invention of gunpowder hastened the decay of feudalism or how two of Henry II's greatest contributions to the judiciary, trial by jury and free courts, going to help me when I'm facing down a skillful enemy pilot or two?* He understood the need for a good grasp of physics and even trigonometry, but how valuable was knowing the statistics of the American population? And he didn't enjoy calculating the statistics of being shot down. *I guess that's exactly why the army advertised "two years of college in six weeks" at Tech,* he thought, *to get us thinking.*

Bill wrote home to tell Frances how miserable both the typhoid and tetanus shots had made him. His head and ears pounded and his stomach heaved, none of which gave him a pass from his classes. Neither did his reaction to the shots or a bad cold exempt him from his physical exams. He stressed and worried over every kind of test he faced in Texas. At the end of those first several months, Bill was even more impatient to jump behind the controls of a North American Mustang than he had been in high school while daydreaming of piloting the P-51. He was eager for the experience he would gain in combat, certain he would both measure up to the challenge and benefit from it. Just like he had seen in the newsreels, he'd climb and dive and shoot and destroy from the cockpit of his fighter plane. He felt edgy, especially knowing he was months away from completing all the required training.

∞

On 25 July, with the Texas heat casting mirages that rippled and distorted the distant atmosphere, Bill once again boarded a troop train loaded with aspiring cadets. They were heading west out of Lubbock before curving north to Santa Ana Army Air Base, just south of Los Angeles, California. It was another three-day trip, but this time everyone on board was in uniform.

The train pulled away from the station and lost no time picking up speed. There were few towns to slow down for between Lubbock and the New Mexico border, just a whole lot of nothing but wide-open land. He found the scene akin to his trip down to Wichita Falls all those months ago—flat and dry—but then he spotted a wooden windmill and, in the distance, what appeared to be mountains. A massive herd of famous Texas longhorns appeared. They were being driven eastward, probably to a processing plant, Bill guessed. When they crossed the state line into the Land of Enchantment, he reached into his briefcase, pulled out his sharpest pencil and a few sheets of Sheppard Field paper, and began a letter to his parents. He titled his missive, "Somewhere in New Mexico."

"Dear Mom & Dad,

Well, we're on our way at last. Please don't mind my writing 'cause the train's jumping around all over the place. I'm the car commander and therefore got a compartment. It really is nuts. New Mexico looks swell to me; it isn't as flat and desolate as Texas. There are mountains and huge hills on both sides of the train now. It really is interesting. We have passed many Indian villages and they are the McCoy too. The people wear bright red outfits and all the works. We're going to get off in a little while for breakfast. The food is the one thing I am sure going to miss about Tech. I hear that the Santa Ana mess stinks."

Finding it impossible to write on the lurching train, Bill folded the letter and slid it into his leather briefing bag. *I'll finish it later*, he thought. Looking up, he realized there was less chatter amongst the boys than the buzz that filled his trip to Texas last winter.

As the train chugged along, Bill and most of the other cadets slept. When awake, he walked the aisles or stared out the window, contemplating the next segment in his training, or listened to the exchanges of the few young men sharing rumors and jokes to pass the time. He was comfortable talking with whoever happened to be sitting next to or across from him at the time. On the second day of their journey, Bill met Yancey. Yancey was from Long Beach and knew the base at Santa Ana pretty well. Bill easily found his nickname for the cadet, The California Kid.

"Have you ever been to Santa Ana?" the California Kid asked Bill after the two young men dispensed with their introductions.

"I have," Bill replied, "but I barely remember it. My father's mother, my grandmother, lives in Beverly Hills. When I was about six years old, my parents and I took the train from Chicago to visit her. It was a big adventure for me at the time. Nana and I write to each other regularly now, and she comes out to Chicago often."

"Well," Yancey began, "Santa Ana is about thirty miles, give or take, south of Los Angeles. The base is a few miles west of town." As he spoke, he pulled out a travel map of the US he'd stuffed inside a book and pointed to where they were headed. He had made notations all over the map, indicating the regions where he had been sent to train, Texas Tech being the most recent. Bill was impressed with the detail Yancey had added to the map: notes on the landscape, historic monuments, the animals he had encountered, the weather he had experienced, and the dates of his arrival and departure to and from each location. *And people tell me* I'm *detail-oriented*, thought Bill.

"I figure the layout of Santa Ana is just about the same as Lubbock," Bill shared his guess.

Yancey quickly corrected that assumption. "Santa Ana Army Air Base is at least five times bigger than the base at Lubbock. It may even have grown since the last time I saw it. There's a tram into town if you find the time off to explore."

"Wow," Bill reacted to the image of such an immense army air base forming in his head. "I hadn't imagined it to be so big!"

"Yep! Texas isn't the only state to do things on a grand scale," replied Yancey. The two cadets shared a hearty laugh.

"I reckon we can expect more marching, book learning, and physical training at Santa Ana too," Bill laughed knowingly. *Surely,* he thought, *the army will throw some new trials at us here.*

"No doubt," Yancey concurred as he settled back and closed his eyes. His part of the conversation was over.

Bill felt a familiar, excited curiosity—his constant companion as of late—and it intensified as the train drew them closer to Santa Ana. With his eyes shut, he rocked to the rhythm of the wheels on rails and dozed until dinner.

∞

Waking from a late-morning snooze on the last day of the journey north, Bill watched lazily as the view out the train car window began changing rapidly. He noticed the lack of shadows on the ground and consulted his watch—the Bulova A-11 his father had given him.

"You need a reliable watch in the army," Bill remembered him saying, "and now that you've activated your deferment, it is only a matter of time before you see how valuable a good watch can be. A matter of time, get it?" his father had laughed.

Bill loved the black dial, the white markings, and the fact that his watch had the hacking mechanism that would make synchronizing with any future crewmates all the more accurate. By the reading on his watch, it was just past 1600 hours, or 4:00 p.m. Bill figured he would have known that just by looking out the window. The sun had lowered considerably, and the deep oranges, purples, and pinks of a Southwestern sunset were gathering amid the clouds, preparing to paint the sky.

The train crossed into California with little fanfare, but when they stopped in Needles for dinner, a sleek, high-end Streamliner came in on the next track and pulled to a stop at the station. The troop train pulled up behind the luxury liner, and moments later, one of the boys in the seats up front shouted, "Mary Beth Hughes just walked off that train. I saw her!" Bill wondered if Miss Hughes knew she had pulled up alongside a troop train. Sure enough, as he stepped onto the platform, there she was, speaking with the station master, pointing in Bill's general direction. All the boys were clustered around their car commander, waiting and wondering what to do next.

"She's coming toward us!" a scrawny kid nearly screeched with anticipation.

Bill was wondering how anyone so thin made it into the cadet program, when he suddenly was pulled into the arms of the lady herself for a big kiss. Then, she handed out autographs, kissed a few more of the boys, and expressed her gratitude and pride before turning and leaving many a star-struck boy behind. *How about that*, Bill thought as he felt the lingering warmth of the kiss on his cheek. *William Powell's wife just kissed me? That'll be something to write Mom about!*

After the excitement of the kiss, it was time for an early dinner. Bill was ravenous. Once his hunger was satisfied at the station café, he jumped the steps back onto the train and headed for his compartment for a lie-down. When he woke next morning and looked out the window, the scene was transitioning from neat rows of fruit orchards to city streets. Elaborately curved iron lamps lined each side and lit up storefronts sporting tawny clapboard siding. After a short while, the engineer began to ease the train into a slow chug, signaling its approach to the Santa Ana station.

Bill moved into the train car and took a seat in front of Yancey. He turned around and announced with a grin, "High noon and here we go! Best of luck to you in your training and wherever you are sent after!'

Yancey saluted Bill, saying, "You'll do all right, Gemmill. I'll see you around base!"

Bill was awash with anticipation as he stood to collect his gear. He was curious and eager for this next phase of his journey. *Each training base is one base closer to seeing action,* he reminded himself, *and each is its own adventure.*

∞

Bill jumped down from the train, landing in a sea of hopefuls like himself. He was concerned about the state of his uniform pants, but there was nothing he could do about that; every uniform on the train appeared to be a bit worn-looking after the ride up from Texas. At least he had removed his jacket and folded it inside out, laying it flat on the overhead rack, the way he had seen his father do on many occasions. That seemed to do the trick in keeping the jacket fairly crease-free. He ran his hands down any wrinkles he could reach on his pants, hoping to smooth them out at least. Then he looked out at the scene before him.

The hot air was blown about by a perceptible breeze, and he imagined he could smell the dryness—something akin to a brown paper bag. Unlike his departure from Chicago's Union Station where all the boys wore civilian clothes, everywhere he looked he saw men of every age in uniform: dark blue train company uniforms with shiny brass buttons, khaki military uniforms with a variety of insignia and patches signifying rank and squadron, and basic khaki cadet uniforms. Each uniform had its own cap. Like all the cadets, the uniform cap he had been issued was shaped much like the popcorn vendor at the ballpark, he admitted to himself. *At least,* he thought, *ours aren't white with the logo of a frank or box of popped corn on one side.* Bill wondered about the standards for how all the other military caps were to be worn. He figured he'd find out soon enough.

Bill had been standing still for too long—in danger of being trampled right there on the platform. He joined the flow of the crowd, the momentum bringing him toward a loose group of cadets. He was amazed at the number of people in action. He spotted a platoon of WACs, members of the Women's Army Corps, going through their paces. Bill had yet to make up his mind about women in the military. Maybe he'd meet some of them and be able to better decide. Just as that thought crossed his mind, his eyes met those of a fetching WAC: a lieutenant, judging from the bars on her shoulder. She wore bright red lipstick and had pulled her dark brunette hair under her kepi cap. Bill had never seen a khaki uniform fit anyone quite so well. The WAC and the cadet exchanged smiles. She winked, then turned back to address someone in her group.

He looked away from the winking WAC and aimed his gaze above the crowd, into the far distance. Bill had thought Sheppard was built on a grand scale, but this base was beyond impressive. He spotted various single-story and two-story structures on the horizon and reckoned the single-story buildings were the barracks. *The remainder must be for administration and classroom purposes*, he considered, noting that they were built largely with buff-colored cinder blocks that blended in with the dry buff-colored earth.

Bill also noticed a few spindly trees dotting an otherwise barren landscape, their leaves not mature enough to provide any measurable shade. Nearby, drill sergeants barked instructions while boys scrambled into formation. The sound of their boots was softened to a dusty scuffle by the cracked arid dirt. *Good grief!* Bill observed. *Controlled chaos.* Yet, just like at Union Station, the volume of activity had an energizing effect on him. He had become accustomed to it. Military training was now part of him; it was in his blood. Distracted by the scene before him, he didn't hear the crusty words aimed directly at him.

"You got cotton in those ears, Cadet?" an army sergeant half Bill's height croaked his challenge. His sunburnt face looked painful, which may have affected his mood and manner. His khaki uniform was starched and pressed to perfection, and his boots wore a recent shine; not a speck of dust or dirt clung to them so far as Bill could tell.

"No, Sir!" Bill snapped his reply. He knew better than to get off on the wrong foot with any sergeant or officer during his first moments at a new camp. He was going to be here for six weeks, and he was prepared to be a model cadet for the duration, whatever that meant.

The sergeant reminded Bill of a small dog, either unaware of his own size or unaffected by it. He stood on his tiptoes in an attempt to look Bill in the eyes. "Then get in line! We ain't got all day!"

"Yes, SIR!" Bill answered briskly, standing at attention and unnecessarily saluting the sergeant. Then he lined up with the rest of the boys standing next to him. *I hope I don't get this guy as my squadron sergeant*, he thought.

∞

Bill soon discovered he was right to be impressed by the size of the base; it was an immense sprawling tract of land that served the Army Air Force as a classification center and training camp. After testing and training, each man would be evaluated and classified according to their test results. He knew full well that some of the candidates, himself included, would be overjoyed to receive their most desired classification: pilot. According to popular belief, pilots got all the girls and glory, but not everyone could fly fighters and bombers.

The sun beat down as hot as Texas here, and the semi-arid air was as dry as the hard-packed ground. Sparse drought-loving vegetation, like olive and sumac trees, were planted among the buildings, with most of the trees and grasses lining the roads that crisscrossed the base. Clumps of penstemon, their happy little yellow flowers brightening the landscape, were planted amid gray-green sage bushes that ringed the buildings. Someone had gone to a great deal of trouble to add some color and make the base as attractive as they could. Hordes of aspiring cadets—Bill had heard that more than sixty thousand had arrived by the spring of 1943—came to Santa Ana with dreams of contributing to the war, and he was one of them. He had mere weeks to learn and excel in everything the Army Air Corps could throw at him. He knew he'd have to undergo additional training and testing to discover his classification, and he knew most cadets would be fiercely competitive.

∞

Anyone who had spent any time at the base referred to it as "SAAAB" and, wanting to fit in, Bill quickly adopted the acronym. He guessed most cadets would be as disappointed as he would be to wash out of flight school and be sent instead to mechanic, bombardier, or navigator school. Any one of them could also be reclassified or, worse, washed out entirely in the next phase of training. He also knew a war cannot be fought and won with pilots alone. Every single member of a fighter or bomb group was as vital as the next, a fact that was honed into every airman flying, be he an officer or enlisted man. But so far, no one he knew ever talked about their fears of losing out on gaining those pilots' wings, including himself.

Bill was aware how important his performance would be at SAAAB. He was determined to do everything in his power to become a pilot, although he told himself he would be just as proud to be a bombardier or navigator; he wanted to be a part of a team. He was most decidedly going to be an officer: it was the whole reason he had gone in for the cadet program in the first place. Only an officer could be a pilot, copilot, bombardier, or navigator. *Eyes on the prize, Gemmill,* he told himself repeatedly. *First, there's preflight!*

Having found his unit and been directed to his barracks, Bill organized his belongings and pulled out the unfinished letter to his parents. He had to add one last thing before he found a letter drop. "Well, I'm here at last. Santa Ana isn't bad so far. At least it has Sheppard Field beat. I only have a very few minutes to write but I'll give you a little news," he scrawled. Then he told them about the kiss Miss Hughes gave him on the train.

∞

From the moment they arrived, cadets were escorted everywhere by drill sergeants or training instructors—referred to as "TIs." Bill found most of them hard as concrete. These non-coms (non-commissioned officers) marched the cadets to class, to the dining hall, and back to their barracks. On his first night at SAAAB and every night thereafter, Bill collapsed into bed and fell asleep with the sounds of TIs marching him in his head. When he woke the next day, he was as tired as when he finally went to bed the night before. *Football practice was easier than this*, he thought.

Instructors ran the cadets through twenty-four classroom hours of refresher courses in physics and twenty in math. Bill was studying harder than ever before, even harder than he had done at Tech. He found the eighteen hours of map-reading classes and thirty hours of aircraft recognition relatively easy. After months of avidly watching newsreels on weekends while still in high school, he was already familiar with most military aircraft found in every country engaged in the war. Another forty-eight hours were tacked on for learning Morse code. There were few gaps in the schedule; most every minute was filled with studying, learning, and perfecting skills. Still, a body couldn't study all day every day. The brain, at least, needed a break.

There were moments of entertainment, mostly coming from Army Air Force Radio. Bill and the other cadets in his squadron enjoyed listening to radio shows: *The New Adventures of Sherlock Holmes* and the comedy *Stop Me If You've Heard This One* were favorites. They rarely had the opportunity to listen to a show in its entirety before falling asleep. He took any opportunity he was given to write home to his parents and friends, filling them in on the few dates he had managed to have so far, training, and anything else about his life he felt like sharing. Most of the time, he just rambled on about his day-to-day, throwing in an occasional request for items like shoes or clothing.

Bill admired his roommate "Chief" and considered himself most fortunate to bunk with him. Chief was Navajo, several years older than Bill, a few inches shorter, and spoke Diné, the Mother's Tongue. A lover of languages, Bill enjoyed hearing Chief speak Diné and tried to learn from him as best he could. The Native American had a solid stance, as if he was connected to the earth herself. He'd take Bill outside on a regular basis to teach him how to wrestle the Navajo way, but Bill never was able to push the man off his feet. "You may need these skills if you are ever shot down," Chief explained to Bill. The value of what he was being taught struck Bill immensely, and he made a point to carve out at least thirty minutes a day to practice his lessons in self-defense. As it happened, his roommate also made the best damn coffee on the base. After a mug of Chief's "Joe," his first taste of coffee ever, Bill was hooked on the bean.

When they weren't studying or crawling under barbed wire or

marching in full gear and loaded pack, Chief would brew up some coffee and speak to Bill about his life before the military. He was raised on a reservation where his elders showed him the importance of honoring the earth and every living thing on it. They shared their rituals with him, his siblings, and all the youth coming up behind them. They kept their language and culture alive. Bill couldn't get enough of Chief's stories, and he was curious about his blanket. Chief slept beneath a colorfully woven blanket every night, folded it carefully, and put it in the footlocker at the end of his cot each morning, lest he be accused of not conforming to army protocol for keeping a tidy bed.

"My mother and sister wove this for me," Chief explained to Bill one evening. "It is to keep me safe in battle."

"Do the symbols have significance?" Bill asked.

"Oh yes," Chief smiled. It appeared to Bill that he was delighted his roommate was interested. "Lightning motifs are woven into the blanket for power, and these crosses represent the secrets of Spider Woman.

"The secrets of Spider Woman? Sounds intriguing," Bill said, genuinely interested. "What kind of secrets?"

"Growing up, my grandmother always told me that Spider Woman gave Man the secrets to make his way in this world. Before that, only the deities knew how to walk among men, so I guess that was a mighty secret she shared," Chief chuckled at the thought.

Listening to Chief's stories fed Bill's wonder and inspired him to one day explore the Southwest. "I've had so little exposure to Native American culture, and what I do know is pretty much Navajo and Apache. I think. Oh, yeah, and Mohican. After listening to you, I reckon there is a whole lot more to the Navajo and Apache stories than Hollywood has to offer," he admitted to his friend.

"Well, Hollywood only distorts and hides the truth about native peoples. Details of events like the Long Walk aren't taught much, if at all, in schools across the country … public or private schools," Chief frowned. "If events *are* taught, the focus is on the sensational, like Custer's Last Stand or the ferocity of Geronimo when what he was doing … what all native peoples were doing … was trying to protect his people. Told in this way, it sells more books and funds big box-office films."

"Yet, here you are," Bill replied, "training to do your duty for your country. Is commitment Big Medicine?"

"Yes, commitment is one of Spider Woman's secrets. It is Big Medicine, as you say," Chief smiled, and it was a serious smile, yet kind at the same time, and its energy bored into Bill's heart. He hoped it remained there for life.

Determined to be the best damn pilots in the army, Bill and Chief were forever firing trick questions at each other.

"You're low on fuel; if you don't turn around and head to base now, you won't make it back. But you see one of your group being pursued by the enemy. Do you engage?" Chief asked one night, testing Bill's resolve.

"You turn back, of course. You have to for the good of the entire squadron, no?" Bill answered.

"Yes, and I imagine it will be a most difficult choice to make," noted Chief.

"Let's just hope we are never forced to make that choice," Bill replied thoughtfully, although the reality was that it was very likely they'd be facing just this scenario. They routinely practiced well into the night, fueled by Chief's aromatic brew. Then, they'd wake early the next day and resume practicing before classes. When Bill's good friend from high school, Danny Shea, showed up at SAAAB, he expanded the private study group by one. The discipline suited the trio, and each one of them excelled at his studies.

Bill discovered that change often comes quickly in the military when, after only a month, Chief was assigned to the Code Talkers in the Pacific. The language of The Mother was impenetrable to the Japanese.

After giving Bill the news, Chief and Bill walked over to Danny's barracks to tell Danny. Along the way, they reminisced about their training together. Chief was more muscular than Bill, his weight distributed over his body differently. As they strolled along, Bill noticed how his roommate walked. How purposeful it was, as if he was literally feeling the earth with his feet. He thought it gave the man a regal bearing, despite the army boots. He wondered why he hadn't noticed this until now. Chief spoke again, interrupting Bill's thoughts.

"All the practice targets I've seen you hit, Gemmill," Chief was saying with a lilt in his voice, "and the number of obscured targets you've managed to spy before anyone else ... I'm convinced you are born of Atsah!"

"OK, I give, Chief. What is an Atsah?" Bill joined in the game.

"Why, it's Diné for Eagle, my friend!" Chief said proudly, laying a muscled hand on Bill's shoulder. Bill was going to miss the spirit of his first native friend, the one who walked as "Chief." He never did learn his true name.

∞

Early on in their assignment to SAAAB, Bill's fellow students elected him cadet commander—and Bill felt honored at the show of respect. He took on the responsibility with gusto, marching his charges, calling cadence, and making sure their uniforms were clean and properly assembled. He listened to their grievances and readied them for review when it was time for a parade. There were endless parades to show off what the cadets had learned about moving as a cohesive unit. At one point, while marching his class to chow, the group passed a man in uniform. He was an officer by the looks of it, or so Bill thought after a quick sideways glance at the man, who wore a standard short-sleeved khaki uniform shirt and a crush cap. Per standard protocol, and with enthusiastic respect, Bill called "Eyes right!" and the entire class saluted … the Coca-Cola delivery man! Arrrgh! Bill cringed immediately upon realizing his gaffe. How embarrassing! The only response he thought appropriate was to laugh along with everyone else, but he feared the mistake would follow him to his next assignment before it petered ou.

Six

THE CADET AND THE MOVIE STARS

*Santa Ana Army Air Base,
July–August 1943*

WHILE IN TEXAS, Bill discovered that entertainment was part of the army curriculum. But for the weekly film, that amusement was mostly self-generated. He happily participated in inter-squad baseball games, glee clubs, and airfield dances where local girls could be found taking a spin or two around the floor with a lucky cadet.

Now that he was here at SAAAB, his entertainment scene broadened. It was also fortunate he was so close to Hollywood. Movie stars, musicians, and the sports elite stopped by frequently to entertain the cadets. Soon after arriving at SAAAB, Duke Ellington and his band showed up on base for a rousing concert that had Bill and hundreds of cadets up and out of their seats, dancing and cheering. Bill spotted Joe DiMaggio among the crowd, jumping and jiving with a clutch of WACs and cadets. *How about that,* Bill thought, *the Duke and Joltin' Joe together in one night! It sure is swell of the brass to keep us happy while we sweat and toil.*

He used his first Saturday pass to hop on a Pacific Electric Red Car and head into Hollywood to pay Nana a visit. Their letters back and forth, which had begun once he knew his alphabet, had strengthened their relationship; they truly got to know each other from the pages written and read.

Nana was lithe and limber. She loved to dance too. Her hair had not yet begun to gray; it was a luxuriously deep chestnut tinged with highlights of copper. She dressed in fine custom-tailored suits and loved wild hats, the bigger the feather, the better. She was thrilled when her favorite and only grandchild walked through the door of her Spanish-style adobe apartment. She peppered him with questions, insisting on being brought up to date on what he had been doing since his last letter, and he, doting grandson that he was, took it all in: the love, the questions, her photographs and objects d'art collected from far and wide and tastefully displayed around her home. He enjoyed the bright colors she had painted the walls and noticed that his most recent cadet photo took center stage on her piano. He found the turquoise kitchen especially welcoming after the drab colors the army chose for every room he had been in since leaving Chicago.

"Your place sure is swell, Nana," Bill complimented his grand-mother. "And something smells good! What have you been up to?"

"Oh, I heard what they feed you on that base over there, Dear, and I wanted to make all the foods I know you like," Nana explained. "It was fun for me to save my sugar and butter rations, knowing I'd be feeding you. I even waited for the butcher shop to open and was one of the first customers to grab his best offerings. Boys like you … excuse me … young men like you, training so hard to defend your country, need sustenance." Nana emphasized her point with a swish of a wooden mixing spoon and steered Bill toward the kitchen table where he filled his plate with roasted chicken, his favorite dumplings, and a healthy heaping of boiled peas.

"I know you don't like anything green, William," Nana said as she scooped them from the serving bowl, "but you're going to eat those peas. I shelled them myself!" She had brought out her set of good Homer Laughlin china for the occasion—Georgian in Eggshell Cashmere. As Nana served, Bill watched the pattern of the plate become obscured by chicken and dumplings and peas.

"That's probably enough, Nana," Bill cautioned his grandmother, hovering his hand over his plate.

"You need all the healthy food you can eat these days, what with all the hours of marching and studying and drilling. I know what you boys go through, and that level of effort requires good nutrition!"

"You sure know how to feed a growing cadet, Nana," Bill teased his grandmother. "And I sure do appreciate the effort to support my health!" Nana sat and watched Bill enjoy the meal. They talked about home and family. "Aren't you going to eat?" Bill asked her with a mouth full of dumplings.

"I couldn't eat a bite. I'm too excited!" she answered.

Bill told her about some of the social calls his father had asked him to make while in California. He thought Nana looked conspiratorial when he told her about his next scheduled escapade into Hollywood— evidently a date his father had arranged.

Following the filling meal, Nana went to the kitchen and returned with a fresh-baked cherry pie for dessert. After the warm conversation waned, the close-knit pair said their goodbyes until another weekend pass came Bill's way.

∽

Soon after his visit with Nana, Bill set out to fulfill a request his father had made of him. He was ready to seize the day and invited Danny Shea to join him in the adventure. He remained mysterious, only telling Danny to be certain to wear a clean blouse and uniform; he made sure his own was crisp and well-pressed. He knew where they were going and who they were going to see, but he wasn't about to spoil the surprise by telling his friend the who, what, or where until he had to, but he did drop one hint as they boarded the Red Car bound for Hollywood.

"Danny, we have an appointment with a star of the silver screen," Bill teased.

"Are you on the level?" Danny asked as they boarded the train and took their seats.

Bill rode backward so he could face Danny. He tried not to smile. "I'm telling you, Danny, we're going to meet a movie star."

"You're from Hyde Park. How would *you* know a movie star?" Danny said as he handed his ticket to the Pacific Electric conductor moving down the aisle.

"I don't know this movie star, Danny. Yet," Bill said coyly. "But in about an hour, we *both* can say we do."

"Know *who*, dammit?" demanded Danny, impatiently.

Bill shrugged, "You'll see." Bill could tell the mystery was beginning to frustrate Danny. Fifteen minutes later, the Red Car pulled into downtown Los Angeles. Bill hailed a cab from the stand at the station, and the boys folded themselves into the back seat. A soft voice drifted from behind the steering wheel. "Nice uniforms. Army Air Force, eh? Where're you two headed?"

Wow, a woman cabbie, thought Bill, *and a pretty one at that!* He noticed the upturned nose, the curve of her lips in profile, and raven locks peeking out from her cap. He leaned forward, resting his arms on the back of the cab's bench seat, and handed the cabbie a slip of paper. She glanced into the rearview mirror at Bill, then down at the paper again. *Now I have her attention*, thought Bill, rather pleased with himself for being so mysterious.

"Are you serious?" the cabbie asked, more than a little incredulous.

Watching her in the rearview, Bill couldn't help noticing the color of her eyes; he couldn't describe it exactly—they were almost violet. He found his nickname for her in a flash: Angel Eyes. *Angel Eyes knows the place*, he thought. "Yes," he replied. "I am serious."

"This is one swell part of Los Angeles," commented Angel Eyes. "Are you prepared for something, or someone, so fancy?"

Now she was teasing him, Bill was certain of it.

Danny sat up, intrigued by the cabbie's reaction.

"Can you get me an autograph?" asked Angel Eyes.

"Sure, if you return for us at eight o'clock and take us back to the trolley so we can be back before base curfew," Bill negotiated for another chance to see Angel Eyes.

"You got yourself a deal, flyboy." The cab rolled out of the taxi line and onto the main road.

"What are you trying to pull, Gemmill?" Danny asked, tugging on the back of Bill's uniform jacket.

"You just have to trust me a little while longer," Bill urged his pal as he sat back in his seat.

"And an honest-to-goodness movie star?" Danny couldn't let his curiosity go just yet.

"Relax, Danny. The person you will be meeting is a regular person, like you and me," Bill reassured Danny.

The cabbie looked in her rearview at the two cadets in her back seat, tossed her head, and laughed out loud. Bill laughed along with her, which left Danny to wonder what was so funny.

As Angel Eyes steered the cab down Wilshire Boulevard, the neighborhoods became more luxurious. She drove them down wide palm-lined avenues and into the North Hollywood Hills, where every yard was well-kept. Manicured bushes mixed with cactus, ferns, and wildly colorful blossoms. *I really do like California*, thought Bill. Finally, she eased the cab into a spacious driveway that wound its way to a tasteful and impressive mansion whose sizeable bay window provided an expansive view of the front yard. With the windows of the cab rolled down, Bill found the scent of fresh orange blossoms intoxicating.

"Enjoy yourselves!" Angel Eyes called out as she pulled away. "I'll be back at twenty hundred, sharp!"

Danny whistled as he surveyed the splendid house and the lush grounds. "Hard to believe you know anyone who lives as swank as this, Gemmill!"

"I told you, Danny, I don't. Yet," Bill responded honestly. He was as curious as Danny to see how this side of America lived.

He gathered himself on the landing, took a deep breath, and stepped to the door. He expected to see a butler, but to his joy and surprise, the "Bond Bombshell" herself appeared, wearing cream-colored gabardine trousers and a matching cashmere sweater. She smiled radiantly and smoothed an errant strand of her dark tresses. Even in casual attire, there was no doubt she was a genuine star. No wonder the government had her selling war bonds—who could resist her plea to support the side of the righteous Allied cause?

"Miss Lamour!" Bill managed to say, all the while trying to collect himself and not act too impressed by an honest-to-goodness movie star.

"You must be Bill. Come in, come in!" Dorothy Lamour said graciously, linking her arm through Bill's. He couldn't have peeled the smile off his face even if his life depended on it. He was in the presence of The Jungle Princess herself, famous for her sultry smile and history-making sarong-wearing breakthrough in the popular film. They sashayed into the foyer while Danny, still star-struck and nearly frozen in place, followed a beat behind. William Howard Ross III, Miss Lamour's husband, strode into the foyer to greet the boys as well. He wore tennis slacks and a white short-sleeved shirt. Bill imagined the fellow had just come off the courts. *Probably have tennis courts out back,* he thought. The famous-in-his-own-right advertising executive and former army captain was known throughout Hollywood for cheerfully supporting his screen-star wife and her wartime efforts. Bill didn't catch a word of what the man was saying, and from the deer-in-the-headlights look on Danny's face, he hadn't either. Bill figured Mr. Ross was probably used to guys like him and Danny, young and incapable of speech around celebrities. Miss Lamour, her arm still linked with Bill's, breezed along after her husband, who led them to the drawing room. Bill thought Danny looked like he was in hog heaven; he could have been led anywhere.

"Tell me, how's your father?" Miss Lamour asked Bill, as if they were old friends.

Variety's top female box office star for 1941 is asking about my father, thought Bill before answering, "Last I heard from him, he is doing well."

"Is he still in North Africa?" Miss Lamour sounded truly interested in Bill Sr.'s whereabouts.

"Yes, overseeing German and Italian POWs," Bill replied. *So, she knows Dad is in North Africa. What else does she know about my family?*

"He is such a good man, your dad. It's so reassuring to have him watching over my affairs, even from as far away as Africa. Do you plan to follow in his footsteps and study law after the war?"

"It's all I really want to do," Bill confessed. "Well, after the war anyway." *Is that the best you can do, Gemmill?* he asked himself. *Is that really it? Now is your chance to speak with Dorothy Lamour and this is your response? What else can you tell her?* "Law has been the family profession for centuries, beginning in Scotland," Bill continued, expanding on his initial response. "I like that sense of longevity, and just like my father, I want to do something with my life to help others."

Miss Lamour inclined her head as she listened to Bill. Nodding in approval, she steered her two guests into a casual dining room. A fireplace filled with an immense bouquet of cut flowers in place of the usual log pile dominated the space. The arrangement reminded Bill of a still life he had painted in art class at school in Chicago. He had added irises and peonies in his interpretation because he liked the contrast between the lush roundness of the peony and the slender stalks of the iris, with its burst of blue-purple and teasing yellow stripe. His mother had the painting framed and hung it in her bedroom. Bill still thought of the iris as a happy flower.

Everyone took a seat, with Miss Lamour pulling up the chair closest to Bill. She regaled the group with tales from some movie sets, beginning with one about Tyrone Power: "Then, Tyrone came around the corner of the set, and a star-struck aide ran right into him. A hank of rope had been coiled up on the side, but no one noticed. Tyrone went tumbling over the rope, and he's usually so graceful, but he wasn't hurt in any way. Well, maybe his pride. The aide started laughing … out of nervousness no doubt … poor thing. It was all Tyrone could do not to get angry, but soon, he was laughing along with the rest of the film crew. What choice did he have?"

At dinner, Miss Lamour asked about Bill's childhood, how he and Danny met, and what had made them friends. She had taken the leaves out of the table so they could all sit closer. Danny, still mesmerized, mumbled something about SAAAB and training to fly.

"Aviation cadets! How marvelous!" Miss Lamour declared.

"It feels good to be doing something," Danny said.

"Yes, it does. Like selling war bonds. We do what we can, don't we, Danny?" Miss Lamour offered graciously.

After a dessert of baked Alaska, Mr. Ross offered to show the boys the grounds, to walk off the meal. Being respectful guests, they agreed and followed him out the French doors in the back of the house. Sure enough, a groomed gravel path led them to two tennis courts. "Do either of you play?" Mr. Ross asked.

"Not really," Bill said. "I'm more of a basketball, football kind of guy, although I wouldn't mind trying the sport sometime," he grinned at Mr. Ross.

Danny spoke up. "I've played tennis," he smiled. "A little."

"Bravo!" said Mr. Ross. "It's known as the King's sport, you know. The French court was especially fond of it."

The light was fading rapidly from the sky, a signal it might be time to start working their way to the front of the house. Angel Eyes would be pulling up before long. *Where had the time gone?* Bill wondered. *Have we really been here for five hours?* For him, the day was over all too quickly. Yet, here it was, 1930 hours, seven thirty in the evening. Miss Lamour was waiting for them as they returned to the house and, once again, threaded her arm through Bill's.

"I believe you are about to tell me it's time for you to go, Cadet. And so soon!" she said.

She's read my mind! Bill thought, amazed. They all moved to the front porch, waiting for the cab to arrive. "Yes, unfortunately. Thank you, Miss Lamour, Mr. Ross. Thank you for your hospitality and for sharing your stories."

"It's been our pleasure," said Miss Lamour. "Dinner is the least we can do for two of our finest cadets. I hope you can stop by again before you head out to your next base."

"That would be swell," Bill said, grinning at the prospect of another evening with Dorothy Lamour. "And I'll look forward to it!" Remembering at the last minute his agreement with the cabbie, he spoke up to explain, "Say, Miss Lamour, we made a deal with our cabbie: if I get her your autograph, she'd come pick us up and drive us back to the station. Do you think—"

Miss Lamour cut him off with a lighthearted laugh. "Of course! William, be a dear and go get one of my autographed headshots for Bill, will you? You know where they are." As Mr. Ross went inside to retrieve the autograph, Miss Lamour said, "A lady cab driver, you say?" Before Bill could answer, Mr. Ross was back with the goods. As she handed Bill the signed photograph, she said delightedly, "How marvelous!"

∞

As the boys got out of the cab at the train station, Bill handed the photograph to Angel Eyes.

"Thank you! You are a man of your word," she said, smiling. And, as she handed him his change, Bill noticed a slip of paper among the coins. He looked at her quizzically. "Hey, I thought you might want *my* autograph. Cab driver, elevator operator. It worked for Dorothy Lamour. Maybe it will pay off for me too! Maybe people will want my autograph one of these days!"

On the train, Danny, who had been unusually quiet during the visit, became a chatterbox. He wanted details.

"Dorothy Lamour is the legal ward of my dad. Don't ask me what that means because I don't know. She needed a good attorney. One of Dad's big-shot clients told her Dad was the best," Bill explained as best he could.

"Oh yeah? And who might that have been? The big-shot client, I mean?" Danny pressed Bill.

"Herbie Kay," Bill replied, matter-of-factly, as if everyone's father had clients like Herbie Kay.

"Herbie Kay. *The* Herbie Kay, big-band leader?" Once again, Danny was incredulous.

"Yeah, pretty swell, eh?" Bill grinned.

"What else haven't you told me, Gemmill?" Danny laughed.

∞

Bill's Hollywood adventures weren't over. Nana had a surprise for him. She called one evening, after his visit with Miss Lamour. "Can you get a pass for this coming Saturday?" she asked her grandson.

"I believe so, Nana. What's up?" Bill asked.

"There's a girl I want you to meet," Nana answered. "Make sure you arrive by four o'clock."

Well, this is interesting, Bill thought. *First Dad and now Nana. I wonder if a flair for intrigue runs in my family.*

Saturday arrived and Bill knocked on Nana's door right on time. "Helloooo Nana!" he said as he gathered her in a big hug. She stood on her tippy-toes as he towered over her.

"William, Dear," Nana said as she relaxed into his hug. Her fresh face and youthful demeanor belied her age. As long as he'd known her, she had worn her clothes well: the folds of her deep navy pleated dress fell easily over her hips and ended at her calves. *I love that I am living so close*, he thought, *even if it's only for a little while.*

Bill cut to the chase. "What's all this about a girl you want me to meet? You were so mysterious on the phone; you gave me zero information," he said as he headed for the kitchen. Nana was baking something sweet; the smell enticed him through the kitchen door.

"It's all set," she said, her eyes sparkling as she followed him into the kitchen. She was excited and eager to reveal the details.

"What does she look like and does she want to meet *me* is the big question?" Bill pressed his grandmother for more information as he swiped a fresh-baked chocolate chip cookie cooling on a wire rack.

"As it turns out, one of my closest friends at school, Dorothy Fraser, is now June Allyson's guardian ..."

"June Allyson? *Best Foot Forward* June Allyson?" Bill interrupted. "You are pulling my leg, Nana!" He almost choked on the cookie in his mouth.

"As I was saying, after you wrote to tell me you were going to be training at Santa Ana, I mentioned it to Dorothy, who mentioned it to June's agent, who mentioned it to MGM ..."

"Ah, the chain of command," Bill joked.

They walked back into the living room and took a seat in a wide picture window. Nana continued with her explanation, "... then your cadet photo, you know the one you sent me? Well, that was passed around, and the next thing I knew, June's agent was calling me wanting to set up a date, then the studio, and ... oh, good, right on time!"

Bill followed her gaze out the window. Outside, a shiny black limousine was pulling up to the curb in front of Nana's apartment. Bill smiled. "Nana, what have you done?"

"You'll be wonderful. Go on, dear, enjoy your evening," said Nana as she gently pushed him out the door.

∞

It was a spectacular evening. *I remember my art teacher showing us Maxfield Parrish paintings with skies like this,* Bill observed. When the limo pulled up to June's house, faint stars were beginning to appear. The driver stepped out and stood at the ready by the passenger-side door. Bill knew the drill. He headed for the front door and rang the bell, his head spinning with thoughts. *It's a blind date, right? I've already been in a movie star's home. This should be a piece of cake, right?* Encouraging thoughts ran together in his head. The limousine ride would be another first. Then, the door opened and the quintessential girl-next-door extended her hand toward him in greeting.

"Call me June," Allyson said as she took Bill's outstretched hand and shook it vigorously. *What is it about movie stars opening their own doors?* Bill thought.

The starlet's voice was like fine sandpaper, more smooth than hoarse. There was a charming squeak to it too—a spunky tomboy quality with a perkiness that thrilled Bill. *She truly is an all-American beauty,* he thought as he took her hand in his. "Bill," he replied with a warm smile. "Call me Bill."

MGM had arranged dinner for the couple at the fashionable Restaurant La Rue, and June's agent had insisted on an inside booth for a bit of privacy, yet accessible to members of the press he had hired to document the occasion.

"May we have a table outside; the night is so beautiful," June, rebellious to any restraints placed on her, asked the maître d'. Then she turned to Bill and said, "I had my heart set on dining on the terrace."

Bill didn't care where they ate, whatever made June happy. As they moved onto the terrace, it was already overflowing with people dining al fresco. There was no room for the couple. Besides, June had told him on the limo ride over that the studio had explicitly stated they were to be seated at an inside table. Reluctantly, her desires thwarted, June allowed the maître d' to escort them to a pistachio-and-cocoa-striped booth where they settled in and listened to the chef's recommendations.

The squab was delicious. They both had ordered La Rue's specialty. Neither had tried anything like it before. Bill was encouraged. *We'll reminisce about this down the road*, he imagined. With dinner behind them, and too full for dessert—another first for Bill—the couple was eager to continue the evening elsewhere.

"Let's get out of here," June flashed her famous squinty smile.

"You read my mind," Bill agreed. "Want to go to the Canteen?"

"Now you're reading mine," June laughed. She had a way of making something coy sound innocent.

The driver turned down Sunset Boulevard, heading for the Hollywood Canteen on Cahuenga. Bill and June exchanged questions along the way. Bill found her energy infectious. Do you like to dance? What is it like to audition for a film? What's it like to audition for the Army Air Force? Soon, he felt he had always known the girl every red-blooded G.I. wanted to come home to.

They danced cheek to cheek at the Canteen to tunes of the Harry James Band. Bill couldn't believe his across-the-board brilliant good fortune. Soldiers and sailors cut in to dance with June, all in grand fun. They teased Bill—isn't the Canteen off-limits to cadets? June enjoyed the attention, handling it in her naturally good-natured way.

"Hi Bill!" a familiar voice called out from the side of the dance floor.

"Hello, Miss Lamour!" Bill waved. She was posing for photographs with a sailor, an airman, and a marine. They were grouped around a large silver "V" for victory cutout. The word "Hollywood" trailed down the left arm of the V and "Canteen" down the right. *A war bond opportunity, no doubt*, Bill deduced. He danced on; his hand firm on

June's back, playing the part of the perfect leading man.

After his exchange with Dorothy Lamour, June stepped back and took another look at her date, most definitely intrigued. "Who don't you know in Hollywood, Cadet?" she asked.

Bill shrugged in answer. *This is going well,* he thought. *If only she knew I'm as surprised as she is!*

The night had to end at some point; Bill was due back to SAAAB before midnight. *Just like Cinderella,* he thought, not a little resentfully. He collected June's wrap from the coat-check girl and steered his date toward the door. Just like he had seen on the newsreels, photographers swarmed the couple as they were leaving the Canteen: bulbs flashing, elbows jostling for a better vantage point.

He hadn't considered the press. *This dating a movie star is no joke,* he thought. *How does a person get used to this?* The limousine was waiting close by and the couple managed to get in without being knocked over by the crowd of eager photojournalists. June instructed the chauffeur to drive directly to the train station. When they arrived, June stepped out of the limo, stood on her tippy-toes, and kissed Bill on the cheek—much to his disappointment. He thought a light kiss on the lips would have been the more patriotic thing to do, seeing as how he was off to the war in the not-so-distant future.

For the next several days, Bill bought every movie magazine and tabloid he could find at the BX. He expected to see images of himself with June Allyson, captions below reading, "Movie Starlet Out on the Town with Lucky Aviation Cadet," but no such luck. Apparently, there wasn't a magazine publisher in the business who deemed a cadet's night out with a star noteworthy enough to mention. *Her publicist must be hopping mad,* thought a disappointed Bill. But, what did he know of Hollywood's ways?

∞

Despite his brush with two of California's most famous women, Bill tackled his training with characteristic vigor. He memorized manuals, codes, and protocols and practiced at night with Danny. On 29 July, he received his long-awaited classification.

"Gemmill, you have been classified as a bombardier," the CO began to explain as Bill stood at attention in the commander's office.

Well, this isn't what I've been waiting and training for all these months, Bill thought. His shoulders slumped visibly as he continued listening to his commanding officer.

"You'll receive your orders shortly. You'll probably be sent for bombardier training in Las Vegas," the CO continued, eyeing the cadet standing before him. "I can see this is not what you were expecting, but let me fill you in on some facts. A bombardier's character, integrity, and trustworthiness must be unimpeachable. Bombardiers are entrusted with the carefully guarded secret of the new Norden—we will win the war with that bombsight, mark my words. And do not doubt that the work of the bombardier requires the highest degree of coordination between a keenly alert mind and a sound body. In fact, the success of every mission is dependent upon the bombardier's precision and skill," he added, making a strong case in favor of the importance of this assignment.

Hearing his commander lay it all out was a comfort. Bill stood a little straighter, and the heavy load of disappointment he was feeling lifted. He felt lighter on his feet. And honored. It was dawning on him that he had been tested and deemed worthy of a critical position. *I'm proud to take up any position on a crew.*

"I have no doubt you will make a fine bombardier, Lieutenant," the CO said, ending the conversation.

"I am willing to do whatever it takes, Sir. Thank you, Sir," Bill replied as he saluted the CO and left the office.

∞

When he had the chance to telephone Nana, she listened sympathetically to his news before changing the subject. "There's a rather large envelope waiting here addressed to you," she informed him. "The return address is that of June's agency."

"Well ... please open it," he instructed his grandmother. Bill had been expecting a phone call from the starlet, at the very least. He thought that they had made quite the connection and was hoping for a second date before he shipped out to his next training assignment. *How did I miss asking for her number?* he mused as he listened to the rip and tear of paper on the other end of the phone.

"Oh my, it's a glossy photograph of June Allyson. And she autographed it!" Nana gasped excitedly.

"What does she say? Wait! Don't tell me. I'll come out Saturday. I want to say goodbye anyway. Looks like I'll be in Las Vegas in a week," Bill said, his voice strong and confident.

At Nana's the following Saturday, Bill pulled out the studio photograph from its envelope, and there in the corner, at a jaunty tilt, June had written, "To Bill, with love, June." It was a very large photo. It was a very large autograph. *Women,* wondered Bill. *Will I ever understand women? And here I thought I showed her a swell time.*

Nana watched her grandson's face for clues about his feelings. Bill felt her watching him.

"How do you really feel about missing out on that pilot classification, Bill dear?" she asked lovingly. "I know you had your heart set on it."

Bill was relieved his grandmother hadn't brought up his recent date with June. "Actually, I feel really good about that bombardier classification, Nana," he responded. He told her all the attributes of the bombardier the CO had emphasized. He wanted Nana to understand the importance of the job he was about to do. "It's pretty swell when I think about it, actually."

"I am so happy for you," Nana gushed. "And I'm proud of you too."

On the day of his departure, Bill was up early, packed and ready in less than an hour for the next leg of his journey. *This will be my first specific training*, he thought. *No more covering every possible position. From now on, I will train as a bombardier and all that entails.* He wished his fellow barracks mates well with their next assignments and checked the mail one last time. His mail slot was empty. As it turned out, that autographed studio photo would have to do. He was bound for Nevada and greater things beyond, never to see June Allyson again.

Seven

CROSSHAIRS

Las Vegas Bombardier & Navigator School, Las Vegas, Nevada, October 1943

THE TROOP TRAIN ARRIVED in Las Vegas with little fanfare. It was Bill's shortest trip in a long list of travel by rails thus far: Santa Ana to Las Vegas in a day. Like some military taxi stand, army trucks waited in line at the depot for incoming cadets, then drove them to the base. Bill hopped into the back of the first truck in line and waited for it to fill up. It didn't take long; everyone on that train was going to the same place. After reporting to the training officer, he took advantage of the remaining daylight and went out for a walk—he wanted to get the lay of the land. The sun was warm and the air was brisk: his favorite kind of weather. He found his way across the base, stopping for directions or just for conversation and clarification. He found the place pretty flat, the earth devoid of any sense of undulation and not a tree or hill in sight. Twenty-four hours later, he officially entered gunnery school—a requirement of every officer.

Bill was ready and eager for this next step, largely because of the encouraging words his commanding officer at Santa Ana had used at the time of his classification. And it was no small consolation knowing that when it came time for him to bomb the enemy, he would be the one flying the plane. As the bomber approached the target, it was the bombardier who took control of the plane for the duration of the actual bomb run, through the device known as the Norden, a sort of early computer with gears and clutches and gyros that required precision computations. Upon dropping the payload, the bombardier then relinquished control back to the pilot. So, in a way, he'd have plenty of chances to fly an aircraft. It might not be from the flight deck of a jet fighter, but a great big Liberator would do nicely.

Bill had heard the skinny on the big bird, or "Heavy," as the B-24 was known in bomb crew circles, both in Santa Ana and newsreels. He also knew the bomber was most famously known as "The Liberator." Apparently, the founder of Consolidated Aircraft Corporation, Major Reuben Fleet, heard Edith Brocklebank, the English nanny under his employ, refer to the aircraft as "The Liberator" in a discussion he was having with his wife, Dorothy, and Edith. Major Fleet liked the moniker, and the name stuck.

Bill quickly learned that gunnery school wasn't just about learning to fire the big guns, or which projectiles to drop when, or which incendiaries to use when the target called for "walking" the bombs: dropping the ordnance in timed and rapid succession to cover a larger target area. It also wasn't just learning how to man a powered turret or a flexible-mount machine gun. The school was in keeping with the rest of his training: discipline, discipline, discipline. *If gunnery school requires more attention and study*, he thought, *just wait until I get to bombardier-navigator school.* The marching never ended regardless of the base. He was marched to and from classes, a specialty of every camp he had attended thus far in his journey, and rather than a barracks, he was bivouacked in a canvas tent, roughing it for the first time in his life. After his first night sleeping on a cot, Bill was grateful this phase of his training was only for two weeks.

Training began on the ground with shotguns. Cadets then moved on to shotguns mounted on the backs of trucks. Bill enjoyed standing in the bed of the truck while it was being driven through a course, shooting at targets along the way. A week of that and he was up in a bomber, shooting at targets being towed by training aircraft. *At last,* he thought, *I'm working from the air.* It was dangerous work.

"You've heard the stories," a cadet from his barracks said, turning to engage Bill on his first run. The kid had wild, thick black eyebrows and a head of hair to match. Bill immediately tagged him as "Wolf Man" and felt empathy for the barber who had to keep that head trimmed to army standards and regulations.

"What stories?" Bill asked.

"You know, the stories of airmen in gunnery training being killed," Wolf Man replied.

"Well, yeah," Bill answered. "It's a lot of pressure knowing you've got to hit the target 22 percent of the time or you're out!"

"Yeah, that pressure is definitely the culprit," agreed Wolf Man. "The week before you got here, one pilot crept too close to the target plane. The collision took out the light bomber, the pilot, and the trainee. The day you arrived, a trainee went ahead and shot his round, even though he didn't have a clear view. Killed the pilot dragging the practice targets."

Bill felt a little edgy hearing about the spate of bad luck he'd walked into. He decided to change the subject.

"I got my schedule from the training officer when I reported for duty. I can see we're going to be kept mighty busy."

"Yeah, it's all business now, with maybe a little goofing off," the cadet laughed.

"My class schedule is packed," Bill lamented. "Higher math and physics aren't going to be easy, but the rest of the courses sound more than manageable. Do you have a favorite class so far?"

"I'm drawn to meteorology and bombsight maintenance," Wolf Man replied.

"It's a wonder they leave us time to get upstairs and practice," Bill said, pointing his thumb to the sky. "What do you think of the instructors here?"

Wolf Man thought for a moment, then said, "I'd say they're top-notch. Sure, they drive us hard, but that's supposed to be how we learn, right?"

"Right!" Bill agreed.

After gunnery school, the cadets moved on to aerial training. Ground school had been fun, but Bill was a lot happier in the air. When he wasn't shooting at a target or strafing a practice plane, he studied. He caught on early to the instructors' penchant for tripping up the trainees on their aircraft recognition skills and doubled down, acing the name of every aircraft, marked and unmarked, Axis or Allied. He refreshed his codes, both Morse and army, and learned about various bombs and how to defuse them.

He was fascinated with the Norden: how it worked and its precision. He understood why the US had to protect this knowledge. The Axis didn't have anything like it, which gave the US a strategic advantage. If it fell into the enemy's hands, the Allies might not win the war.

The day Bill first faced the challenge of the pressure chamber, he was one of twenty bombardier trainees crowded into the small room.

He experienced no adverse effects from the pressure, but sixteen of the trainees passed out.

"I got a little dizzy, sitting for twenty minutes at twenty thousand feet with no oxygen," he confessed before they headed to the mess hall for dinner. "But I didn't pass out."

"How'd you do at thirty-eight thousand feet?" Wolf Man asked Bill as he followed him out the door to dinner. They were joined by another cadet walking into the mess.

"Same, only ... less dizzy, actually," Bill answered, wondering why he was less lightheaded at the higher altitude.

"How was the gas?" Wolf Man pressed on, a sly smirk on his lips.

"Have you ever been in the chamber when twenty guys let fly at once?" Bill asked, laughing loudly.

"Hey, any gas will expand at thirty-eight thousand feet. You have to get rid of it somehow," the bunkmate said, laughing out loud, his eyes tearing up at the thought.

The cadet who had joined them chimed in. "I never want to go into another pressure chamber again!" he declared. "I blew lunch in there!"

Bill winked conspiratorially at Wolf Man. They didn't know each other well, but Bill deduced neither of them would let a little vomit get in their way.

∞

Immediately following gunnery school, with its sparse aerial training, Bill entered bombardier and navigator school (B&N School) on the same base in Nevada. There, he learned the art of bombsighting. It was a delicate balance between lining up the Norden's crosshairs, then calculating wind speed and drift. While he was busy computing, he also needed to feed airspeed, wind direction, altitude, and angle of drift to the navigator. Considering that the outcome of any mission would be dependent upon his accuracy, it was imperative he get those numbers right. The words of his base commander at Santa Ana came back to him: "the trustworthiness of the bombardier." The bombardier also served as the armament officer on the aircraft. In addition to knowing everything about the bombs the B-24 would be carrying, he'd also have to know everything about the ten Browning machine guns as well as the guns on the turrets. *I will be busy*, Bill thought.

The classrooms were rough—barely heated in the winter and stifling hot in the summer. Since Bill arrived in the fall, he figured there was a good chance he would experience the winter scenario. It might have been October, but he was sweating through his classes. He felt like he was being cooked.

"So, Gemmill," a cadet Bill called "Philly" said as they were dressing for the day, "did you always want to be a bombardier?" Philly was Louis Engleman, Bill's closest friend in class. He was also assigned to the same barracks. Bill called him Philly as a nod to the kid's hometown of Philadelphia.

"Not at all. I was going to be a fighter pilot, like Eddie Rickenbacker," Bill answered, fidgeting with his tie.

"So, what happened?" Philly asked, obviously wanting to know more.

Reflecting on preflight, Bill hoped it would be the last time he had to spell it out for someone.

"Well, I managed to clip the wing of the AT-10 I was flying. I was lining up to land, and my right wing connected with the roof of the hangar. It ripped the wing right off," Bill said, demonstrating with his hands the position and trajectory of the aircraft.

"It's hard to realize you've just made the biggest mistake of your life," Philly commiserated.

"Yes, it is. I had nailed everything else, the takeoff, the taxiing," Bill agreed, "but landing was always difficult for me." *Now I'm practically a bombardier*, he thought. He was learning everything he could to become the best, an ace bombardier even. He had the nerves for it, and especially the eyes. Ever since he was a little kid, he'd been able to see for miles and find the tiniest detail. He figured that ability would stand him in good stead once overseas.

"How about you, Louis? Did you have bombardier in mind when you signed up?" Bill asked his friend.

"Actually, yes!" Louis answered. "But that's probably because my brother is a bombardier over in England. It's a tough position, so much responsibility riding on your calculations, but he loves it. He's always going on about it in his letters to me."

Talk like this energized Bill: he was chomping at the bit to get going already. But he still had weeks to go. Most of the guys in his barracks had already been in Vegas for at least a month.

∞

Bill had met a lot of pilots, navigators, and bombardiers at preflight, and many of them were here in Vegas with him. He knew them well enough to nod a greeting when they passed each other or to chat when they sat next to each other in class or at mess. Mostly, they'd discuss studies like the mechanics and physics of flight and how tough their most recent exams had been. Like every other cadet in Las Vegas, Bill endured ten hours in a flight simulator, dubbed "The Blue Box." He decided if the crudeness of the structure didn't put you off flying, and the simulated deep dives and steep angles in the thing didn't have a similar effect, you might just make it as an airman yet.

Perhaps because it was the next-to-last stop in the string of training camps before assignment to a crew, Bill found there was less downtime here. The thought didn't disturb him; he was determined to earn his lieutenant bars, and he wasn't afraid of hard work. Besides, he always managed to find a way to have fun. Vegas was no exception.

His biggest laugh arrived each payday when he'd cash in his military chits for coins at The Hotel Last Frontier, one of the casinos cropping up on what would become "The Strip." He'd stuff all of the coins into one of the pants pockets of his khaki uniform, then walk out of the casino. Once on the sidewalk, he'd purposely list to the coin-heavy side, as if this was a normal way to navigate the world. Passersby looked him up and down, and he'd politely touch the tip of his cap and smile as if all was right with the world.

"You are too much, Gemmill," Philly said as he laughed at Bill's antics, encouraging him all the more. The foolery was his coping mechanism, his way of lightening any tension or drama. He prided himself on being able to find humor in almost any situation.

∞

Las Vegas proved to be a real boost for Bill because it was here where he met a man of inestimable influence: Sgt. Neville Kinzie. Sergeant Kinzie saw something in this nineteen-year-old lad, a talent or, perhaps, a gift of perfect vision and quick reflexes. Add to that the fact that the boy reveled in his Scottish heritage, which greatly pleased the transplanted Scotsman.

Neville Kinzie was the Norden bombsight instructor at Las Vegas Gunnery School. It was his duty to teach his students everything he knew about the art of raining terror down to the ground. Bill thoroughly enjoyed learning from Kinzie—or "Mac," as the cadets referred to the tall, brawny instructor—and his distinctive Scottish brogue. And Mac enjoyed keeping a close eye on all his charges and seeking out the talented in each new batch of cadets. He kept Bill and a handful of others within his sphere of influence, often revealing more nuanced details of the analog computer.

Bill quickly ticked through all the lessons his mentor had taught him in just a few short weeks: how the Norden was hard to use and how it broke down a lot what with all the gyres and pulleys and ball-bearings. He learned that the most important thing the bombardier needed to do, above all else, was to make and keep eye contact with the target, which, in the clear skies above Nevada, wasn't a challenge. Mac stressed that the experience in Europe or the Pacific—with their skies alive with smoke and FLAK—would be a lot more challenging. The aircraft defense cannon, Flugabwehrkanone in German, or FLAK as it came to be widely known throughout World War II, was treacherous, and once up in the air in the thick of it, unrelenting. The Nazis filled missile shells with shards of sharp metal fragments, which were loaded into the cannon and shot above the target. The shells detonated at altitude, creating a field of treachery for Allied aircraft to maneuver through, often with tragic results. It was a terrifying deterrent.

"Knowing how to find the target, that's your biggest challenge," the B&N instructor was fond of saying. "Correct calculations and a keen eye for the unexpected are your greatest assets, Gemmill."

The numbers associated with the bombsight staggered Bill's imagination: each of the ninety thousand Nordens cost the US $14,000. They were considered so valuable that the Army Air Corps devised a security protocol for their delivery: they were escorted to the bombers by armed guards—wrists cuffed to the black, custom-made leather case containing an incendiary device, should the case be tampered with or the bomber shot down. Bombardiers were made to swear an oath to protect the device with their life.

It was an unwieldy and heavy thing, the Norden bombsight:

a network of clutches, drives, and levers, all manufactured in two connecting charcoal-gray parts. The first time Bill held one in its case, the heft of it surprised him. It weighed more than forty pounds when fully assembled. Maneuvering the telescope eyepiece into position over a small window on the bomb deck took a deft hand. Bill would sight his target via a mirror that tracked the target electronically as the plane approached it. He would wait until, according to the calculations he fed into the analog computer, both the vertical and horizontal crosshairs were aligned before simulating a bomb drop.

The crosshairs determined the exact point, some twenty miles more or less from the target, at which to release the bomb load. This was the IP, the initial point, and from here on, the formation had to fly straight and level and take no evasive action with the bomb bay doors open—a most vulnerable moment, to say the least. This was the time the bombardier would take over the plane for the duration of the bomb run. Even in simulation, it was nerve-wracking.

Bill learned that not every bombardier had a Norden—those went to lead and deputy lead bombardiers. The other bombardiers in the formation watched for the lead bombardier's payload to drop before flipping a switch that released their bombs. The switch was called a toggle, and the bombardier, a "toggelier" for the moment.

In early December, Bill started thinking about going home for Christmas. *Wouldn't that be swell?* he thought dreamily. His father had returned from North Africa and been reassigned to a post with the War Department in Washington, DC. Bill planned to start out on 15 December for a brief furlough to DC—his parents had bought a house in Bethesda to be close to Bill Sr.'s work with the Army Air

Corps—before heading to Albuquerque and advanced bombardier school. But all plans to spend the holidays at home evaporated when he received orders to report to Kirtland Field—the "West Point of the Air"—on 24 December.

"I felt bitter towards the army and all that goes with it at first, but it just can't be helped," Bill wrote Frances, resigned to his fate. He asked his mother not to take it too hard. "Think of it this way," he wrote encouragingly. "The next time you see me, I'll be a first lieutenant!" As this was a joint letter, he reminded his father not to forget: "GEMMILL & GEMMILL, ATTYS. AT. LAW." He pleaded with them to save up their money because more than anything, he wanted them to come to his bombardier graduation in New Mexico. "Dad, will you pin on my bars, and Mom, will you put on my wings and insignia?"

∞

On a most nondescript, average day, with only a handful of cadets in attendance, Bill graduated B&N School. Having completed all of his courses, gunnery, bombardier, and navigator with high marks, he was moving on. *At least the sun is shining*, Bill thought as he stood in formation on a chill day for a brief presentation parade. He had fallen asleep to thunder and lightning, the sky an impure purple. That morning was a blaze of light, the clouds streaked the sky pink and orange, and a dusting of snow lay softly on the ground.

The flight officer called the parade to begin, and the graduates began to march their last march in Vegas. The CO stood at attention as they moved past, as did the handful of officers behind him. A frosty wind picked up and sent Bill's squadron flag flapping wildly. When his turn came, he stepped up to the CO who handed him his insignia and certificate, and that was that. *Definitely less pageantry than at preflight*, he noticed, *with its parade and significantly larger crowd*. He now reveled in the classification of bombardier. He was prepared for Albuquerque. All that was left for Bill to accomplish was advanced bombardier school: his last fifteen weeks of training would lead to his commission of first lieutenant.

Eight

ROMANCE ON SANDIA PEAK

*Advanced Bombardier School, Kirtland
Army Air Field, Albuquerque,
New Mexico, December 1943*

ON A COLD AND CLOUDY Christmas Eve, Bill reported to the Army Air Corps Advanced Bombardier School at Kirtland Field in Albuquerque, New Mexico. He had always thought of the Southwest as perpetually warm, but his time in Texas had proved him wrong: even Texas could be cold in winter. He rubbed his hands together to thaw his frozen digits. *Why didn't I remember to keep my gloves on the top of my duffel?* he wondered. *At least I thought to keep my wool uniform cap handy.* He hated hats, but this time he made an exception.

Kirtland was overrun with young bombardiers, everyone missing their first Christmas away from friends and family. Bill wiled away some time waiting in line for his bunk assignment, talking with a boy from Colorado.

"Geez, am I going to miss my mother's roast leg of lamb, our family's traditional Christmas meal," Bill said, his mouth watering at the thought of the spread.

"I love lamb. We raise tasty sheep in Colorado," said the Colorado Kid. The Kid's words were a cloud of crystallized vapor as they hit the air, and his uncovered ears were red as fresh roses.

"Must be all that high mountain air!" Bill responded, still imagining the aroma from the meat roasting in his mother's oven.

"Did you hear the president's fireside chat last night?" the Colorado Kid asked Bill.

"No, I was traveling by troop train all night. What did he have to tell us?" Bill responded, sincerely interested.

"He said that General Dwight D. Eisenhower is going to command the Allied invasion of continental Europe during the coming year."

"So, looks like FDR believes this war is going to carry on a while," Bill mused.

"Looks like," said the Colorado Kid with a tilt of his head.

"This maybe sounds strange but I sure will be disappointed if this war ends before our training does," Bill confessed.

"Oh boy, that isn't strange at all! I've been worrying about the same thing for months!" replied the Kid.

"Well then," said Bill, "we just have to light a fire under our superior officers and tell them they have two patriots here ready to get a move on!" Both boys belted out loud laughs, which caused the quartermaster to look up from his papers and glare in their direction.

For the first three weeks, Bill diligently pursued more ground school activities. He drew equipment, field manuals, logs, Mercators, bombing tables, notebooks, calibration cards, and maps from the quartermaster. For eight hours a day, he was plied with an aerial education on the ground. When the day came to take to the air, he was excited to put into practice his newly gained tricks of the trade. He had large ideas and was eager to crawl into the nose of an AT-11, complete with navigation facilities. He planned a 0–0 mission: zero Allied casualties, zero aircraft down. While airborne, he juggled pilotage logs, spun computers, wondered which state he was in and, lastly, hoped he was still in the States. After six weeks, he dropped his first bomb. He gazed patiently at the target—a shack—awaiting its destruction. *My calculations must be faulty*, he thought as the first bombs landed off range. He recalculated his numbers, and as the training bomber circled around for another run at the target, his bombs hit square on or close enough to it most of the time.

The brass knew the boys were restless at this stage, so close to being part of a crew, closer still to the perils of war. They encouraged the boys to take downtime on the weekend, to air out their over-taxed brains. Bill's class of students had been studying and training intensely for nearly twelve months.

Now that he was receiving monthly pay, Bill was ready to spend it on something. Or someone. He needed a break, time to refresh his brain cells. On one particular weekend, he caught a ride into Albuquerque with a couple of flight instructors who were headed for the Old Town Square.

∞

The Jeep skidded to a halt in front of the canteen, and the instructors jumped out. As they peeled off, Bill hopped over the side and surveyed his surroundings. A sign indicating The University of New Mexico beckoned, and he followed. Soon, he found himself on what could only be sorority row; every house flew a Greek-lettered flag of one sister organization or another to his Deke house. He considered this to be as good as any other day to get acquainted with one of these women's groups. As he made his way down the street, he couldn't help but notice how quiet the well-kept front yards were, especially for a Friday afternoon. Feeling spontaneous, he decided to knock on one of the houses' doors and see who answered. He chose the Kappa Kappa Gamma House.

"Hello!" Bill said to the woman who answered the door. "My name is Bill Gemmill. I'm in advanced bombardier training at Kirtland. I was a Deke at DePauw before I activated my deferment, and I thought I'd stop in to pay my respects," Bill offered in his most courteous manner.

"DePauw, you say? Fine school, fine school. Come in. I'm Mrs. MacMurray; the late Mr. MacMurray was also from the Midwest."

Mrs. MacMurray led him through a foyer lined with muted impressionist prints and shapely vases of cut sunflowers. The orange-yellow glow from the large buds spilled their saffron light into the hallway. The chaperone guided Bill into a drawing room, indicating they should sit in chairs that looked remarkably similar to the two in his own foyer back home, which made him feel briefly nostalgic. The clear-eyed widow listened politely while Bill elaborated about his training and how he was eager to bomb the hell out of Germany or wherever they might send him.

"All the men in my family have been in the law profession. That's what I'll do after the war: finish college and go to law school. Then I'll join my father's law firm," Bill shared, voicing his intentions for when he returned to civilian life.

"So, you have plans for after the war. That's a good thing," Mrs. MacMurray nodded approvingly. "We like to support our boys any way we can and want to see you all come home and resume your lives."

The windows filtered the last of the afternoon sunlight onto pale blue walls. From his vantage point by the oversized fireplace, Bill watched several sorority sisters glide by and slip a solid surveying eye his way. A lanky coed sauntered into the sitting room. She walked deliberately, purposely avoiding eye contact with Bill or the house mother. Still, Bill figured she had to be curious about him, had to wonder about his purpose at her sorority house. Why else had she come into the room?

She looked up for a brief moment and their eyes met, his so gloriously blue and hers a grounding hazel. The coed chose to sit near the window, folding herself casually into an overstuffed chair. She picked up a *Ladies' Home Journal* and began flipping through the pages. Bill felt compelled to break the ice and sought her out, talking across the room.

"Hello," he directed his salutation to the silent green-eyed enigma. She turned her gaze on him: it was challenging, territorial, and unsettling. She glanced away at a few friends who had entered the room, making no reply.

After several minutes, Mrs. MacMurray decided Bill was harmless and left the room, moving on to other duties.

A sultry brunette approached him. "Thirsty?" she asked Bill.

"Now that you mention it," Bill answered, and a tray of Coca-Colas materialized. He chose a cold bottle of the sweet liquid and air-toasted the room and the brunette with it. "This sure is swell," Bill said as a thank you.

More girls came into the room. It was as if the whole sorority had been waiting for this moment. A bit of normalcy in an uncertain time for the country and for the coeds.

"Do you like to dance?" the brunette asked enticingly, swaying her hips side to side as she switched on the record player and placed the needle down on the spinning acetate plate.

"I love to dance!" Bill jumped to his feet and began moving his feet to "I've Got a Gal in Kalamazoo," courtesy of Glenn Miller. Bill knew the words to the song by heart, too, and started singing along. Within minutes, ten Kappas and one lucky cadet had a dance party going.

The lanky coed remained seated at first, until the beat got to her. Her toes couldn't stop tapping, and she was up and dancing with a couple of other girls before the tune ended. In his best Hollywood style, Bill made it over their way. He bopped into their circle and, for a moment, the statuesque girl with the hazel eyes forgot herself and let go her reserve.

That Friday ended all too quickly when Bill looked at his Bulova.

"Time for me to get back to base," he announced reluctantly. They'd already danced to several Dorsey, James, and Shaw tunes—"Begin the Beguine" was an absolute must, as was "Tangerine," and what better song to end an impromptu afternoon with than "You Made Me Love You"? Several of his dance partners escorted him to the door; he was encouraged that the silent one was among them. He walked to the square and caught a ride with a passing Jeep heading back to Kirtland. The image of the lanky girl with the mysterious eyes lingered on his mind the whole ride home.

∞

Bill found himself back at The University of New Mexico the following weekend. The second week of the New Year had warmed some, and now, at forty-seven degrees and sunny, it was downright balmy. As he approached the sorority house, Bill saw a few familiar faces and was inspired by their smiles. Even Mrs. MacMurray was cooperative.

"Hi Mrs. M!" Bill said with a smile when she answered the door. "I wonder, can I please speak to that girl who came into the drawing room last week? The tall blond?"

"Oh, do you mean Phyllis?" Mrs. MacMurry replied.

"She never told me her name, but, yes, if that's the girl you remember," Bill said.

Phyllis, it seemed, was at home right there in Albuquerque for the weekend. As Bill headed down the walk, his newfound friend called out, "Roberts! Phyllis's last name is Roberts!"

"Right! Thanks!" Bill called over his shoulder. A few inquiries and a short walk later, he was at the Roberts's front door. On the way over, Bill had been toying with what exactly he wanted to say to the girl he found so irresistible. *She has only two choices: to ask you in or to tell you to take a hike*, he told himself.

Bill lifted the brass lion knocker and let it drop hard on the door panel, once, twice, and then twice again. Footsteps sounded in the inside hallway, then the door opened.

When Phyllis saw the fair-eyed visitor, she tossed back her head and laughed, and Bill forgot everything he had planned to say. "Whatever brings you out here, Lieutenant?" she smiled politely.

As if she has to ask. Bill left the remark unspoken. "Uh, good question. I think maybe we got off on the wrong foot."

Her attention trailed after her voice, "Oh, I see ..."

"Let me guess," Phyllis recovered. "Mrs. MacMurray told you where to find me?"

"Ah, your house mother and I are in cahoots and found out," Bill feigned regret.

Phyllis laughed again and opened the door wide. "Come in, come in. You've come this far. We can't have you walk all the way back to the square without hot chocolate for all your trouble. I was just making some."

"Actually," Bill said, "I was thinking we might take a stroll. How can you stay inside on a morning like this? Unless it's too cold for you, of course." He swung his arms wide, as if to take hold of the cool, sunny day.

"We'll have to come back so you can meet my parents."

"That'll be swell!"

"Dad, I'm going for a walk! Tell Mom I'll be back in a little while!" Phyllis called out as she grabbed a marine blue wool coat and a pair of matching gloves.

"Uh-huh." The voice that came down the hall was all leather and sagacity.

The sun's warmth rose through the desert cold. Anything in its path that was covered in frost—grasses and tree limbs, the sides of wooden railings—released its thin blanket of ice in a gauzy breath. Bill and Phyllis moved in tight formation, hands and shoulders brushing from time to time. After a while, they retraced their steps, but when they reached her house, Bill explained that it was probably best that he head back to base.

"But what about Dad? He'll want to meet the man who got me out of the house!"

She was being polite; Bill liked that. They reached the graceful entry, done in hacienda style—all arches and adobe. The skeletons of bougainvillea climbed the curved gateway.

"Shall I call again?" Bill asked. "Your folks can size me up then."

To his surprise, she agreed. "I'd like that very much."

"Then, tell your mom and dad that I'll be back." Bill turned and started his walk to town. He nearly skipped as he reviewed the outcome of his gamble. How lucky can a guy get?

∞

Mr. Roberts had taken to Bill immediately and soon made it a habit to lend Bill his car when he had a full tank of gas and ration coupons for a refill. The couple would go for drives into the mountains, the cool air refreshing Bill. With Phyllis's head on his shoulder and the radio breathing tunes from Glenn Miller, Sammy Kaye, or the Dorsey Brothers, Bill could dream for a while. Once atop Sandia Peak, they had fierce snowball fights and created snow and ice sculptures. On one outing, Bill fashioned a seven-foot Mohawk brave, watered him down, and let him freeze solid. Much to their amazement, a good portion of the sentinel was intact and waiting for them on their next visit.

Bill's favorite thing to do was to take Phyllis dancing. Moving to the beat and rhythm with his girl in his arms was the closest thing to bliss he could imagine. A musician himself, playing drums and standup bass, Bill appreciated the subtle nuance of a riff here and there. The notes and bars seeped into his pores. He pictured the music as it scatted along his bloodstream, engaging a genetic code that inspired him to move with the beat. Phyllis seemed to enjoy a rollicking swing, too, or the acceptable sensuality of a slow languorous number. If she only knew how unnerved he was when they danced cheek to cheek.

The days of training and classroom work intensified. Inspired by his commitment to the cause, Bill was testing near or at the top of each class, but an inner voice was growing louder, cautioning him: *Phyllis is fun and sweet, but you have a greater priority*. He wondered what the heck he was doing, letting himself fall so deeply when he was heading off to war.

∽

"So, graduation is coming up," Bill said on one of their last weekends together. "Will you be there?"

"I wouldn't miss graduation for all the world," Phyllis answered kindly.

In an attempt to bring their time together to a heartfelt close, Bill lifted her chin gently to meet his gaze. "When I leave Albuquerque, I'll be assigned to a crew immediately and sent overseas soon after. If I'm given time to see you and say goodbye, I will."

"There's still time for fun before you leave, isn't there, Bill? Mom and I are planning a graduation party for you and your friends."

"Great idea, Phyl. A party it is then, with dancing and all the food we flyboys are going to miss when we get to our assigned bases!" Bill said, sounding much happier than he felt.

For now, he would dig into the last of his classes and enjoy these fast-dwindling days in the Sandias and the enthralling scent of Shalimar lifting from Phyllis's soft skin.

∞

The days hurried along, news of the war continued to reach the cadets, and Bill became increasingly eager to seek his destiny. He'd been voted cadet commander again, and he took his duties seriously, striving to set as good an example as possible. No more saluting the Coca-Cola delivery man! He had learned early on at Vegas and again at Kirtland that a bombardier must have more than the ability to drop bombs correctly. As an aerial gunner, he had drilled on stoppages and malfunctions on the heavy .50-caliber machine guns and could strip down and reassemble them blindfolded.

Calisthenics, wind sprints, and scaling the obstacle course in gas masks continued. Football, volleyball, and other assorted games and exercises kept the cadets in top physical shape. As precision training drew to a close, he knew that he'd soon be shipping out. The war would be a test of his courage, training, and commitment. Reflecting on the weeks and months of molding himself into a proper airman, Bill thought, *I've made it. I've made it through everything they could throw at me.*

∞

It was with great pride that Bill stepped onto the podium on graduation day—the sixth cadet graduating class of 1944 at Kirtland. He was now a fully commissioned officer in the Army Air Corps. Despite the warming April air, an excited chill raced along his spine as he heard his name announced, with honors. He had envisioned his father pinning on his first lieutenant bars and his mother attaching his bombardier insignia on his collar, but that had been a hopeful dream on his part—his father was far too tied up with his work with the Provost Marshall General in Washington, and his mother felt obliged to remain by her husband's side. Being in high spirits, he chose to look at the positives: he had hope and youth on his side. He had Phyllis, for a moment longer, there on the parade ground, beaming as she pinned his silver wings and insignia into place.

The graduation party at the Roberts's was bittersweet; each friend he had made would soon be off to far-flung places. *Heck, I'm excited too!* he realized. *We'll all be entering another world.* He had stuck to his plan and gone through all the steps—OK, falling so hard for Phyllis had definitely been *unplanned*—but he worked hard for his wings and commission. Scanning the room, he found himself assessing his feelings about the past fifteen weeks and was surprised to realize he was relieved to be heading out.

"Thanks for everything, Phyl," he said as the party drew to a close. "This was a swell send-off."

"It was good for us too, Bill," Phyllis answered as she walked him toward the door where they paused and embraced. Looking up to meet Bill's gaze, Phyllis suggested she'd come to the depot to see him off on Monday.

"That's OK, we're leaving before first light and … it's better this way, don't you think?" Bill offered. Phyllis nodded in agreement. He was surprised to find he was already moving on. His focus was locked on his immediate future, and Phyllis, her scent of Shalimar notwithstanding, was moving into his past. There was room for one last kiss, their final goodbye to the great love that might have been, before Bill disengaged and walked out the door. He had one day to pack his duffel bag, write a letter home, and maybe even relax.

Dawn the next day was streaked with those now familiar western stratus clouds tinged with dark lavender and an ever-brightening pinkish orange. Military personnel swarmed the lobby of the old Alvarado Hotel, the air static with a mass of expectations. Standing across from the train depot, taking in the scene, Bill reflected on last night's party and beyond, to his experiences with the movie stars of Hollywood and their glamour. He was grateful for the taste of the swell life, but he found it wanting. His was a mission that had nothing in common with the high life. He sauntered over to the rail platform as the troop train pulled slowly into the station. As the newly minted first lieutenants grouped into their respective units—for they would travel as units from here on—Bill followed and stored his gear while considering the reality of training: what it meant and what it required. At every stop along his way to war, every new base of training, he'd checked in with himself and found his commitment to fight the war reinvigorated.

Once on the train, Bill chose a seat by the window so he could gaze out toward the horizon and take in the scene. The growing morning light spilled onto the spring desert. It reflected in his eyes and, for a moment, all he could see was a bright spot, as if someone had taken a flash photograph of him. When the spot faded, he turned to scan the crowd of officers, families, and well-wishers milling about on the platform, and thought, *Look out, Hitler, here I come. I'm going to help sink the Axis.*

Into The

Wild Blue

Nine

BOMBARDIER TO CREW

Albuquerque to Biggs Field,
El Paso, Texas, May 1944

IT WAS BACK TO TEXAS for Bill, by way of Nebraska. He had been assigned to his first crew and they were assembling in the Cornhusker State. When he arrived, he reported to the flight officer, who in turn directed Bill to a barracks. Four young men stood outside, each one dressed in identical khakis.

"Are you the bombardier?" one of the officers asked, one hand resting on his hip and the other tipping back his crush cap.

"Sure am, I got here as quickly as the Air Corps allowed," Bill said with a smile before introducing himself to his fellow officers. He was excited; these boys were going to be his family for the duration of the war. The young officers nodded their recognition and shook hands as they introduced themselves. The entire exchange took less than five minutes. He wasn't surprised; they appeared to be as excited and ready for action as he was.

Bill understood the sense of impatience he felt here, the urgency. He was ready to roll, too, to get over there—wherever "there" would be—and do something to bring an end to the war. Perhaps that's why he and his new crew were given a mere forty-eight hours to board a trainer B-24 and get up in the air. Their most immediate task was to come together as a crew. When those two days were up, the crew hopped aboard a transport plane for the flight to Biggs Field in El Paso, Texas.

Bill's crew arrived at Biggs Field by early afternoon. Almost immediately, they were airborne for a practice run with Major Cavanaugh, the director of training. The major was tasked with observing each member of the crew and assessing how they handled their jobs. The run proved fateful for the pilot. Halfway through the flight, squirming in agony, the pilot confessed to the major that he was miserable due to a case of hemorrhoids. How he had gotten this far was a mystery to Cavanaugh, who wasted no time in dismantling the crew. Once they were back on the ground, he gathered all ten men around the aircraft.

"Boys, the members of this crew are being reassigned. I can't tell you much at the moment, but I'll send for each of you as soon as we receive a request for your position," the major explained. Bill wondered if the disbelief he was seeing in nine other faces reflected his own.

∞

The next morning, after a shower and a shave, Bill stepped outside of his barracks, still adjusting to the fact that his plans had changed. He was beginning to consider breakfast when, as if on cue, a Jeep drove up full-tilt and the driver motioned him over. He was tan and blond and slim, and by the looks of it, his voice full of drawl. Bill noticed captain's bars on the shoulder of the uniform.

"Hop in! Major Cavanaugh wants to see you," the driver called to him amiably. Bill sprang into the passenger side.

"By the way, I'm your new pilot," the driver revealed over a grind of gears, then floored the gas pedal, the Jeep's tires leaving a cloud of gravel and dust in their wake.

"Drive on, Pappy!" Bill grinned because that's what you call your pilot. He thought as he held onto his cap, *Pappy, as in the leader of the group, the father figure.* Things were moving fast—especially at the moment. Like in a Looney Tunes cartoon, a pile of dust hung suspended where the Jeep had been seconds before.

"Before my reputation precedes me, let me tell you that you'll be my third bombardier," Captain's Bars called over the whine of the Jeep's motor.

"What happened to the first and second?" asked Bill, wondering what he had gotten himself into.

"I fired 'em!" the pilot roared with laughter. All Bill could do with that revelation was laugh along with his new pilot.

As they came to the large, buff-colored clapboard building that housed the director's office, the pilot slowed just enough to park the Jeep, kicking up more dust. They walked up a few steps and through the door. The scent of fresh paint cloaked the corridor. Bill dabbed lightly at a glob of celery green coagulating at the edge of a wall. He figured the building had been a tad shabbier earlier in the day; there were still some areas sorely in need of a fresh coat of paint. They reached Major Cavanaugh's office. A highly polished brass nameplate on the door read: Director of Training.

Once inside, Bill and his new pilot stood at attention while the major sat at his desk and revisited the purpose of Bill's reassignment: the pilot in Bill's crew had been hiding the fact that he was "in agony from the piles." Major Cavanaugh had no choice other than to reassign the rest of the crew. The major was brief and direct—an attribute Bill appreciated.

"At ease, Lieutenant." Bill relaxed his stance a bit as ordered.

"Hemorrhoids. Geez, poor guy," Bill was still pretty disappointed in the abrupt change of plans, but it was clear from the major's demeanor that this was no joke.

"That's just the way it is," the director continued. "So, you got yanked the first day of an assignment. So, you liked your pilot, had plans; every airman has visions of grandeur. Don't you worry, we're the best!"

"It's just that in a mere two days we were really coming together as a team, Sir," Bill thought it only right to express his thoughts on the subject.

"Well, you'll just have to continue that work here with your new crew, Lieutenant," the major replied patiently from behind his standard-issue desk. Bill scanned the view immediately before him: President Roosevelt looked on from his framed painting on the wall, a model P-51 was positioned prominently front and center of the desktop, an assortment of dark manila folders collected on the corner, and a silver picture frame stood on top of a heap of loose papers, the photo of a young man beaming through the glass. Bill thought the face looked familiar, but what really got his attention was the file in the major's hand: it had Bill's name on it.

"Powell here will be your new pilot. He's one of our best," Major Cavanaugh nodded to the tall, sandy-haired young man standing off to the side of the desk. "He's got a top-notch crew. You'll just have to find that out on the way."

On the way? Bill found himself wondering where he was going now and how soon. The major held his gaze, shifting in his chair.

Discussion over.

He's been here before, thought Bill. *Guess this isn't the time to start questioning the Director of Training!*

Powell stepped forward.

Bill extended his hand, formally introducing himself. "William Gemmill, Chicago, at your service," he said politely. "I go by Bill."

"Wesley Powell, Texas. You can call me Wes," said the gangly pilot accepting Bill's hand in a firm shake. He said "Texas" like there wasn't any need to designate the town—the state was all he needed to know.

"Let's go meet the rest of the crew; they're all anxious to get to know the new replacement," Wes said. He then saluted Major Cavanaugh and moved for the door. Bill saluted as well and waited for the major's return salute before tracing the pilot's long-legged steps.

Pilot and bombardier walked out into the bright sunshine. Bill relaxed under Wes's shy, faint smile. He looked to be about twenty-six—pretty old by Bill's standards. His manner was calm, his moves deliberate. Bill figured the guy wasn't easily rattled, a good quality for a pilot to have if he was going to bring his crew home in one piece.

"Honestly, what happened to your last bombardier?" Bill asked again, squinting into the sun's brightness. He wanted to know if there was anything he should be aware of not doing. He didn't like the idea of being bumped to another crew yet again.

"He wasn't getting along with anyone," explained Wes as he leaned against the hood of the Jeep. "That boy caused strife wherever he went. I just couldn't have that where we're going. I recommended him for a desk job."

"Your navigator must be pretty happy the guy is gone. How'd he get so far along in the program?" Bill still needed to satisfy his curiosity.

"Just lucky, I guess," Wes drawled and smiled.

Wes is obviously a man of few words, thought Bill. Hell, when he considered it, he wouldn't want to miss the war on account of a bad attitude either.

Wes shifted the conversation back to Bill. He was curious about this latest bombardier to come under his command. "You train here at El Paso?" he asked.

Bill rested his foot on the front bumper of the Jeep and rattled off the route his training had taken: "Wichita Falls and Lubbock, actually. Basic at Sheppard and college credit at Texas Tech. Then Santa Ana, Vegas, and Albuquerque, New Mexico, for advanced bombardier school."

"Yes, sure, New Mexico. I was there for a spell myself," Wes reminisced.

"You got a pretty big state down here," Bill was warming up to the lanky, soft-spoken man from the Lone Star state. "Where do you call home?"

"Houston. Maybe you'll visit me after we finish this business. I'll show you some good ol' Texas hospitality."

"Maybe I'll do just that," Bill said, flattered by the invitation.

"Might as well start over at the club," Wes suggested.

They left the Jeep parked and strolled the short distance to the officers' club: a gray metal Quonset hut. Inside, the interior was sparse: a few chairs and a credenza that served as a bar. An American flag stood stagnate in one corner, no breeze to salute its colors. The dull scent of stale beer permeated the air.

An energetic first lieutenant with a wide grin approached Bill. "Who says size doesn't matter?" he said. "Look at the two of us. Who better to fit into that broom closet of an office they give us up there?" he asked, pointing to the sky. "Joe Parkin's the name. Iowa's my home state; we'll be sharing that broom closet. I'm your navigator!"

Bill could see Joe had a point; the two young men were sized like the comic book characters Mutt and Jeff. Bill was lanky and tall; Joe was short and muscular. Their section of the B-24—the "office" where bombardier and navigator worked—was cramped under the best of circumstances.

Leaning over the credenza, a tall muscular lieutenant watching the scene poured himself across the bar. "Jug Kell," he said as he shook Bill's hand. "Your copilot from the great state of Georgia." Jug rolled an unlit cigar stub he'd been chewing to the other side of his mouth. "Good to meet you."

"Likewise, Georgia," Bill felt instantly at ease with the nonchalant flier.

"You can call me Jug. I came down here to fly fighters. Not even sure I can fly a beast like this here big-ass bird we're about to go over, but I'll shore give it my all," drawled the crew's copilot.

"I had the same notion, but I couldn't nail landings no matter how I approached it. At least we're both still in the air," Bill commiserated with Jug.

"Yeah, I reckon. Say, what do most people call you? Bill, William, or just plain Sonny?" Jug eyed the new bait carefully, then grinned over his cigar stub. *It looks like I'll be the youngest on the crew*, Bill surmised. *Jug must be at least twenty-four. Judging from this introduction, I'm in for more teasing.*

"Bill. You can start with just plain Bill," he said.

Wes stepped in. "We've been assigned a bomber for our get-to-know-you escapade. Let's go take a look at her, boys. The rest of the crew is going over her before tonight's run, and I'd like to check their progress."

"Lead the way, Pappy," Bill said, as he fell behind Wes, his legs matching the pilot's stride for stride.

The rows of B-24s parked on the tarmac impressed him: the most he'd seen collected on any one airfield. Up until now, he had seen maybe ten Heavies on an airfield at any one time.

"Is that us?" Bill pointed to the closest B-24 on the tarmac. Several uniformed men were crawling out of, under, and into the aircraft.

"'Tis," said Joe. "Ain't she purty?"

As the officers walked up to the plane, everyone inspecting it turned their eyes to Bill. They were all smiling. The first to approach him was a gawky kid even taller than Bill or Wes.

"You must be the new bombardier," said the kid. "Howdy, name's Mike Stohlman. I'm the engineer."

"Howdy back," Bill replied, nodding his head in recognition of the engineer. "Bill Gemmill, and you are correct. I am your new bombardier. Where's that accent from, Stohlman?"

The crew's first engineer was thoughtful for a moment. "Louisiana, but I've traveled around. Rode the rodeo circuit a good while. Do you like to read? I can't get enough of Louis L'Amour. Read every one I can get my hands on, twice at least."

So, Bill thought, *we have a genuine cowboy among us.* "I'd like to hear some of your traveling around stories sometime."

"Oh, don't get him started!" a distinct voice boomed. "You'll never hear the end of his tall tales!"

Bill turned to find a big-eared fellow extending his hand.

"Charles Oltarzewski, chief engineer and crew chief," said a rather short man with the big voice as he came forward to greet Bill. "Everyone calls me 'Murph' 'cause they can't get their tongues around the name. Jersey's home for me." Murph's hands enclosed Bill's in a double greeting.

Thick blond hair slicked back with Brylcreem sprouted from the top of the engineer's head. Murph also had the largest ears Bill had ever seen on a man and, for being not more than five feet four, his hands were enormous. For a moment, the hair gel's advertising jingle floated through Bill's head: *A little dab'll do ya!* Watching Murph, he was certain that the man's smile wrapped around both sides of his face—it was that wide. "Good to meet you, Murph," Bill smiled back.

"This here's Bill Hill," Murph continued, pointing his thumb at the guy to his right. "He's a good man to know, even if he is from Brooklyn and opinionated as hell! We mechanics stick together, eh, Bill?"

Bill Hill stepped up. "I watch your backs from the tail. You're in for it now, Lieutenant, hooking up with the likes of us!" Hill let out a high-pitched laugh.

"Good to meet you both," said Bill, shaking Hill's hand.

Murph came across as good-natured, and his sidekick Hill amusing. Bill was well aware of the double duty engineers and mechanics would be pulling once they were airborne on a B-24. Their teasing attitude and blunt jibes would serve as a foil for those dangerous times behind the guns at the tail, the nose, and the waist.

"Murph," Wes interjected, "you never told me what a great host you are!"

Ignoring Wes's comment, Murph continued. He was on a roll. "And bringing up the rear there is the rest of us: George, Bob, Loren ... meet your new bombardier!"

All three men whose names had just been called came forward and shook Bill's outstretched hand.

"Hi. George Harvey. I'm your radioman," said a leggy young man with a bright smile. Bill thought those teeth worthy of a Pepsodent advertisement.

"And I'm Loren Rittenhouse. You can call me Ritt. I have the nose. Say, how old are you, Bill? You look like you're still wet behind the ears!"

"Twenty," Bill replied, and felt his face warm a notch. *Yep, the baby in the group*, he thought.

"Ha!" Ritt nodded. "I still hold the record. I'm the oldest here by far, even older than Pappy here by a few years!" Ritt cackled at Wes.

One more member of the team stood ready to meet his new bombardier.

"Bob Belding's the name; family's Canadian, but I must've taken a wrong turn somewhere on the way to the war. Ended up with this motley crew. I'm the gunner in the ball. Whatever you want to know, just ask. I'll tell you even if I don't know the answer!" said the cordial young man from up north.

"Happy to meet you, Bob," Bill said with genuine interest. He'd heard great things about Canada and Canadians, and now he'd have a chance to know one.

"Well, that's everyone. Now, let's go bomb the hell out of Phoenix!" Joe chortled.

"Phoenix?" Bill wasn't certain he'd heard Joe correctly.

Joe picked up on Bill's confusion. "I've plotted courses for our night training runs. You know … training?" he laughed. "We bomb cities. Practice bomb, of course."

"Didn't you beauty queens on the other side of the field ever pull night duty?" asked Jug.

"Cute, Georgia Boy," responded Bill. "And, no. This will be my first night run with a full crew."

"We'll see what power plants we can take out tonight. It's good practice for wherever we wind up," Wes stepped in to explain.

"Phoenix it is then. What's the weather report?" Bill asked.

Joe sighed, "Mild and more of the same. You and I will be the only birds actually working on this run!" With a glance to Belding, who had joined them, the plucky navigator added, "It'll be good to get overseas and watch everyone else have to join in and stay awake for a change!"

Bill had a thought. "Say, do you all tune in to the radio on these runs? I'm a big-band man."

"Do we ever!" Joe called out. "You'll see after the exercise."

The young men had been walking casually in a cluster. As they left the tarmac and neared the camp, the enlisted men peeled off, leaving the four officers to proceed to the briefing Quonset hut where they'd receive instructions on the evening's training mission.

Bill took notes at the briefing, eager to have a good first session with his new crew. The competition among the crews at El Paso was as legendary as that of the bomb groups overseas, and he had been anticipating this moment for months. He stepped out of the meeting and into the cool night air.

Back on the tarmac, the planes and crews paired up and were airborne in a matter of minutes. These night training sessions had become routine for the rest of the crew. Playing "catch up," Bill got busy calibrating the bombsight.

After a while, in their "office," Joe asked, "You locked in there, Bill?"

"Just about. We're real close to right on." Bill was confident with his figures, having made thousands of calculations over the course of his training.

Joe seemed ready for some action, any action. He told Bill, "Let's head upstairs when you're done then. The guys will have Dorsey on the radio."

The plane droned on. Wes was keeping her steady, making it doubly easy for Bill to make his computations. After "bombs away," Bill inched forward on his stomach to see the lights of Phoenix below. An alarm bell rang, piercing the engines' steady murmur. Joe and Bill both tried their intercom but couldn't raise anyone on the deck. They had to climb up there to find out what was going on.

Bill popped his head into the deck and saw Wes scratching his head in wonder. "I stood up to stretch. Must have hit the dang switch. Sorry, boys, false alarm."

Stohlman, the engineer, looked at Bill and shrugged his shoulders in an awkward plea. He had been slouched half asleep in his seat behind Wes, enjoying the big band sounds on the radio. The tunes played on through Wes's embarrassed explanations.

"And they thought I was too tall to be in here," Stohlman cackled.

His comment got Bill's attention. If he were to add up the cumulative height, theirs might qualify for tallest crew on the base. Joe and Murph, of course, would be the curve killers.

After returning to Biggs Field, the crew deplaned and made an unusual discovery. Nose Gunner Ritt was missing. The mystery was that no one had seen him leave the plane or jump on the Jeep for the ride back to the debriefing.

At breakfast the following day, a gloomy, close-mouthed Ritt reappeared.

Jug started in. "What's eating you, boy? Tell old Jug where you've been."

"You'll find out soon enough," Ritt managed to say.

An hour after breakfast, Jug, Bill, and Joe were over at the officers' club drinking coffee and considering the mystery of their missing nose gunner. Wes strolled in, laughing in his quiet way.

"Well, are you intending to tell us what's so funny, or are you going to keep us in suspense?" asked Jug.

Wes looked at his officers and grinned. "Listen to this, y'all. Last night, when I accidentally hit that alarm … well … Ritt was asleep in the midsection. Apparently, he shot awake at the sound of that bell and looked around. He couldn't see any of us, of course, since we were all up on the deck at that point catching the Dorsey show. Well in his sleepy stupor, old Ritt thought the worst, grabbed a 'chute, and bailed!"

"Well I'll be," Jug whistled. "But we weren't all that quiet. We were all giving you heck about that alarm bell. And the music *was* playing."

Bill chimed in and said, "Hey, a clanging bell will jar anyone, especially if that someone was sound asleep toward the back." He was working to put the pieces together and thought that Ritt had shown everyone how seriously he took his training … and his naps!

Jug mused, "That's one hell of a deep sleep!"

Joe couldn't resist. "Talk about getting your bell rung."

"There's more to the story," Wes chuckled. "I had us so close to the Mexican border that Ritt sailed right on into Mexico. He had to drag his 'chute across the border and get the border guards to radio El Paso!"

Joe chuckled. "That must have been some sight for the boys at the border: seeing this bundle of silk and khaki stumbling out of the brush toward them."

Wes warned him, "Go easy on Ritt, Joe. That could have been you."

Bill was moved to go check on Ritt. He left the club and stepped out into the heart of an already scorching Texas morning in search of the embarrassed gunner. As he walked toward the enlisted barracks, he realized he had no idea what he'd say to the guy, but he knew that Ritt was sure to have a story to tell.

Ritt was in his bunk; it wasn't a stretch to find him. He was lying low, waiting for this humiliating storm to blow over. He wasn't happy to see the "new guy" and turned his back to him.

Bill sat on the bunk opposite Ritt and began speaking calmly to the nose gunner, sharing his own story of humiliation.

"Back at flight, I just couldn't land a plane," Bill said, his voice soft. "I had visions of being a fighter pilot; all those same visions of glory so many of us have coming into this war. I even came close to crashing once because of that one inability. I felt pretty bad about it, too."

With no response from Ritt forthcoming, Bill continued his tale. "I was convinced that I'd be washed out. They're pushing us through so fast now. It's hard to develop instincts and reaction times, yet I'm told that they are the best tools we have to come home in one piece."

Keeping his back to Bill, Ritt said, "Both the CO and the director want to see me, said they'd send for me. Do you think they'll wash me out?" Then he turned over and faced Bill. His entire being seemed strained and taught with worry. He remained curled up on his bed.

"What, and rob you of your patriotic duty? Nah," said Bill. "You've been training hard. You were lulled to sleep by the engines' drone and the peacefulness of it all. Where we're going, it'll be too noisy for a nap."

Ritt appeared to take comfort in the bravado. "You're right, you know. I was dead to the world on that stack of parachutes stowed in the back. Once you get them adjusted just right, it's not that bad a bed. When I heard that damn bell, it was like I was shot from a cannon. I was alone … no one was in the waist with me, some of you were up front on the flight deck and some of you were at the tail. I wasn't even thinking, really; reacting was more like it. To me, that bell meant alarm and none of you answered when I called out. I figured everyone assumed I had bailed with the rest of you!"

Bill was curious. "How was it, bailing out in the dark?"

"After that initial shock, you know, when the 'chute opens and you're yanked like a human puppet, it was really peaceful. The lights from below twinkled; there was only half a moon. I couldn't gauge how long before I would hit the dirt, but the rush in my ears told me I was descending pretty fast."

"Yet you managed a safe landing, eluded the enemy, didn't break anything, and made it back to base," Bill said, trying to lighten the mood of the room.

Ritt conjured a smile. "Nothing broken but my pride. This will be a tough one to live down, let me tell you."

Judging from what he already knew about their copilot, Bill figured Jug would for sure ride Ritt on this for a good while.

Wes slipped into the barracks.

"Here we go," sighed Ritt.

"They're ready to see you now," Wes's voice was calm.

"Yeah, OK," Ritt said, resigned to what he perceived as the inevitable. He stood and straightened his uniform, then turned toward Bill.

"Say, Lieutenant … thanks."

Bill didn't know what to say. "For what? I haven't done anything."

"Yeah, sure. Well, thanks just the same," Ritt said as he followed Wes out of the barracks, the screen door slamming shut behind the nose gunner and pilot.

"You're welcome," Bill managed to say a little late. Maybe the mesh screen was distorting the view, but Ritt appeared to be standing straighter with each stride.

This was his new crew, these men his family. They would train together, fight together, and bring each other home. *Anyone can make a mistake*, Bill thought. *Anyone*.

Ten

SHORT SNORTER

*Texas to Nebraska, Nebraska to New
Hampshire, New Hampshire
to Newfoundland, Newfoundland
to the Azores, May 1944*

ONCE THEIR BRIEF TRAINING was over, the ten-man crew left El
Paso and flew to Topeka, where they received orders to continue on
to Lincoln Army Air Field in Nebraska to pick up a brand new B-24J.
Having studied aircraft for so many months, Bill knew the 24J had
an improved autopilot, stronger guns, and a larger munitions capacity than the earlier iterations of the bomber. She was a very heavy
aircraft. Empty of her short- and long-range bombs, she weighed
36,500 pounds. When fully loaded, she weighed twenty thousand
pounds more.

The crew considered themselves lucky not to be heading to a port town on the West Coast because they knew that meant they would likely be sent to the Pacific Theater. Speculation was rampant as they made their way to Lincoln.

"Picking up a plane is a good sign, don't you think?" Joe asked Bill.

"Well, sure. It *has* to mean that we're going to be flying wherever they're sending us," Bill teased. "It could be we're going to Europe. Either the 8th or maybe the 15th?" he continued. The US 8th Army Air Corps was based in England. Most war correspondents were based there, too, so Bill and the others had plenty of opportunity to read about their exploits. They didn't know much about the new 15th, other than it was headquartered in Italy now that the Allies had cleared Axis troops from the region, and the weather was dicey there.

"Well, let's hope it's the 8th. No language barrier. And pretty little WRAFs to wake us for dawn missions," Jug encouraged the group.

"What else do we know about Italy and the 15th?" pondered Bill.

"I hear that it's bogged down in mud 80 percent of the year," Joe mused.

"How come we never hear about our flyboys in Southern Italy? Why is it those guys are never written up in *Stars and Stripes*?" Bill asked.

"No personalities visiting, no movie stars or USO—" Murph began to answer.

"Well, I'm feeling lucky. The 8th it is!" Bill beamed as he interrupted the crew chief.

"Slow down y'all! We can't take anything for granted just yet; the brass keeps us on our toes with all the changes they make at a moment's notice," Wes interjected.

"I'm still looking at this as a good sign," Bill insisted.

"Ever the optimist," Joe chuckled.

∞

Wes and the crew took the new plane up for a few familiarization flights in and around Lincoln. After acquainting themselves with her personality, Wes, Jug, and Bill felt that they had been flying her forever. With the sun glinting off her pristine aluminum skin, Bill dubbed her "Silver Beauty," and the name stuck.

The trial runs ended after three days, and life on the base became as quiet as the lull in the air before a big thunderstorm. Bill knew their departure was imminent when, after their last practice mission, Wes received orders restricting the crew to base: no outbound phone calls, no trips into town, no visitors allowed in. Bill settled in to review his maps and practice calculations. Joe studied his charts.

Word came down twenty-four hours later. Wes was reclining on his cot when there was a knock on the barracks door. A sergeant entered, asked the pilot to identify himself, then stepped forward and handed Pappy a manila envelope. Without a word, the sergeant saluted, turned on his heels, and made a quick exit. Bill held his breath as Wes slid the directives out from the envelope.

"Off we go!" Wes called out after reading his orders. "Round everyone up; I want them on deck in one hour!"

"OK, Pappy!" Bill was halfway out the door before Wes could finish his sentence.

Once again, a familiar four-by-four army truck drove the young men, officers and enlisted men alike, out to the airfield. Stowing their gear in the bomber, the crew settled back for the flight.

"Shall we see what else this baby can do?" Jug asked.

"How about we fly at treetop level as much as we can from Lincoln to New Hampshire? What do you think about that?" Wes asked his officers.

"Well … since you put it that way, Wes, guess you can say it's pretty clear we aren't flying west," Joe said. "Thanks for keeping us in suspense until the last possible moment!"

"Army regs, Joe," Wes shot back to his navigator. "You know how they insist on keeping everything on a need-to-know basis."

"I think flying at treetop level will be swell!" Bill threw his head back and laughed, which got all the young officers cheering. They were full of bravado and daring—kids in a shiny, life-sized toy.

∞

Fueled up and geared up, the crew climbed aboard the new bomber to begin their flight to Europe. Once airborne, Wes eased the bomber low, skimming the treetop canopy. When he spotted a farmer plowing his field, he nosed the plane a little lower. She lumbered up and over a rise and caught the farmer off guard. Bill was sitting in the nose gunner seat, swinging the machine guns back and forth, tracking imaginary targets. The farmer stared wide-eyed as Bill lined up his sight on him. The farmer jumped from his tractor and started running for his life, tripped and fell, then flattened himself into the dirt just as Wes pulled the nose up and continued on, engines roaring.

"Ha! Did you see the look on that poor bastard's face?" Joe shouted into the intercom.

"He won't be forgetting us anytime soon," Bill predicted.

Wes touched down in New Hampshire in plenty of time for a brief meeting with the flight commander. He joined the rest of the officers for a meal before they all turned in early.

The next morning, a second sealed envelope was delivered to Wes. Its instructions sent the boys on to Gander, Newfoundland. By now, everyone had settled into a more serious attitude; each leg of the journey was taking them closer to their purpose. Wes flew the plane at the briefed altitude and refrained from showing more of the airplane's skills to the locals. The entire crew breathed easy—the CO at Grenier hadn't mentioned any complaints filed from the farmer back in New Hampshire.

Gander boasted the worst early summer weather Bill had ever seen, and he was from Chicago with its notorious foul, lake-effect winters. The fog was so thick that it enveloped Bill's hand when he extended it into the soup. The fog then changed to a wet snow that soaked through every layer of clothing that he was wearing whenever he walked from his quarters to the mess hall. In the five days the crew waited on the weather before they could continue their journey overseas, Bill smoked his first cigarette and learned to lose at poker.

He was disappointed in the coffee. He had become somewhat of a coffee aficionado while rooming with Chief, but this sludge, for that was the only word he could find to describe the drink, required heavy doctoring to alter the taste. To add to the insult, there was no milk to be found to alter the dense flavor. Bill loved milk in his coffee.

∝⊃

Bill and Joe had each member of the crew sign a crisp one-dollar bill, excited to begin their "Short Snorter." They'd heard it was a way to commemorate their journey to war and were eager to commence. After the crew signed, they donned their foul-weather gear and roamed the base, looking for Allied crews from other countries to add their names and currencies. Bill envisioned one long string of bills, taped together, and added to the scrapbook Frances was keeping for him. He came away with British, Polish, Australian, and Russian currency in exchange for his US dollar bills.

∞

Wes and Murph went out to the tarmac every day to inspect *their* bomber. Bill often accompanied them, having nothing else to do.

"She sure is a beauty, even in this," Bill said, indicating the dense curtain of mist and snow. As he walked up to the bomber, he glided his hand along the wet metal skin of the plane.

"Yeah, she does grow on you, doesn't she?" Murph sighed.

"Let's start her up!" Wes ordered. They started the bomber every day, checking the fluid levels and hydraulics.

At last, the weather lifted. Wes received sealed orders with instructions to consult his navigator after reading the contents—*before* they were airborne. Sitting in the briefing room with the other officers, he scanned through the papers, then turned to his navigator and shared the identity of the destination for their next leg.

"Whoa, the Azores! That's going to be like finding a needle in a very wet haystack!" Joe commented. The Azores were part of Portugal. The North Atlantic Ferry route, their route, took air crews to the war in Europe via the Azores to French Morocco. At this stage of the war, Morocco supported the Allied Air Forces in the Mediterranean Theater of Operations.

"Yeah, we'll head straight out over the Atlantic. You ready?" Wes asked.

"Just give me a crack at it, Pappy!"

"Let's go over the details of the route a few times, Joe," Wes suggested. The two men poured over the maps and the potential for having to make quick changes due to rough weather over the Atlantic. Bill and Jug also had a look at the maps. Satisfied, they headed to their bunk room to collect their belongings, anticipating an early start.

Morning broke and Bill couldn't believe he was finally leaving the continent. As he and Joe walked up to their "baby," a sliver of sunlight shining on the bomber's nose reflected the brightness in Bill's heart. The aircraft gleamed as if she was as eager for her next adventure as he was. Joe was grinning, too, as he entered the bomber and slid in next to Bill.

"So, we're traveling across the Atlantic. Have you ever navigated across this much water, Joe?" Bill asked as he considered the route. He did his best to rein in his delight and focus on the trip ahead because he was still amazed he was even here: the reality of all the months of hard work leading to this moment.

"Not exactly, but we did simulations in navigator school and made a few flights over Lake Michigan. The Azores sit about 1,230 nautical miles from Gander, and the weather could play a factor. I may need your help," Joe revealed.

They were airborne in minutes, ten young men heading east toward certain adventure. Bill's imagination raced: heroic images and the daring deeds to come paraded through his head. Once they were over water, he took a seat in the nose and wondered at the route. Everywhere he looked was gray-blue with an occasional streak of sunlight adding depth to the sky, beckoning them onward before diving into the ocean.

∞

They'd been flying for six hours and Joe had them right on course. On the approach, they flew over Lajes, the largest of the islands in the archipelago that made up the Azores. It was also where they had been instructed to refuel. When Wes brought the plane in for a landing, the entire crew found the scene unsettling.

"Are those German planes?" Bill asked, incredulous. He felt his stomach drop.

"Yeah, look, the Luftwaffe Cross is clearly marked on that whole lot parked to one side," Joe said. "We're landing on a German-occupied island? I must have overshot our target," he said dejectedly.

Wes called out, "Pilot to crew, we're low on fuel. We'll have to land and take our chances as POWs."

Bill's stomach dropped again. "Hell, you mean to tell me that we're going to be taken prisoner before we even get into the war?" he snapped.

The wheels hit the tarmac and they taxied in, following directions from the tower that led them to the opposite end of the field, far away from the Luftwaffe planes. As they passed the enemy aircraft, the crew watched as their German counterparts busied themselves with what looked like routine maintenance.

Wes reached the end of the island, then tailed a "follow me" truck right into the village, slowly taxiing between two houses until he was instructed to stop.

"We'll park here," Wes instructed with a smile.

"You have to be kidding," Bill said, looking over at Joe.

"She'll be fine, y'all," Jug chuckled into the intercom.

Bill took note. No Nazis surrounded the bomber. No Luftwaffe police shouting, *"Hande hoch!"* appeared to menace them.

With the bomber parked, Wes and Jug deplaned first and spoke animatedly with the American liaison officer who had approached the plane. Jug was gesturing wildly.

The liaison officer understood their distress and calmly explained the presence of the German planes. Prior to 1943, the Portuguese government allowed the German navy to dock and refuel their U-boats in the Azores. Sometime that same year, British diplomats persuaded the Portuguese government to lease the bases on the islands in the Azores to the Allies. When the Nazis pulled out, they abandoned a handful of Luftwaffe aircraft—mostly Ju-52s. Portugal refitted, re-marked, and used these aircraft to provide Allied convoys with air cover as well as to conduct meteorological flights. A modest crew of Luftwaffe mechanics had remained on the island to assist in the refits. That was who the boys had seen, Portuguese and German flight engineers dismantling and repairing the abandoned aircraft.

"So, that's the situation on the island," the liaison wrapped up his end of the conversation.

"You didn't think to warn us we'd be landing next to Luftwaffe aircraft and their maintenance crews?" Wes insisted. "We should have been told."

"Agreed," the liaison chuckled. "But you know now."

Wes turned away from the liaison officer and waved to Bill, who dropped down to the tarmac and walked together with Wes and the liaison to the mess hall. They ate their fill of pork and beans, and as an after-dinner treat, the liaison officer handed Wes his orders. He instructed that they were not to be opened until they were airborne the next day. Bill got Wes's attention with a head-bob.

"Before we call it a night, Joe and I are going to find someone with Portuguese dollars for our Snorters," Bill said.

"Don't venture off this end of the runway, Gemmill," Wes ordered. "You either, Parkin."

"Right, Pappy." Bill saluted his pilot. "No sweat." In only a matter of minutes, Bill had exchanged several American dollar bills for currency from Canada, Poland, and Russia—signed, of course. Joe fared equally well.

Shortly after dawn the following day, the crew awoke refreshed and ready to proceed. The bomber taxied to the end of the runway, then turned and gained speed, lifting off the island. When they reached the ordered altitude, Wes opened the now-familiar envelope, their destiny sealed in manila.

Eleven

THE BAZAAR

The Azores to West Africa,
May 1944

THE GERMANS WERE LISTENING. Wes was under orders to fly low to avoid detection, and minimum altitude gave Bill better than a bird's eye view. Sitting in the nose of the bomber once again, he felt he could reach out and touch the waves as they teased the belly of the plane. Joe's ability to read the aircraft's speed off the waves was impressive. Reaching land, they cruised at treetop level over West Africa, the bomber scattering wildlife and causing confusion and distress among a band of Bedouins. Bill was enchanted.

They landed on a hard-packed runway just outside Marrakech. The sandstorm created by the bomber's rotating propellers blew a filmy curtain around the plane. Jug shut down the engines and locked the controls, and he and Wes dropped down to the runway. With the flight deck empty, Bill climbed up from the turret and stuck his head out of the cockpit window. The desert breeze tasted nothing like Las Vegas or New Mexico. This air was ancient, old, and baked. It drained any semblance of moisture from his eyes.

Bill couldn't get over the fact he was in Africa. It amazed him when he considered just how far across the world he had come from Chicago. He reached for his Ray-Bans, turned, and shimmied over the catwalk to the bomb bay doors, sliding through the belly and onto the ground. The exertion was a relief after the long trip in the cramped nose turret, although it was his favorite seat for viewing the world below and ahead of him.

He felt the sun instantly frying the skin on his prominent nose and high cheekbones. Heat hit the metal surface of the wing, bounced off, and gyrated around him. Bill could hear the heat, he was certain of it: a high-frequency vibration like thousands of cicadas seeking their kind of love.

"You sure do like riding up front, Lieutenant," Ritt chided Bill as the bombardier stepped down on the hard-beaten earth. "You afraid you're going to miss something?"

Bill laughed as he replied, "Best damn seat in the aircraft."

"You can have it, Sir. I'll be hanging out there all too soon, firing away at Gerry," Ritt hadn't even been reprimanded for prematurely bailing back in El Paso, the Air Corps being that keen on keeping every man in the ranks they could at this stage of the war. He'd sat in the waist of the bomber with the rest of the gunners the whole ride over the Atlantic.

"Yeah, don't forget that Gerry will be firing at you, too," Bill called over his shoulder as he caught up to Joe.

Joe had been first to reach terra firma and had already wrapped his shirt around his head in a makeshift turban. *Two minutes landed and already our compact navigator is trying to fit in with the locals*, Bill laughed to himself. The breeze disturbed the dry heat, setting waves of hot air to gyrate. Joe had his hands on his hips, arms akimbo in hopes of some immediate air-conditioning.

A liaison officer stepped like a ghost out of the swirling dust kicked up by the zephyr. His head was covered by a black-and-white checked *shemagh keffiyeh*, the practical scarf used by locals in the Middle East to shield themselves from the sun and blowing sands. His head, nostrils, and mouth were covered by the blue-and-white checkered material, but he had left a slit for his eyes. He wore uniform shorts. Bill found the combination of the man's USAAF fatigues and colorful scarf exotic. The liaison didn't bother to introduce himself to the boys. He also didn't offer any advice on how they, too, could escape the grinding sand. They were covering their noses and mouths with their forearms and shielding their eyes with their free hands. He watched them struggle for a moment before addressing Wes.

After having been greeted in the Azores by a genuinely happy contact, Bill was surprised by the demeanor of the first American they met in Africa who was so inured to his surroundings he wasn't even bothered by the sand pelting his bare, skinny legs. Bill and Wes leaned in to hear what the dusty figure with the sand-scrubbed shanks had to say.

"This is North Africa. You and your crew will remain in Marrakech until further notice," the army captain droned. He handed Wes the anticipated envelope containing instructions for the next leg of their journey. *Of course, we're in North Africa*, Bill silently chided the captain. *Our navigator knows how to read the waves. We aren't stupid.* "You know the procedure. You are not to open the packet until you are airborne. I will notify you when this is to happen," the liaison cautioned Wes.

The liaison then barked a short briefing about the utterly unfamiliar customs of the area and how under no circumstances were they to ever look any local woman in the eye.

Hearing this, Bill mused, *How oddly liberating it is to travel without knowing where you are going, just waiting to be told the details.* In the end, they were headed to war; that's what mattered most to him. And as for the local women, he had no intention of causing an international incident and every intention of exploring Marrakech. His time in Africa was limited; he was more than happy to oblige the customs he was certain to encounter.

"This military stuff is all right," Joe chortled. "As long as we keep checking in, they're happy to tell us where to go." He unwound the uniform blouse he had wrapped around his head and was trying to wrap it more like the liaison officer's, to little effect.

Even the ever-serious Wes laughed at the double entendre, but the quip appeared lost on the Air Corps officer standing slump-shouldered in the midst of a gritty screen of dust, his eyes looking through the slit in his *keffiyeh* past the newly arrived flight crew. The only thing Bill could figure was that the man was weary of his assignment. Perhaps the desert heat and swirling sand had beaten him down. Bill was glad he had trained in the Southwest; the experience had given him a taste of what dry heat feels like.

"Can't you give me an idea, at least, how long we can expect to remain in North Africa?" Wes, not ready to be dismissed, asked the captain.

"Until further notice," huffed the liaison through his scarf. He turned his back to Wes and the rest of the crew without another word and headed back through a sandy veil from whence he'd come.

"How can that guy breathe with all the dry dirt coiling around his head like that? Scarf or no scarf," Bill noted.

"He looks as parched as the ground," quipped Joe.

"He's been here too long. It must be tough sitting out here, watching crews come and go, missing the action," Wes offered assuredly.

After drawing up a guard duty roster for the plane, they left tail gunner Hill on the tarmac as first watch. The rest of the crew rode a sand-blasted army six-by-six—grateful the canvas cover had been deployed against the elements—to their temporary quarters: a former French Foreign Legion post. The enlisted men were dropped off at a group of wooden barracks; the officers were deposited in front of whitewashed mud bungalows.

Murph helped Bill carry his flight bag, heavy with maps, E-6B slide rule, calculation books, and pencils. The wisecracking sergeant took a look around the officers' quarters and piped out a soft whistle.

"You officers have it pretty cushy. The real men of this outfit can tough it out in the barracks," said Murph.

"It smells of centuries and dirt, that's about all, don't you think?" Bill asked.

"Yeah, dirt and heat. I'll never complain about New Jersey again. See ya, big shot," the engine wizard laughed as he sauntered out the door, dancing down the steps.

"Take care of our baby, Sarge," Bill called out.

"Will do, Lieutenant," Murph tossed the words over his shoulder.

With the enlisted men rotating guard duty, Bill, Jug, Joe, and Wes were free to discover the old town's wall mosaics, stained glass windows, and intricately carved cedar doors. The exotic-robed people and endless bazaar fascinated the boy from the Windy City. He shared the streets with the milling throng of small nations, people from all over North Africa and the Middle East, as well as saddled camels, belled goats, and loose cattle. Everything was going on at once: bartering, trading, steal-ing, butchering. Merchants were busy weighing, measuring, selling, roasting, wrapping, and tying. Children were collecting animal dung in baskets. Nothing was wasted; the animals provided fuel for heat and cooking as well as meat and milk for eating and drinking.

American visitors saw few women and Bill noticed their absence. Those women who did venture out were covered from their heads to their feet. Black kohl eyeliner defined the one feature visible to outsiders, although Bill remembered that eye contact was not advised. Every few hours a voice called men to prayer, the accent insistent and mesmerizing.

Over the days they waited in Marrakech, Bill took to tasting and negotiating, trying on the language for size. He laughed with the vendors at his own naiveté, his accent, and attempts at pronouncing their words. He was a goodwill merchant, making friends with all sorts of characters in the marketplace.

In contrast to the merchants and traders were the beggars of every size, age, and gender. Bill deduced by the systematic way he was approached that begging was big business.

Often a small band of giggling children tailed the tall bombardier, trying, and failing, to match his stride. He pretended not to hear them for several steps before turning around and confronting them with a great big smile.

"Hello, OK," the youngsters would chime repeatedly, laughing and tugging at his pants pockets, looking for candy or coins. Bill always kept a few coins in his pocket. His height, blue eyes, and easy smile were like a magnet for the reserved locals. They didn't appear to smile often.

The colors of the clothing, the speech, and the foods reminded him of a carton of crayons. Gradations of blue, red, brown, and orange provided depth to the sandy tan dust of the streets and the desert beyond. Awnings of hand-woven rugs, veils, and scarves sheltered the vendors from the already too-hot morning sun. Removing his Ray-Bans, Bill shielded his eyes from the brightness, and for the first time he noticed the depth of the antique sky. A bouquet of cumin, cinnamon, coriander, and braised lamb led him down narrow winding corridors in search of the source of the remarkable smells. The herbal aroma from continuous cooking melded with the stench from open sewers, creating a cacophony of odors. Luckily, he was never quite able to distinguish one fragrance from another.

One day, while on a journey through town, Bill heard a loud pinging sound coming from a shady side street. He followed the jangle, peeked through what he thought was a shop door, and bravely began communicating with the apparent owner, a gentleman long in the tooth. The feel of Arabic on his tongue, the way it was harsh and soft at the same time, pleased him, but Bill wasn't confident he had the meaning and intonation down yet. The old man was pounding a silver plate with a small ball-peen hammer. A sort of production line had been devised, with the patriarch smoothing out the metal, a regal elderly woman gracefully dipping it in some watery solution, and two younger women busy polishing. Gleaming trays, goblets, and platters reflecting shy, smiling faces lined shelves or collected on the floor.

The head of the house gestured for Bill to enter. The man wore a flowing robe, and his whiskers reached his chest. He handed Bill a small hand-worked sterling box. Turning it over with his fingers, Bill was moved by the skill the artisan brought to his creations. Dancing around the outside of the rectangular box were camels, some with packs, others with riders. On the lid was a deftly wrought palm tree that played in an unseen breeze. Bill grinned at the shopkeeper, and the bartering began in earnest. He left the silversmith's with his prize, happy with his purchase, considering it a good omen.

At a favorite stall visited often by American and Canadian fliers, the Berber proprietor prepared gyros. The smell of lamb broiling over the grill drew the foreigners in from their haggling with the rug weaver, tinker, and wool dyer. Bill enjoyed the greasy sandwich and eventually mastered a technique of devouring it without getting the oily drippings on his uniform. Stretching forward, he leaned over the sandy street and savored the foreign flavors and non-regulation seasonings. The awkward posture made everyone laugh, but he was happy not to have to do more laundry than necessary.

∞

The following morning, Bill and Joe paired up for a foray into Marrakech away from town and the bazaar. They weaved and wandered their way past the Allied POW camp where German soldiers and fliers were held. Bill approached a prisoner standing close to the wire fence that ringed the perimeter of the camp. He could see the entire yard through the large open weave of the metal barrier. A young Luftwaffe lieutenant was selling souvenirs and held up a handmade ashtray that looked to have been fashioned out of the headlamp of a Jeep or maybe the front-end corner of a tank; Bill couldn't be certain. The kid offered it to Bill through the fence. It just fit through the wires.

After examining the ashtray, Bill dug in his pants pocket and handed some coins to the German. Bill's father had told him how, although the food was good in the North African camps, it was not plentiful. Many prisoners crafted items for sale out of parts from crashed planes, disabled jeeps, and tanks collected by the army and piled in a heap in a corner of the camp. Perhaps the kid could buy some chocolate, dates, or cigarettes sold by the merchants stationed strategically outside the gates of the prison. With a little English and German, shoulder shrugs, hand gestures, and a grin or two, the young men made an exchange through the enclosure. Bill watched the POW call to a young Moroccan boy and give him the money. Moments later, the German was feasting on a steaming, rolled-up sandwich. He beamed at Bill as he chased each bite with a plump date. Bill understood now why Axis soldiers hoped to be interned by the Yanks. He looked more closely at his purchase. A camel in bas-relief posed at each corner of the square receptacle, and although not as neatly wrought as the silversmith's, the work was more personal somehow.

"Maybe they don't have it so bad after all," Bill mumbled aloud, turning the ashtray over between his hands. He and the prisoner mirrored each other in many ways: the German kid looked to be Bill's age and he was about the same height. They both were tall, dark-haired, and blue-eyed. Bill wondered if the kid truly believed in what he had been fighting for, because one thing that might set them apart was the fact that Bill knew he was on the side of justice and freedom.

"Look at these guys, Bill," Joe said as he wandered up the embankment, curious about the exchange. "They have sunshine, palm trees, food to eat, enough water to drink, and Air Corp lieutenants to buy their junk." Bill shrugged as Joe continued, "Better a prisoner of the Allies in sunny Marrakech than freezing in a POW camp in Des Moines."

Thanks to newsreels and papers, most Americans were well aware that thousands of captured German soldiers and airmen were shipped to the US to wait out the war in internment camps, the primary camps being in North Carolina and Georgia. The men being held in Marrakech were awaiting transport to the US.

Bill considered the distinct possibility he might land in a POW camp himself before this war was over. From what he had heard, the Germans were not so kind to captured American airmen. Sometimes both the Germans and the Japanese ignored the Geneva Convention.

The thought crossed his mind that whatever his final destination, he bet no friendly German flier would buy an artifact from him. No runner would deliver fresh, hot food. Bill was finally close enough to smell the war.

∞

Five days after their landing, ten more B-24s arrived from the States. Bill was certain this is what they'd been waiting for.

Each pilot and crew of the 24s were met by the same humorless contact who gave the same monotone speech Bill and the crew had heard less than a week ago. He mingled with the new crews to learn what he could about them: Where were they from? Did they have news of friends gone ahead or left behind? But Wes kept his bombardier busy after the new planes began arriving, checking out the armament and maintaining a level of readiness with his gunners, leaving Bill little time for socializing or going back into town.

Two days later, after a dinner of Spam and beans, Wes called the crew together outside the officers' quarters. "Pack up your gear, gentlemen!" he instructed the crew. "We lift off at 0400 tomorrow morning, and we'll be flying with the squadron that arrived yesterday."

So, this is it, Bill thought to himself. He was excited their journey was proceeding and moved quickly. His slide rule and protractor were already stored in his leather bomb equipment case. He had stuffed his clothes in his duffel and replaced all of his maps, paper, and pencils in his briefcase for the duration of the flight across Africa. Everyone saw that their personal items, reading material, and shaving kits were packed after getting ready for bed. It took hours for Bill to fall asleep, his mind racing over what lay ahead.

The crew assembled at Silver Beauty at 0300 the next morning. The sky was crystal clear. Bill had never seen so many stars; they looked like diamonds sparkling on black velvet. Murph and Mike drew the tarp off of the nose of the aircraft while Bill watched and held his breath, but she didn't look too badly battered by the ever-present blasting sand.

Joe followed Bill as the two young men tossed their gear up, then pulled themselves into the belly of the plane, making their way toward the cramped nose turret. When everyone was in position, they checked in with Wes who had Silver Beauty's wheels up in moments.

"Bombardier to pilot," Bill called into the intercom as they gained altitude and leveled off. "When are you going to open that packet?"

"I just did," Wes answered. "We won't be getting off this continent, not yet anyhow. Now keep off that intercom."

"Roger," Bill replied as he left his "office" on the bomb deck and took a seat in the nose.

They pierced the African skylight, colors dissolving within colors, instant storms dissipating as quickly as they appeared, flying just above green umbrella treetops. Their destination was a closely guarded secret until Wes could speak face-to-face with Bill and Joe about their course. The Germans were listening, after all.

Twelve

THE SANDWICH

*From Marrakech, French Morrocco,
to Tunis, Tunisia, Spring 1944*

AS SOON AS THEY REACHED cruising altitude, Wes handed over the controls to Jug, then climbed down from the flight deck. Before takeoff, Wes had given Joe only the basic coordinates to get them headed in the right direction. Now, he'd let his officers below know they were headed to Tunis. The capital of Tunisia was 1,097 miles from Marrakech, just 503 miles shy of the Silver Beauty's range. Wes laughed to see Joe on the bomb deck, stripped down to just his boxer shorts. The navigator was going over his collection of plots and charts, speculating about the route. When Wes revealed their destination was Tunis, Joe immediately began consulting his map of the area. It had been sitting on top of all the other maps.

"Once you turn us east, I'll just keep that big blue blob of water on our left, and we'll be right on target," Joe teased.

"That's the Tyrrhenian Sea to you, wise guy," Wes said as he leaned over Joe's shoulder to take note of the route. Then he headed up to talk to Bill; he knew where to find his bombardier.

Sitting in the nose, Bill's lungs grappled with the heat and his face tingled, as if too close to an open blast furnace. His summers working in Indiana at the steel mills, stoking fires and stacking rods and ingots, had toughened him up for football. He thought he knew what intense heat was. Until now.

"I see you've resumed your favorite viewing spot, Gemmill," Wes said as he poked his head into the nose gunner's compartment. "And you've made yourself comfortable."

"The view from the nose continues to be spectacular, Pappy," Bill said, stating the obvious. "As for being out of uniform, well, it's just too damn hot in here to wear the full gear."

"I don't have a problem with you being out of uniform," Wes replied. "If you ever visit us on the flight deck, take a gander at the other guys. You'd think I'm running a ship for nudists."

"Then I'm in good company," Bill grinned.

All Wes could see was the side of Bill's head. "I came to tell you we are heading to Tunis. We'll refuel and probably spend a night or two before the entire squadron heads out again. Similar to Marrakech."

"Tunis, you say?" Bill asked his captain. "I've got a feeling we're headed to Italy."

"Could be," said Wes. "We'll find out when we get to Tunisia." Wes patted Bill on the shoulder as he headed back up to the flight deck.

Bill raised his hand in a long-armed salute and resumed his vigil over the scene before him. He watched the desert unfold itself as he considered every step he had taken thus far to get to the war. He had been in history class when news came over the intercom that Japan had just attacked Pearl Harbor. He immediately felt the outrage of millions of Americans added to his own. His greatest fear was that his home would be invaded and occupied like the countries and towns he had seen in newsreels. He was now making his way to the thick of it—the killing, the maiming, the destruction.

There might be, right now, some German or Italian kid making his way there, too, paralleling Bill's trajectory. He reflected on the fact that a great number of men fighting the air war, regardless of sides, would do a lot of killing. He wondered what the deaths of so many people, done remotely and with precision, would make him feel after the fact. He wondered, too, if all the exercises built into his training to assist him in remaining focused and do his job would give him an advantage. But these days, before he actually got to toggle that bomb switch or be honored with a Norden, Bill couldn't help but consider the consequences of his actions. Or the losses.

He was going into this war with the combined might of the Allies: the US Army Air Corps joined with the armies and air forces of the British, Canadians, Russians, Yugoslavians, Poles, Belgians, Australians, Chinese, Danes, Greeks, Netherlanders, New Zealanders, Norwegians, South Africans, and the untold thousands of local partisans and patriots fighting their own stealth battles in towns and hills scattered across Europe. He imagined those people, too, men and women willing to risk their lives, as they rescued the persecuted and caused as much damage as possible to the Axis troops invading their homelands. Some of them might end up at or near one of his targets.

∞

His eyes stung from salty rivulets of sweat flowing from the top of his head. Even the hairs on his arms and legs stood at attention, as if they couldn't bear to touch his skin. The nose gunner's compartment was too small for a tall young man like Bill to wriggle around much. He had stripped down to his government-issued, cotton, khaki skivvies before climbing up into the nose. The effort his body was making to regulate its temperature stained the back of his undershirt and pooled under his arms. The interior of the bomber was nothing but metal, which conducted the heat and the cold with excellent precision. Bill was not alone; the entire crew shed as much of their clothing as they could in the face of the heat. Their captain chose to remain in uniform to present a measure of discipline within the ranks of his men.

The panoramic view while sitting in the nose turret gave Bill the sensation of being suspended in midair, separated from the sub-stratosphere by panes of plastic glass. "This is like being in a movie!" he called into his headset.

"Yeah," Jug's voice drawled, crackling back at Bill. "Hey, y'all, I think I can see Rudy Valentino!" Jug's teasing laugh mingled with the static over the intercom and crept into the sweltering, cramped dome with Bill.

Below, Silver Beauty's shadow stretched over a wide expanse of the Sahara. To Bill's left, the aqua shimmer of the Tyrrhenian danced like a mirage. He followed the bomber's shade as it passed over a long caravan of camels carrying piles of silks and leathers, inching its way through the sand drifts toward a distant ring of palm trees. The robed camel pullers glanced up and waved as the bomber passed overhead. Bill waved back, wondering if they could see him as clearly as he saw them. He thought he detected a glimmer ahead; the men and camels were aiming right for it. *An oasis*, he deduced.

Bill sensed the bomber bank right and shifted his gaze to the blue above. He squinted at the sun, which was angled straight at him, the convection intensified through the Plexiglas. He closed his eyes, allowing a whisper of sleep to coax him into a doze. Nearly an hour later, he woke with the realization that he was hungry.

It was next to impossible to adjust a six-foot-three-inch frame in a four-by-two-foot capsule. Noticing the warmth most when he moved, Bill did his best to remain still. His skivvies were soaked, and his legs stuck to the black leather seat, his sweat like an adhesive. He was careful to avoid the scalding metal ribbing of the turret and the lethally hot twin fifties. *If those guns are hot now, how hot will they be when engaged? Ritt will have to be careful once we're in battle,* he concluded. Bill's hands were greasy wet from swiping his forehead. He rotated the guns ninety degrees away from the front of the nose so he could expose a small vent, thinking that if he let in some air, the heat would at least be moving.

Bill mindlessly unwrapped the paper from around a standard inflight Spam sandwich while panning the scene below. He liked spiced ham, but he resented the stale bread. *Couldn't they give us a decent lunch for all our trouble?* he wondered as he took his first bite. Then Wes's voice screamed into the headsets of every crew member on board.

"Who's the dumb bastard who threw that crap into the engine?"

Stunned out of his drowsy *long view,* Bill looked around the close quarters of the nose turret. His sandwich wrapper was nowhere to be seen. He felt the left engine shudder and cough.

"Maybe it was a bird," Jug said. "Damn, something sure as hell's been sucked into that left inboard engine!" The copilot's words heated up the nose compartment more than a notch, and the bomber's struggle with the jammed engine rocked the flight deck.

"I'm going to feather the prop; maybe whatever is in there will blow out." Wes was cool as the engine continued to run rough, the plane shaking fiercely, like some wild animal with its prey between its teeth. Wes feathered the bomber's engines, shutting down the left engine and aligning the propellers with the airflow.

Bill screwed his body into a left-hand turn as much as the tight space allowed and watched as the propeller slowed to a stop; its feathered position now cutting directly into the wind, reducing drag. The illusion of a few final counterclockwise spins mesmerized him. He shook his head to synchronize his eyes with his brain, then crossed his fingers for luck. Then he heard the engine shut down. The cold, tight ball in his stomach was not just Spam. Bill was counting on Murph. Although he knew that if the flight engineer couldn't restart the engine, they probably would be able to limp into Tunis on three engines. Brand new plane too. He had no doubt that Wes and Jug would blame him for any delay. *Way to go, Gemmill. Sonofabitch! Come on Murph baby, work your engineer's magic.*

Bill knew he had to say something; everyone would figure it out sooner or later. He was sure Wes already had. After all, the pilot sat right above and behind the nose turret—a perfect position to notice a brown blur swoop past his windshield. And Wes, ever alert, had asked who had thrown something out of the plane. Bill was the logical guilty party since he took the seat in the nose most often. He clicked on his mic.

"Must've been my sandwich wrapper ... I ... opened the vent. Sorry!" No reply was forthcoming. "I said I'm sorry, for Chrissake!" A sudden roar from the lame engine smothered Bill's voice. He was elated.

"Shit, Gemmill! Have you any idea what you just did?" Wes was incredulous and angry. "You're lucky I don't haul your ass up here for good. Keep your head about you or the only bombs you'll be dropping will be the ones in your dreams. Sonofabitch!"

Laughter, low and steady, streamed through the bomber, reaching a crescendo in the nose turret. The guffaws of the crew leapt through the intercom, pelting the raw bombardier hunched in the bubble.

"Way to go, Chicago!"

"What were you doing up there, Gemmill, dreaming?"

"Shit, boys, we got ourselves a saboteur!"

"Knock it off, y'all. Enough of this chatter. Let's get on down to Tunis, then you can have your laughs," Wes wanted to direct everyone's attention back to the serious job of flying.

Red-faced, Bill endured the crew's merciless teasing as he allowed himself one more look over the multitude of tans and browns, the verdant oasis vanishing with the Valentino images he had been imagining.

Thirteen

TUNIS, THE PARIS OF AFRICA

Tunisia, 1944

BILL HAD LEARNED SOMETHING about Tunisia in his high school history class. Historically, the capital Tunis was a glorious conglomeration of cultures and peoples from the ancient Egyptians and Romans to the Phoenicians. Later, the Berbers and Arabs influenced the region with their politics, art, and inventions. Then the French came along and created the Protectorate of Tunisia.

By the mid-1940s, Tunis had become a bomb-ravaged village where the inhabitants rummaged through war materiel left behind during a hasty Nazi retreat. From time to time, Nazi pilots cruised by for a look-see and to strafe the airfield. It was this unsettled environment into which Bill and the crew arrived. Wes parked Silver Beauty and attended the required meet-and-greet with the liaison: a jovial, walrus-mustachioed British major dressed in his summer uniform of khaki shorts, calf-length tan socks, and pith helmet. Afterward, the major directed the crew to their barracks and the mess. What Major Mustache failed to mention were the erratic flybys the enemy was so fond of performing. When Bill, Wes, Jug, and Joe walked into their quarters, they'd no sooner plopped down on a bunk than Bill got them right up again.

"Let's go find the mess," he nudged Joe on his booted foot dangling off the end of the bed. "I'm starved."

"You are always starved, Gemmill," Joe mumbled as he roused himself. He was a tad hungry himself, now that he considered it.

"You too, Pappy, Jug," Bill insisted. "The food will do you good." Wes and Jug rallied as well, and the four officers headed for some grub.

With their bellies full, the quartet walked back out to the plane for one more check before turning in for the evening. As they crossed the tarmac, Wes kept looking for the liaison officer, hoping the man would appear with orders for the next leg of their journey, but the jolly man was nowhere to be seen. Disappointed and tired, the four flyboys headed back to their barracks. Bill was betting on one of his famous deep slumbers.

∞

In the dark Mediterranean night, Bill awoke ahead of everyone else at the sounds of aircraft above him. It was the crash at DePauw all over again. Just as in Indiana, he headed toward the source of the commotion. Joe trailed sleepily behind him, tugging on his uniform blouse, followed by Wes and Jug. After hours of extensive training, Bill had learned what it meant to be a target. He waited to be hit, to be wounded, to be dead. He imagined the whistle of bombs through the air, the thunder of steel casements impacting earth, the screech of metal twisting and tearing.

Bill ran to the airfield, noticing that several more US bombers had arrived in the night. They had parked staggered and far apart to create a more difficult target in the case of an attack. Apparently, one lone Luftwaffe pilot had decided to surprise the defenseless airstrip in Tunis with a low pass overhead, guns blazing. The Nazi pilot had sprayed the side of the control tower with bullets on his first pass. A tornado of concrete and siding flung into the sky, then came crashing, clanging, and banging to the ground. Banking for his second pass, the German was apparently targeting the newly arrived aircraft. Bill could see him coming head on, straight for him. Incensed, he stood at the edge of the airfield, screaming up at the enemy, "You bastard!" The pungent odor of burning fuel and metal melting surrounded him; his eyes stung from the fumes.

"You're crazy, Gemmill!" Jug ran up to Bill and yelled, but Bill couldn't hear his words above the din of projectiles slamming the metal sheeting of Allied planes.

"Come on, you bastard!" Bill continued to scream at the ME-109, firing his GI Colt .45 in defiance and frustration. He even locked eyes for a second with the Nazi pilot, almost willing the German to come within range of his pistol.

"We have to get to the plane. That popgun can't do shit! Let's find a way around this mess," yelled Jug, who was now in Bill's face. This time his bombardier heard him loud and clear. Then, Murph, Joe, and the rest of the crew ran past Jug and Bill, aiming straight for Silver Beauty. Stohlman and Belding grabbed some of the camouflage netting piled next to the tarmac and began to drag it over to the bomber. Bill and Jug arrived and pitched in, climbing up onto the roof of the flight deck to tug the netting over the windscreen. Wes and Ritt positioned themselves at both sides of the aircraft, and the two of them stretched several squares of camouflage up over the wings, pulling with all their might.

The extra muscle power mixed with adrenaline helped immensely, and soon the aircraft was covered from nose to tail. The group moved as if they were in a drill, mechanical and full of purpose. It helped them feel they were doing *something* to thwart the German pilot.

With Silver Beauty protected, the crew had regrouped at the edge of the tarmac as the reverberation of the Daimler-Benz engines in the Messerschmitt faded away. Joe took out his .45 and cocked it. He was ready for battle. "If they come for us, I'll take out a couple of Luftwaffe bastards on our way down," he assured Bill and Jug.

Bill knew a single plane could do a heap of damage. The Nazi had a fighter, a slender speedy Messerschmitt. Their crew had a lumbering tank of a bomber. It was pointless for them to fire up the engines and pursue the enemy. Frustrating as it was, pursuit was also against regulations. They had little recourse but to protect what they could. Besides, the attack was over almost as soon as it had started.

Bill watched as a member of Hitler's air force, the fearless Luftwaffe, left the scene. Anger spread red across his face and seized the muscles in his jaw. He had been hogtied, unable to defend his friends or himself. All any of them had managed to do was to throw some nets over their bomber. Fortunately, the Nazi had been a lousy shot, but it sure sounded like he had torn up the entire airfield. *Or is it on purpose?* Bill began to wonder. *Is this merely a nuisance mission, meant to intimidate and frighten the greenhorns and the war weary?*

∝

In the morning, Wes returned to the officers' quarters after meeting with the British liaison officer. He had news about the previous night's adventure. "We can consider ourselves initiated, boys," Wes began to explain. "Seems Gerry likes to pay the airfield a visit when he gets wind of new arrivals." Bill had been right to question why the brief attack concluded with little damage done.

"That's not all," Wes continued. "Because of the large dumps of wrecked aircraft and reclaimed vehicles strewn across the area surrounding camp, we've been warned not to venture too far." The Nazis had left land mines rigged to aircraft engines and acres of burned-out tanks, making it doubly dangerous to poke around.

"Did you happen to get our orders?" Joe asked.

"The liaison did not mention any orders, Parnell," Wes replied.

Curious, Bill went out to walk the perimeter and get a feel for the danger Wes had spoken about. He noticed that the ruined equipment included Allied as well as Nazi war materiel. The upper right corner of an American flag painted on the remnants of a Mustang's wing, a painted Union Jack scraped up but fully recognizable on a large tank panel, a partial Iron Cross from the fuselage of a Messerschmitt. He determined it would definitely have been an easy task to rig explosives among the detritus; there were so many hidey-holes to be found.

To occupy themselves while they waited, all the crews played baseball on the hard clay soil or card games on metal tables they found in the airfield's hangar. These they dragged into the shade of the bomber's wing for some relief from the intense midday heat. What they all really wanted to do was to continue on, but they needed orders to do that, and nothing was forthcoming as of yet. Still, American B-24s continued to arrive on a daily basis.

∞

After two weeks in Tunis, the boys were ecstatic when Wes returned from another meeting with the liaison, holding orders to continue to Gioia, Italy. He hadn't had to wait to open the ubiquitous manila envelope; the major had told him to his face as he handed them over. Two days later, with the crew on board, Wes started up the engines and taxied to his position on the tarmac. Their motors humming, the crew headed for the 15th Air Corps staging base in Gioia, Southern Italy.

So it's the 15th, Bill realized, *and the Italian mud*—although he had heard that the infamous sludge and mire arrived with the winter rains, and it was barely June. It wouldn't have mattered what time of year they arrived; he just wanted to receive an assignment to a bomb group and get cracking. The enemy would soon find out there's a new bombardier coming their way. *Gerry,* he sent out a silent message, *you're about to see this American's spirit.*

Fourteen

MEDITERRANEAN SPRING

*Gioia, Italy, D-Day,
June 6, 1944*

FOUR HOURS and fifteen minutes later, at 0630 hours, Wes and Jug brought Silver Beauty in for a landing at the Gioia del Colle Airfield in Gioia, Italy, headquarters of the 15th Air Force. The spring sun had begun its rise, throwing shades of golden pink and orange ahead as if to light its climb. At roughly the same time, and unbeknownst to the crew, over in the European Theater of Operations, Allied troops had launched their attack on the Nazis entrenched in Normandy, France. D-Day was on.

The 15th—a gathering of pilots, copilots, bombardiers, navigators, radio operators, mechanics, and engineers—was largely responsible for reducing the potency of the Luftwaffe and Wehrmacht,

Nazi Germany's air force and army, in Northern Italy and Southern Europe. Because of frequent inclement weather in England, home of the 8th Air Force, it was hoped squadrons flying out of Italy could take up some of their missions.

While the Gioia ground crew was busy blocking the wheels of the plane, Bill crawled back to the bomb deck to grab his duffel and flight bag of maps, notebooks, and photographs of practice targets. Joe gathered up his own set of maps, plus his sextant and other navigational equipment.

Bill decided to head out. "You coming?" he asked Joe.

"Give me a few minutes," Joe replied, waving Bill off.

Bill weaved through the bomb bay, dragging his bags with him, and jumped down through the crew hatch in the belly of the bomber to wait for Joe. His stomach rumbled. They had finished their standard inflight sandwiches—without incident—three hours earlier and had breakfast on their minds. Bill was excited to be in Italy, the home of classic history and a language of romance, although he wondered if he'd have an opportunity to experience either of them. He surveyed the airfield and tasted the breeze: it was warm and salty. Bill took a moment to stretch. Standing at the wing, he leaned every which way to unkink his back, then folded over his legs, touching the hard cement ground with flattened palms. Feeling more limber, he slipped back into his khaki uniform blouse, which he had removed during the ride from Tunis, and tucked the tail ends into his trousers.

He looked up at the crew hatch just as Joe's head appeared. Joe called out, "You ready to receive?"

"Toss 'em on down, Joe," Bill answered. He caught Joe's bag with both hands and watched as Joe lowered himself down.

"Did you notice that sunlight on the water as we came in? It reminded me of sparkling diamonds," he said to Bill as he watched his buddy resume his limbering-up routine. Then he smoothed back his hair and straightened his blouse. Looking each other over, the two boys decided they were presentable enough.

"I did and thought the same thing: diamonds," said Bill. Changing the subject, he added, "What do you think the odds are of us getting a swim in while we're here?"

"Dunno. If we do, I sure hope to hell it isn't because we were shot down over the drink," Joe responded.

Unlike the hints and shadows of conflict Bill had seen in the Azores and Tunisia, there was no mistaking he had arrived in an honest-to-goodness war zone. The base at Gioia was overfull with dull green military vehicles being driven in a hurry by men in sandy brown or olive drab uniforms. More Army Air Corps personnel hoofed it on foot—clipboards and briefcases in hand—going about their assigned tasks and duties. Overhead, the vibrations of aircraft engines rattled the sky as transports, bombers, and fighters took off and landed.

"Did you hear Wes say to head on over to the officers' mess and grab some chow?" Bill asked Joe who nodded his response. "And did he say anything about what to do with our gear?"

"Come to think of it, no," said Joe. "Looks like we'll be dragging these bags around awhile because I want some grub before we go hunting down our quarters."

"Roger that," Bill agreed.

They hailed one of the many Jeeps crisscrossing the tarmac, tossed in their bags, and grabbed a ride across camp to the mess, too hungry to wait for the rest of the crew who would soon follow after they had secured the bomber and assembled their gear.

When they entered the lively officers' mess hall, they deposited their bags near the door. Bill's nostrils filled with the familiar scent of American food and … coffee. The place was packed with young men talking, laughing, and loading their bellies for the day. Bill imagined each of the men and boys here were either passing through on their way to their assignments, like he was, or worked at the base. He also imagined that, unlike training camps, they probably weren't fed at regular intervals in a war zone, so they ate whatever they could, whenever they could.

Joe and Bill grabbed a couple of metal food trays and joined the line. They worked their way through the queue to find the cooks—huge steaming metal vats before them—slopping mounds of corn mush, mashed potatoes, meatloaf, and a healthy helping of peas onto everyone's tin plates. *What is it with peas?* Bill was, and forever would be, not a fan of vegetables, and he was certainly unaccustomed to greens at breakfast. He lamented as he eyed his tray. *American food for the Americans*, he thought, when tasting authentic Southern Italian cuisine might have interested him more. *When in Rome.*

He was picky, a meat-and-potatoes kind of guy, and figured he had no choice but to eat what was given him, even if it was the very same he had eaten at every base of training. He and Joe grabbed four cups of coffee for Wes, Jug, and themselves. Bill found a cup of the brew to be the perfect pick-me-up after a long flight, and this particular water-to-bean ratio was the best he'd tasted since Chief's hair-on-end version.

Leaving the line, the boys found a long wooden table and claimed it as their own. Bill listened to the chatter of the surrounding groups of men; it was hard to ignore. The talk at the table nearest them was intriguing.

"Well," one first lieutenant was saying to another sitting next to him, "you've heard how the higher-ups are splitting up the crews now."

"Yeah," the second kid replied. "'Cause of heavy casualties, right?" *So*, Bill thought, *a replacement draft is underway.*

Stateside, he had heard about these drafts; every trainee had heard about them. Replacement pilots, copilots, bombardiers, and gunners were desperately needed by some of the more seasoned crews who had suffered the loss of many airmen. Newly arrived crews who had trained together in the States, green and fresh, were vulnerable to the unofficial yet necessary draft. Bill and Joe dug into their chow and glanced at one another from time to time, silently sharing the unspoken concern that any one of their crew might be reassigned.

Wes and Jug came sauntering up with their own trays of breakfast hash. Both of them looked as fresh as when they had left Tunis at four that morning. Bill wondered how they had pulled that off. Wes had even managed to wrangle an entire carafe of fresh-brewed coffee as he passed through the mess line. He leaned over and topped off Bill's aluminum mug before sitting down. Joe put his hand over the mouth of his cup, declining any more. Their astute pilot sensed the somber mood of the table.

"What's bugging you two?" he asked, pushing his crush cap to the crown of his head and out of his way.

"We just overheard they're splitting up crews," Bill answered honestly. "And we don't want any of that."

Jug heard Bill's answer to Wes but ignored it. Instead, he chimed in, "Boys, I have *news from the flight deck*." He paused to allow room for a response. Bill and Joe just looked at him without comment, waiting for what he was about to say. "Our first casualty is Silver Beauty." Jug waited. Nothing, no bites; neither Bill nor Joe found their voices to speak up. Bill was waiting for the other shoe to drop. "Well, just after y'all left, Wes and I began helping Murph secure the bomber when some sergeant major climbed up into the flight deck and handed Wes requisition papers. She's gone, boys."

Bill realized he had been holding his breath the whole time Jug had been telling his story, afraid to hear the next bit: that he was being drafted to work with another crew. He had to admit, he was relieved that so far it was just the plane that was being reassigned. Bill took another bite of meatloaf and chased it down with a long gulp of coffee.

Jug was matter-of-fact as he continued on, explaining how all of their gear had been removed from the bomber. Officers who hadn't already taken their personal belongings could reunite with their things in the temporary officers' quarters, and enlisted men would likewise find theirs in the enlisted men's quarters. Bill was both sad and relieved. Then Jug shared the news that Silver Beauty was being sent to a squadron that had suffered heavy aircraft losses in the recent escalation of Allied attacks on the oil fields of Ploesti, Romania. Bill was getting the feeling he would be saying goodbye to more than one 24J before his war was over. He hoped it was just the planes he'd be saying so long to and not the crews he was bound to get to know.

He figured he spoke for both himself and Joe when he asked the most important question on his mind. "But we're still intact as a crew, right?" he said, looking at Wes for confirmation. "What we heard about breaking up new crews, that's not happening to us, right?" A few other officers sat down at their table. Bill gave them a smile and a nod before focusing his attention on Wes.

"They've just got to keep us together, Wes," Joe demanded. "The plane is one thing, but we're family now."

Calm as ever and consulting his watch, Wes said, "We'll know more once I meet with base command in about thirty." He continued, "Let's think the best until we know our status for certain." He pushed himself up to standing, readjusted his cap, and asked Jug to accompany him. He turned and said to Bill and Joe, "You boys go find our temporary quarters."

"Aye, aye, Pappy," the two lieutenants chimed back.

As the boys stood up, one of the officers who had recently joined their table spoke to them. "You all talking about that new directive? We heard that too when we got here yesterday. We got lucky; all ten of us are still together. I wish you the same."

Leaving the mess hall, Joe and Bill hoisted their duffels and flight bags over their shoulders and went looking for their quarters. By now, Bill had determined all army air bases looked and smelled the same. The air was thick with the funk of burning jet fuel, oil, and rubber aircraft tires. Everywhere he looked, Bill saw men in uniform moving at a purposeful pace—whether on foot, in a truck, or Jeep. And each one of them appeared to know precisely where he needed to be.

He and Joe were in search of the ever-present signposts—every base had them—and the directions they needed to navigate the layout. They soon found their quarters and the enlisted men's as well. The exercise in locating their housing worked to dispel the are-we-going-to-be-split-up jitters. While Bill and Joe were checking out their quarters, two sergeants drove up to deliver Wes and Jug's gear. Bombardier and navigator stored their bags and duffels on top of the cots they'd chosen, then went back outside to resume their walkabout. Mike, Murph, and the rest of the crew were nowhere to be found, so they turned back and walked to the tarmac.

Bill was content. The sun was shining and the sky was an azure blue dotted with cotton-puff cumulus. He was exploring new surroundings and considering the fact that he was in yet another country. Until he had embarked on this journey, he had never lived anywhere but the United States; he'd only read about Africa and Italy. He couldn't help but be excited, regardless of the serious nature of his presence here. Each new country he landed in was different than the one before and had experiences for him to remember. The air in Newfoundland had been frigid and the sun strong. In Lajes, the atmosphere had been heavy with the humidity of an island nation. The part of Africa he'd seen was hot and dry. When the wind blew strong enough, the sand could strip the skin from a person's face if he wasn't wearing protection.

Each location had its traditional foods, the smells sometimes enticing and often off-putting, but Bill liked to think of himself as the adventurous type: he'd try anything at least once. He planned on eating as much pasta as he could, plain with oil maybe, as he avoided tomatoes at all costs. And oh, the languages he had heard along the way; the nuanced manner in which the locals communicated with one another was very different than how they expressed themselves to him. He was curious about everything before him, and when it was all over, he'd have countries to reflect upon and adventures to tell.

The now-familiar scent of creosote beckoned the two young men to inspect the bombers awaiting their crews and their next missions. Bill felt an intensity here on the tarmac, both in activity and aroma. He recognized the fumes and undertones of fuel and oil as he stood admiring a freshly painted "Vulgar Vulture" on the tail of one B-24. A caricature of a drooling, black-winged vulture gripping a yellow bomb in its talons graced the tail of the bomber, the same model the boys had flown over from New Hampshire, a "J."

"Why do you think some bomb groups have art on the tail and others on the side of the nose?" Joe asked.

"Beats me, Joe," Bill answered. "Standing out is part of the competition I guess."

"Sounds about right," Joe agreed.

"That tail art is swell, don't you think?" Bill asked as they began walking again, searching for their friends.

"It's pretty impressive," replied Joe. "Almost like a professional painted it."

"Say, Joe," Bill began, "how do you feel about the 15th?"

"Well, I like what I've heard about it so far," Joe answered. "It's brand new, and we'll be part of opening up a whole new route to Nazi territory."

"Yeah, our army on the ground can take a load of credit for that," Bill said. "Those guys held the beachhead at Anzio to make the 15th possible." Prior to their leaving the US, he had seen newsreels of dramatic scenes of the Allied fight to cleanse Southern Italy of all Axis activity. That same news was covered extensively in local and national newspapers.

"I think I'd rather be in the air," Joe commented. "Away from the barrage of those Nazi panzers."

"It's only been over a short while," Bill said. "The battle, I mean. Did you hear those guys talking at breakfast?"

"I did," Joe said with a smile. "Our timing is impeccable."

Around noon by Bill's Bulova, with the sun higher in the sky warming the day quickly, most of the crew had found one another on the tarmac. Spotting an open field off the side of the airstrip, they headed for it with physical activity in mind; they needed to let off steam. Mike appeared with an off-duty maintenance engineer he'd met on the airstrip. The kid had been tossing a football from one hand to the other when Mike spotted him. Being a quick thinker, Mike suggested a pickup game of tag football. The engineer agreed, and they set out to join the others they could see gathering on the field.

While the boys stripped off their blouses and tossed them to the side, they drew up sides. Because there were nine of them, they agreed one player at a time would sit out a quarter. The engineer insisted on playing quarterback. "My ball, my choice," he quipped. He ended up on Bill's team. Ritt took up the quarterback on the opposing team, but everyone had to more-or-less play all the positions. The barely green, dried-up patchy grass tripped up more than Bill; the flight engineers, gunners, and Joe all took hard tumbles, yet came up laughing. The boys reveled in the exertion, teasing and joking one another as they ruled the field. When Wes and Jug came strolling up, they watched the scrimmage until Bill's team scored.

Then Wes stepped forward and called over, "Well gentlemen, we've got orders!"

Bill tossed the ball back to the kid. "Thanks for the game. Hope your orders come in soon."

As the crew made their way back to their barracks, Wes explained the assignment. They had five days to report to the 304th Wing of the 740th Squadron of the 455th Bomb Group "H."

"What's the 'H' for, Cappy?" Belding asked.

"Heavy," Wes replied before continuing his explanation. The 455th was based near Cerignola, about a two-hour ride from where they were now. They'd remain in Gioia for a few days of orientation before heading east, almost directly across the ankle of Italy's boot and a bit north to reach the base at Cerignola.

Bill was relieved. Wes hadn't mentioned anything about the crew being broken up.

∞

On Wes's orders, the crew met at the airstrip immediately after breakfast the following day. They now had four days to be combat-ready. They had proven themselves a good team so far, but there was always room for improvement. Bill looked forward to real-time aerial war training before their first mission. Luckily, they were assigned a veteran pilot who knew both the terrain and the enemy for a practice run. The vet was trim and businesslike, his white-blonde hair, shorn as short as peach fuzz, accentuated his very square jaw. Bill dubbed him "Lantern Jaw." While the crew assembled at the bomber, the vet handed Bill the heavy case containing a Norden bombsight. Grasping the handles, he was momentarily transported back to training: the weight and heft of the device was comfortingly familiar. He hadn't forgotten how critical the machine was.

"Ah, my tools," he said to Lantern Jaw. "Now, I feel right at home."

Wes and Jug pulled themselves up into the plane, followed by the rest of the crew. Bill, Joe, and the vet climbed in last and headed for the bomb deck. Bill set down the case, opened it, and removed the device. After a brief inspection of all its parts, he carefully lifted the ponderous black metal contraption and positioned the Norden over a small Plexiglas bubble just off the compartment.

"Looks like you know what you're doing," Lantern Jaw said to Bill approvingly. "I'll leave you to it."

"Roger that," Bill said as he found himself thoroughly focused on his task.

Back up on the flight deck, the vet took Jug's seat while Jug sat in the jump seat behind Wes. They prepared to take off from Gioia to practice "bombing" an area of Italy only recently vacated by the Nazis. Back in their office, Bill and Joe focused on any and all information coming in through their headsets from the officers on the flight deck, taking notes and memorizing landmarks before having to get to work. In moments, Wes had the bomber in the air.

After his practice at two bomb schools, Bill learned that the most advantageous position he could take on the bomb deck was actually on his stomach—his legs stretched out on the floor behind him, and his head poised over the eyepiece of the Norden. He assumed his preferred stance on this run too. It gave Joe room to stand before the pulldown desk and consult his maps. During the run, Bill made constant adjustments on the course knob and drift scale in addition to calculations from the directional clutch. He was ready for Wes's command.

"Pilot to bombardier," Wes's calm voice eased its way through the intercom to Bill. "She's all yours."

Bill took control of the plane through the Norden and practiced "releasing" the virtual load of incendiaries before handing the controls back to Wes by way of the universal signal, "Bombs away!"

The vet assessed Bill's accuracy of aim, Joe's navigational skills, and Wes's ability to react, jotting his findings in a small notebook. Two hours later, they were heading back for Gioia.

"You'll get more practice once you reach Cerignola," the vet assured them as Wes dropped the bomber down to land. "But you and your men couldn't be any more ready."

Once on the ground, Lantern Jaw took Wes aside to say how impressed he was with Bill's ability to "hit" the designated targets. He informed Wes that when he reported to the base commander, he was going to recommend that they watch to see if Bill fit the requirements for lead bombardier. Although proud of his bombardier, Wes asked the vet to keep this bit of news quiet, at least until the crew reached Cerignola.

"Flying lead would mean a lot to Bill," Wes explained to the vet. Pappy knew it would be a confidence booster for his green bombardier.

Fifteen

THE WAIT IS OVER

*Gioia to Cerignola,
Italy, June 1944*

THE CREW ASSEMBLED at the motor pool, loaded down with all their gear for the move to Cerignola. Soon they were bouncing along the Italian countryside in the back of two open GI six-by-sixes headed to the 455th; the officers and their cases and bags in one truck, the enlisted men and their bags in the other. The weather was clear and warm, and the drivers had taken the tarps off the trucks. The open sides of the vehicle allowed Bill to follow the path of destruction the Germans had left in their wake on their retreat north.

He had seen some of the torn and lacerated earth and the collapsed houses and structures from the air on their approach into Gioia. He saw them again on their first practice runs around the area. He'd found the carnage impressive, yet at altitude, he felt somewhat removed from the destruction. It was more dramatic at ground level. Old farmhouses, stone walls, and wooden barns had been spitefully reduced to rubble, and buildings had been set ablaze, leaving a black smudge of a footprint where they once had been. Once-verdant farm fields had been plowed up and left to dry out and die; no living crops were left to grow. Bill imagined the hard-fought struggles that had occurred here: battles to reclaim the land, to push out the invaders. The scuttlebutt in Gioia was that the Germans were still strongly entrenched along a line straight across the Mediterranean to the Adriatic, about a hundred miles north of Rome. He felt the enemy's presence; they no longer were an ocean away. One hundred miles was not far by air, but he was confident in the Allies' ability to rout the Nazis, and he would have a hand in that.

∞

The olive drab six-by-six rolled slowly through Cerignola, a ruined, bombed-out wreck of an agricultural town that now housed double the number of people it had been designed for: a mix of USAAF personnel and refugees fleeing cities and villages further north, making their way to the safety of an American-occupied area. The truck rolled past Cerignola's town square—just as a spring rain began to fall. It dampened the dust and temporarily sent the ever-present flies and mosquitoes packing. Bill welcomed the sprinkle; he was feeling a little dry. When the truck arrived at the airfield, it stopped at headquarters so Wes and the three other officers could report to the CO, Major General Nathan F. Twining. They then would meet with the flight surgeon for their wing, the 304th. Wes motioned to the rest of the crew to hang tight.

As they approached the surgeon's office, Bill recalled a conversation he had overheard in the officers' mess in Gioia: the flight surgeon he was about to meet was famous for referring to Cerignola as a "reservoir of malaria and dysentery." The sheer number of pests in and around the area caused diseases to spread throughout the town and the base. The official stance from HQ was to drink only coffee and boiled water, regardless how many inoculations they had received prior to shipping out. Bill didn't like germs much; he kept himself as impeccably clean as conditions allowed. All this talk about disease caused him to vow to double his efforts when it came to personal hygiene. The doctor spent time getting to know the officers, which Bill considered a good thing; after all, he would be the one determining the fitness of their health, both mental and physical, to fly.

Next up was the officers' briefing with Major General Twining, during which he informed them that the 455th had lost over 100 percent of its strength in the past year. That got their attention. It meant their casualties were high. Bill felt his spine twitch a bit. Then Twining instructed them on the more mundane details, like housing and basic routines.

After the officers had been brought up to speed, they filed out of the building and collected around their awaiting truck. Murph and the boys had been milling around smoking cigarettes and shooting the breeze when Wes called them over to remind them about their conduct and direct them to their quarters.

"OK, back on the truck!" Murph called to the rest of the enlisted men.

"Roger that," Bill said, as he jumped into the truck with Wes, Jug, and Joe. They rocked along with the ruts in the road, the six-by-sixes navigating neat rows of drab brown canvas buildings along the way.

A former vineyard outside Cerignola stood as runways for both the 455th and the 454th bomb groups. The US Army Corps of Engineers had razed what little the German army had left untouched of row upon row of Italian grapevines and laid down steel mats to stabilize the ground for aircraft. Each group had four squadrons, and each squadron was supposed to have twenty B-24s, but with their heavy losses, the 15th often managed with fewer than the ideal. New bombers couldn't come in fast enough: planes were consistently being shot down, lost to combat, or were missing parts, rendering them useless regardless of the heroic effort on the part of the ground crews to get them back up in the air. Looking out over the airfield, Bill wondered where Silver Beauty was by now.

∽

Home for Bill and the officers was a surprisingly spacious tent in a pasture set aside for, and occupied by, the 740th Squadron (H). The pasture was fondly referred to as "officer country." The six enlisted crew members shared an even larger tent about two hundred yards away. An open-air shower stood between them; it was canvas-sided and roomy. Most of the men used old, rinsed-out "Jerry" gasoline cans to draw washing and drinking water from two large tanks that had been erected near the shower.

The previous occupants of their assigned tent had gone down on their last mission. The unofficial five-day waiting period had passed and their personal effects had been sent back home. This left Wes, Jug, Bill, and Joe the task of reinhabiting the place. Anything that could make a tent more comfortable had already been stripped by other officers looking to enhance their own spaces and make them easier to live in. All that remained were four folding cots, two folding chairs, and their duffel bags. The boys decided it was time to get scavenging themselves.

Bill went in search of something to write on and dragged back a marred pine desk plus a third folding chair. Wes contributed an actual coat rack, some wooden slats he thought could be useful, and a bent bronze gooseneck table lamp. Joe also retrieved a desk. It kept leaning to the right; its legs were wobbly and in need of reinforcing. He eyed Wes's wooden slats. Jug added a piece of art: a current pinup calendar he hung with safety pins on the side of the tent over the more stable desk. Bill's desk. Turns out, Jug had several pinups that he rotated through every few days. Once they had agreed and arranged every-thing to their liking, they stepped back to admire their handiwork and ingenuity. They dubbed their tent, "The Manse." But they weren't finished enhancing their space just yet. Within a few days, Joe and Bill, with Murph's assistance, had rigged an unofficially "requisitioned" drop tank from a fighter plane outside the tent.

Murph "laid claim" to a tank with some remaining fuel and devised a way to top it off as needed: he'd "lift" aviation fuel from the depot. This would give the officers both heat and hot water in their tent. Bill was already anticipating his first shave in weeks with hot water—how soothing that was going to feel. They thought themselves geniuses, but Murph had words of caution for Bill and Joe.

"Look, a lot of officers have gone with a similar setup," Murph explained what he'd learned in his first short hours on base. "It's against regulations and dangerous, but it works, so I'll help you get it up and running. A couple of other engineers kindly demonstrated how they've been doing it," he said with a wink.

Several tents equipped in similar fashion had gone up in flames in the past, but when Southern Italy's infamous cold soggy winter arrived, the accidents didn't deter others from rigging heating systems of their own. How was this danger any worse than that of being thirty thousand feet in the air dodging FLAK and enemy fighter attacks?

Bill was impressed with how many original ideas were surfacing out of the most basic human desire to be comfortable. And once the setup was operational, Murph dropped by frequently to take comfort in the warmth of the officers' tent.

∞

At dinner in the officers' mess on his first night in Cerignola, Bill learned where the 455th's moniker "The Vulgar Vultures" originated. He was speaking to a copilot seated at an adjacent table and mentioned the tail art he had seen in Gioia. It turned out the copilot was with Bill's wing, the 704th.

"Glad you like it," the guy said. "We all do." He explained that the art had been a collaborative effort between an air force intelligence officer and the 455th bomb group. The specs for the drawings had been sent to artists at Walt Disney Studios in Burbank, California.

"In the case of the 455th, the artists created a black-and-white cartoon vulture riding a yellow bomb, its talons dripping red blood," the copilot continued. "I'm not certain why the intelligence officer chose a vulture as our mascot—perhaps because our bombers look like vultures and we look down from lofty heights—but those artists took the idea and created our symbol."

Whether meant to create fear in the enemy or a sense of might and victory, Bill approved of the art and was itching to get up in the air in a bomber with the Disney markings.

"Is there a reason the 455th chose to decorate the tails of the bombers?" Bill asked.

"Just to be different from the squadrons who have the name of their planes or other art painted on the nose. Disney doesn't create art solely for the 455th," said the copilot. "They create the artwork for many bomber groups and squadrons."

"Not all of our 24s have tail art," the copilot warned Bill, unwittingly dashing his hopes of flying in a bomber bearing their symbol. "Sometimes, the tail is shot off by enemy machine guns or the art is scraped off by a burst of FLAK. Sometimes our talented ground crews haven't had the time to get to painting. That's been pretty true as of late. We keep those boys pretty busy patching up the planes we limp home in."

Listening to the copilot speak, Bill realized he was already a Vulgar Vulture, tail art or no.

∽

On their second day in camp, Wes had the entire crew up before breakfast. He'd been informed they had twenty-four hours to learn the terrain. Pappy kept a tight schedule; he announced they would fly at least two practice runs before lunch. Bill's stomach rumbled in anticipation of a skipped meal.

Similar to their experience in Gioia, a veteran pilot sat in Jug's seat for their morning runs, acting as copilot, guide, and instructor while the crew learned the landmarks, judged distances, and practiced "bombing" the immediate area. Bill and Joe, back in their office, tried to impress another veteran pilot with their skills: Bill with his accuracy on the Norden and Joe with his ability to memorize critical landmarks, like the Romanesque spire of the Church of Saint Mary of Foggia, his signal they were nearly back to Cerignola. With hundreds of churches and as many spires dotting the towns of Italy, picking out the right one became critical when approaching a landing, especially if the plane had been shot up or crew members wounded during a run.

After a break to refuel and eat some lunch, the crew was up in the air again with the instructor pilot, this time over the Adriatic. Bill practiced dropping bombs over the sea and watched mesmerized as they hopscotched above distant teal water, sending snow-white ribbons of foam several feet into the air before plunging into the drink. Once Bill locked in the target on the Norden, the bombsight took over and kept the target in those crosshairs. Then he programmed in the plane's speed and altitude as well as the type of "bomb" he'd be dropping. The Norden even calculated the path the ordnance would follow and made any necessary corrections due to the wind, heading, and altitude. Bill visualized it all going to plan.

The gunners—Belding, Ritt, and Hill—tested their .50 caliber guns. Murph, Stohlman, and Harvey had a go too. The gunners were Bill's guys, the bombardier's guys; he was their armament officer and checked in with each gunner to be certain their machines and intercoms were in good working order.

As they rumbled along in the safety of the airspace surrounding San Giovanni, Foggia, and Cerignola, Bill's imagination raced ahead to the day when they would receive their first mission orders. *This is definitely the calm before the storm*, he reckoned, *the eye of the hurricane.*

Missions, and the makeup of crews scheduled to fly those missions, were posted on the squadron bulletin board before a bomb run, usually around five every evening. A rough mission might not be posted until as late as nine at night. Bill figured that was to lessen the impact of concern and worry on the crews scheduled for that mission. Any mission could go south, but some were more dangerous than others. The board was set up just outside the briefing bunker, a former wine cellar. He'd read these notices since arriving, waiting for the day he'd see his name up there. He didn't have to wait long—orders came down after their final training run of the day. His first wartime briefing was scheduled for 0400 the next morning. *This is it*, he told himself, *I'm going to war.*

Yonder

Sixteen

FIRST MISSION

*Lead Bombardier, Double Sortie,
Italy to Hungary, 26 August 1944*

BILL WOKE AT PRECISELY 0240 hours the next morning, over an hour before having to report for the mission briefing. He got out of bed, pulled his sheets and military blanket tight, walked over to the door of the tent, opened the door, and peeked out. Dawn had not yet come, and the air was slightly warm. He reveled in the quiet. No sound of reverberating aircraft engines above or tires crunching on the dirt roads broke the silence. Bill looked up to the stars again, making out what constellations he could remember: Cassiopeia, Ursa Major, Ursa Minor. From this angle, they looked different than he remembered back in Chicago: foreign. Returning to the tent, he closed the door and began to dress. The rest of the officers slept on, but they would have to wake soon.

He reflected on last night's dream. He was on a bomb run, the target heavily defended. Clouds of destruction in the form of FLAK buffeted the plane. Only static was coming through his headset, yet Bill knew to stay on task in his cramped, vulnerable position in the Plexiglas nose of the bomber. He glanced up and saw the back of a head bent over a pull-down desktop—Joe. Recognizing his friend in the dream, Bill began to wake—recent images still fresh in his mind. He began to consider how close to his future reality his dream might be. He was considering the certainty of dreams when he was drawn out of the scenario by the distinct sound of a Jeep's motor and vulcanized rubber tires on hard-packed earth.

"Up and at 'em!" shouted the charge of quarters as he knocked on the tent door. "It's glory time, boys!" It was 0300 hours.

Wes got out of bed and dressed calmly but quickly. He walked over to Bill as he was pulling on his white athletic socks—his lucky socks. Lucky because he'd brought his football team to victory countless times wearing socks just like these.

"Gemmill, you know those aren't allowed." Wes fumbled with his uniform blouse as he chastised Bill and pointed down to his bombardier's feet.

"Tell me about it, Pappy. Do you want to talk about that scarf you keep tucked under your suit?" Bill countered.

"You got me, Bombardier," a sheepish grin grew across Wes's face as he tucked his non-regulation, faded red bandana beneath his regulation khaki shirt. He let drop the matter of proper military gear and never mentioned it again.

Called to mission briefing, squadron officers poured down the steps of the cool hundred-year-old wine cellar for the pre-mission briefing. Bill, Joe, Jug, and Wes were among the first through the door. Bill counted: twenty-five steps down. He ducked his head under the lintel and scanned the room. One hundred and eighty boys—eighteen crews—would be flying on this mission. Seventy-two officers were in attendance to hear the day's target. Bill reflected on how everyone in the cellar had his own fears, dreads, prayers, and wishes, and their own way of dealing with emotion. Bill was outgoing yet reflective, Joe talkative. Jug was uncharacteristically solemn, and Wes was his customary silent, no-nonsense self. They sat in the front row for the briefing.

Once all squadron officers had assembled, the squadron leader dropped the drape over a huge horizontal map of Northern Europe hanging on the wall. A collective groan rose as the target was revealed: Ploesti, Romania, the oil refineries critical to the Nazi supply line. Postures adjusted, jaws clenched, and greenhorns like Bill sat staring at the map, trying to get a sense of what they'd be facing. Of course, Bill had heard of Ploesti—they all had. The combined air forces of the Allies had been pounding the place for months. The target was infamous for taking down bombers with their heavy anti-aircraft defenses. The heavier the fortifications, the heavier the Allies' losses were expected to be. It was the cost of attacking Hitler's major source of fuel. Hitler's precious oil refineries were notorious for their near-insurmountable defenses and subsequent casualties. Yet despite the heavy toll the effort took, the fliers of the 15th—in particular the 455th and 454th bomb groups—kept going back, motivated by the fact that without oil, the Wehrmacht couldn't move its tanks, troops, or supplies, and their exalted Luftwaffe couldn't fly.

Army meteorologists stepped forward to give updates on the weather in and around the target. Then the intelligence officer updated the intel on enemy armaments and defenses, like FLAK and fighters. He outlined escape and evasion information, instructed the men whether any Partisans or Chetniks had been seen in the vicinity of the target, and shared other information gained from recent crew debriefings.

"Pilots, you'll see a number printed on the upper right corner of the coordinates we just passed around," the squadron leader announced as the briefing was wrapping up. "You'll find that same number on the tail of your assigned bomber. Good luck." Satisfied that all bases had been covered, including the formation of the run, the squadron leader dismissed everyone save the group bombardiers and navigators, often referred to as "B&Ns," who were told to remain for a second briefing designed specifically for them.

Bill and Joe remained in their seats in the front row. Before diving into the details for each primary and alternate target, the squadron leader gave another quick overview for the benefit of anyone who had missed the details, then introduced the meteorologist once again in order for him to answer any questions the men had. By listening to the more seasoned bombardiers' questions—and the answers they received—Bill was learning that there was nothing like hearing the direct experience of others to help you shape your sense of a situation. At this special briefing, bombardiers and navigators were given time to study the photographs, drawings, and maps of the target area. They might not have much time to consult maps and photographs once in the air.

"Gemmill?" the squadron leader called his name, not butchering the pronunciation too terribly. Bill never understood how people tripped over saying his surname properly; how hard could it be? It's like Campbell, with a hard "G" and no "B." Bill stood up and responded, "Yes, Sir!"

"You will be flying deputy lead. Normally, you and your crew would be way back in the back of the last box, but we're accessing a few of the newly arrived bombardiers on this run," the squadron leader began his instructions. "Your pilot, Powell, will fly second seat. I'm sending your second seat to another crew who lost their copilot. Your pilot for this mission will be Captain Fred Wilde. He knows the route better than most." At this, a square-jawed redhead stepped forward and extended his hand to Bill.

"Good to meet you, Captain Wilde," Bill said as he shook the pilot's hand.

"Likewise, Lieutenant," the pilot returned the greeting.

The squadron leader continued to address Bill. "You understand this means you'll be flying up front with a Norden. I hear you're pretty good on that machine in practice. Show me what you can do with it when the shit starts to fly."

"Understood, Sir," Bill said, not at all surprised by the energy he heard in his own voice. He knew he was up to the task, and the more he thought about it, the better he felt. Being a new crew in the squadron, they could have easily pulled the most dangerous and vulnerable position to fighter attack in the whole damn formation: Tail End Charlie. *No*, he thought, *I'm happy with the number-two slot.*

After the B&N briefing concluded, Bill and Joe climbed back out of the cellar and walked over to the mission board where Wes was waiting. Jug had already left to join up with the crew he had been assigned for this mission. Bill was relieved they'd be flying as a crew, with the exception of Jug, and the familiar names on the board made the war more real: Fred Wilde, Pilot; Wesley Powell, Copilot; Joe Perkins, Navigator; Bill Gemmill, Deputy Lead Bombardier. Bill was still a bit stunned at being designated deputy lead. He had assumed, this being their first mission, that they'd be in the back of the formation with no Norden, or maybe somewhere in the middle, where he would toggle his bombs off the lead. Talk about a trial by fire. He looked over at Wes. The pilot gave Bill a wry smile and a slight tip of his cap. *So this is it*, thought Bill. *We're going up and getting into it at last.* Murph and Ritt and Hill approached Wes impatiently, while Belding, Stohlman, and Harvey hung back a bit in silent anticipation.

"So? What's it to be? An easy milk run or Hell?" Murph pressed Wes. He had taken a wide stance with his hands on his hips, and looked up at his pilot.

"We're being baptized by fire, boys," Wes drawled before turning to the rest of the crew gathering around him. "Time to get this show on the road. I'll fill you in on the way out to the airfield."

"Aye, aye, Cappy!" eight voices cheered in unison.

When Bill and Joe arrived at the crew's assigned bomber, a security officer approached them and asked for the bombardier. The man was carrying a black leather Norden bomb case that was attached to a metal chain that led to a silver bracelet cuffed to his wrist.

"That would be me," Bill said.

"This is for you," said the security officer. He unlocked the bracelet, detached the chain, and turned the case over to Bill. "Good luck," the officer said before turning and walking back across the tarmac.

"Well," Bill sighed as he looked at Joe, "this really is for real, isn't it?"

"Looks that way," Joe said as he helped hoist the case up to Bill through the hatch.

∞

Once they reached their designated altitude of twenty-four thousand feet, and while they were still over friendly territory, the squadron bombers maneuvered into a combat box formation, also known as a staggered formation. From the ground it looked like a series of triangles flying tightly, one plane behind and slightly off the wing of the one in front of it. The "box" was designed to provide the maximum amount of protection for the bombers; enemy fighters normally attacked from the rear or front because that was where the aircraft was most vulnerable. Pilots were instructed to keep the formation tight, which meant that the planes were buffeted about by turbulence from the other aircraft within the box. Three or four bombers formed the box, but a squadron could contain as many as six box formations when other bomb groups joined the same mission. Many a box was scrambled after an encounter with FLAK.

The Germans were creative in hiding the heavy 88-mm aircraft defense cannon. They could be situated in the open, camouflaged under netting designed to look like dried grass; hidden in barns with a hole in the roof; or, in the larger German cities, on the top of towers. The guns were capable of reaching thirty-five thousand feet, and they were accurate. The cannons would fire; the load would reach its set altitude, then explode in midair. Every pilot did everything he could to weave around a field of FLAK. The pilot's and copilot's seats were armored, yet that wasn't much insurance from being maimed, or worse, if a burst from one of those guns pierced the flight deck from the front. Bits and shards of metal tore through an aircraft, shattering instruments, hydraulics, landing gear, radio equipment, and the protective jackets, headgear, and bones of thousands of airmen. The weather added additional factors of concern.

Wilde positioned his aircraft slightly behind the lead bomber's left wing. As deputy lead bombardier, instead of watching the planes in front and toggling his bomb load off of their drops, Bill would work with his Norden as backup to the lead bombardier. He cautioned himself: *First time up and chances are good that all the guys will end up toggling off of me, so no screw-ups, Gemmill.* He felt energized; a steady throb pulsed through him as he realized he was about to fulfill the promise he had made to the downed crew in Indiana over a year ago. And he was particularly happy with the weather report: good flying in all sectors. He was less enthusiastic about the smell of the plane: grease and oil and sweat.

The squadron flew north over Italy before turning east and entered Yugoslavian airspace, keeping the mountains to their left. The lead bombardier ordered the squadron gunners to test-fire all their machine guns. Spent casings pinged off the metal skin of the plane, interrupting Bill's calculations, and for a moment, scared him right out of his white, non-regulation socks. After that initial jolt, he settled down and resumed configuring the necessary calculations on his notepad before entering them into the Norden. Precision bombing relied on his ability to get his figures as accurate as possible.

"Guess you won't be able to hide any mistakes you make now, Gemmill, seeing as how we're up front," Joe cracked. Like Bill, he used a joke to hide any jitters he might be feeling. Also like Bill, he leaned on his training, put aside his nervousness, and did his job. The intercom squawked and the situation changed.

As they approached Ploesti, cloaked in cloud and smoke, the squadron leader ordered the box to turn south toward the first alternate target: a large military barracks in Bucharest, Romania. Scrambling to recalibrate the information in the bombsight, Bill forgot to be nervous, forgot that it was his first air combat run, forgot to worry that everyone from the flight deck to the other bombers was watching him. The skies cleared as they reached Bucharest, and the target loomed large in the Norden's sight. Then the FLAK started up from anti-aircraft guns concealed in haystacks and woods on the ground. It was intense and accurate. Pieces of shrapnel rained down on the plane, causing a ruckus like heavy hail on a tin roof. Bill remained steady, watched the velocity as the bomber closed in on the target, and waited for the crosshairs to align. With all systems go, he released the payload for the first time in real combat.

"Bombs away!" he called into the intercom, and the bomber was back in Captain Wilde's capable hands. Bill was too concerned about the job, the FLAK, and his accuracy to think about the weight of the moment *in the moment.*

As the plane banked away from the drop zone, Bill lay on his side to watch the bombs hit. The FLAK never let up; in fact, Bill felt it had grown more brutal.

"Tail gunner, tell us how we did," Bill's request charged through the noise.

"Looks like those beauties met their mark, Lieutenant. We hurt 'em good!" came the reply from Ritt in the tail.

The initial explosion had grown like black ink in liquid, blossoming in slow motion into the sky. Although they were now moving out of range, Bill continued to watch the results of his work until he could no longer find the target in his viewer. Later reconnaissance photos confirmed what he and his tail gunner had seen: he had hit his first target in combat. If everyone had managed to stay on course and toggle at the same time, the bombs would have "walked" over the target area, devastating the troops and supplies awaiting transport out of Bucharest.

"Well done, Bombardier," Wilde said into the intercom. His kudos were cut short when, as they lifted out of the FLAK cloud, enemy fighters appeared.

Wes called out, "Fighters at one o'clock!"

The gunners began firing their mighty .50s. Belding released a barrage of bullets from the ball turret while Ritt was giving the enemy his all in the nose. The relentless, almighty noise ricocheted through the aircraft. Bill's nerves of steel deteriorated in the Plexiglas bubble where he felt vulnerable and unable to take cover, until a P-51 escort appeared after the enemy's first pass. The US fighters forced the Nazi ME-109 and ME-110 pilots to give up and peel away from the formation of bombers. Like an irritating mosquito, the escort was all over the challengers. Bill watched, mesmerized by the aerial dance, and designated his first hero of his war as he watched a particular P-51 dodge, dart, and taunt the German planes. Every pilot, friend or foe, was making split-second decisions. Bill's heart pounded and he shouted encouragement as several more American fighters joined the fray. Wilde was doing a great job of maneuvering the heavy B-24 through the engagement, keeping their course steady despite the FLAK, machine gun fire, and turbulence stirred up by the number of aircraft occupying the same airspace.

One by one, German planes exploded, burst into flames, or broke apart on their way down. Parachutes emerged from one ME-109, momentarily suspended in the battle-scarred sky before beginning their drift toward earth. Puffs of FLAK hung suspended in the air like dark impenetrable clouds that continued to present a hazard. It was over. Bill waved his thanks to their "Little Friends," uncertain that their pilots could see him.

He had been initiated. He had dropped his payload and survived a barrage of FLAK. Most importantly, he had survived an enemy fighter attack. *Not bad for my first day of combat,* Bill thought. He settled in for the ride home, replaying the dogfight in his head and discussing the details with Joe.

∞

The dome of San Giovanni Cathedral came into view. Bill was elated to see the familiar spire and was consumed with gratitude. When they touched down on the airfield, the seven-hour-and-ten-minute mission was complete. Bill felt they had been gone for days. He would find out at the debriefing and official photographic confirmation if he had passed muster and held up his end. But he knew he had. Relief and a sense of accomplishment enveloped him. He was satisfied with his training, thrilled that he had been accurate, and honestly just damn glad to be alive.

Seventeen

READING L'AMOUR

Bomb Runs to and from Cerignola, Italy, 1944–1945

OF ALL THE ENLISTED MEN on his crew, Bill worked with his engineers the most. Their screwdrivers, pliers, and expertise kept the bombers flying. Murph and Stohlman were genuine characters: one wise and physically close to the ground, the other a tall drink of water, lithe and imaginative.

Charles Oltarzewski, "Murph" to the boys, was the self-imposed leader of the enlisted men in the crew. He was an outspoken kid from New Jersey, but Bill saw through the rough language and recognized the kindness in the guy. Murph's frame was topped with a head of blond hair thick enough to match his Jersey accent. He owned a huge personality, was reliably ready to bend the rules or lend a hand, and always looked on the bright side. Bill admired him immensely.

While flying over the Atlantic on their way to the Azores, Bill and Murph had a chance to talk a bit. It seemed his chief engineer had been a cadet.

"You were in the cadet program?" Bill asked Murph incredulously. "Why didn't you stay in?"

"I got in the habit of buzzing the town one too many times," Murph replied. Bill nodded his understanding.

"What'd you think when Wes buzzed that farmer in New Hampshire?"

"I got a huge kick out of that," Murph laughed. "Especially coming from our rules-and-regulations Pappy." Bill laughed, too, thinking of some of the stunts his training pilots had been involved in.

"He's not the only pilot to bend the rules," Bill began. "One of our instructors at B&N School took us *through* the Grand Canyon after a day's practice bomb run. I bet that was against regs too."

"Now that must have been something," Murph exclaimed.

"Oh yeah, my jaw sure did drop at both the feat and the scenery," Bill agreed. "It left me wanting more, that's for sure."

Positive, capable, and loud-mouthed, Murph kept the engines running. It had been Murph who quickly deduced where the sandwich wrapper had come from as they flew across the desert on their way to Italy, and Murph who had rigged up the heating system at the officers' tent, his pride and joy. He was also relentless when manning a machine gun. And when doing so, his engineering skills told him just where to aim to make the most damage to enemy aircraft.

Mike Stohlman was Murph's assistant engineer. The introverted Stohlman had been a rodeo cowboy in his prewar life, and Bill figured the world was one big rodeo arena to him. His thick, callused hands were permanently rope-burned from working the ranch and training for competitions. He sat behind the pilot on the flight deck so he could be at hand should any equipment malfunction.

The B-24 was an engineering wonder. It could limp home on one or two engines, a gaping hole in her side, or a shot-out stabilizer better than any other aircraft. Both engineers knew their plane inside and out: from the dependability of her four Pratt & Whitney engines to the toughness of her pressed aluminum and molded plastics. Like reading a roadmap, they read the wires that connected the flight deck to the rest of the crew, as well as the electrical system that commanded the bomb rack and the four tons of bombs.

Bill had come to count on Murph to invent his way out of a mechanical tight spot and for Stohlman to make swift repair of the armament rack or the hydraulics on the nose turret. The guy could literally find a fix for most anything on a bomber.

It wasn't until their first mission to Bucharest that Bill discovered Stohlman's passion for Western novels. The rodeo-riding engineer was a true fan of the gritty tales of love and loss out on the range, and they filled the space between base and bomb runs, as far from the scene of his novels as he possibly could be. With everything in working order, he could afford to escape the cold and the engines' din for a few hours. He could have poured through a book a mission, most missions taking upward of seven hours, if he wasn't frequently being called to man the upper turret or one of the guns at the waist of the plane. Even then, as the bomber turned and headed for home and the guns were left to cool, Stohlman would take his seat and pick up where he had left off, the book's pages fluttering in the breeze moving through the aircraft. If Bill hadn't seen it with his own eyes, he wouldn't have believed it.

∞

On his second mission, Bill and his crew took out a railroad bridge critical to the German supply route in Lago di Garda, Italy. After Wes had brought them all back to Cerignola and the officers had been debriefed, Bill stopped by the Salvation Army donut stand. Stohlman was standing by the table, gobbling up a few cakey delights and washing them down with hot coffee.

"What were you reading this trip?" Bill asked, himself an avid reader of all things history.

"*The Towns No Guns Could Tame,*" Stohlman smiled, pulling the paperback from his jacket pocket and waving it at Bill.

"Grey?" Bill guessed. He'd read Zane Grey's *Riders of the Purple Sage* in high school as part of his Classic Literature class.

"L'Amour," Stohlman replied. "Do you know he's over in Europe somewhere? I heard he's a quartermaster or something in the army. Wonder if he's still writing?"

"Do you read to forget that you're airborne when you get into a story?" Bill was genuinely interested.

"It's not that I forget. See, as the story gains momentum it drowns out everything else," explained the engineer.

"Don't the engines make it hard to concentrate?" Bill asked, incredulous. He heard every sound wherever he was, but the engines on the B-24 were the definition of deafening. Louder even than the open hearths of the steel mills he had worked in during his high school summers; a rumbling thunderous base tone. Those headsets weren't just for communicating.

"Not after the first few minutes," the engineer shrugged his shoulders. "You get used to it."

"Where do you go? In the books, I mean. Where do they take you?" asked Bill.

"Oh, I go to Big Rock, Arkansas, and Little Gulch, Nebraska, and Dodge City and San Antonio. Podunk places that have no recognizable names," said Stohlman, rattling off some familiar and not-so-familiar names. Bill hadn't heard of most of them.

"Sounds like the locations of these books travel around like you did before the war," Bill said.

"Come to think of it, they do. The rodeo circuit is kind of crazy," Stohlman laughed softly. "Oh, the places you go," he nearly whispered, mostly to himself.

Bill recognized the hint of nostalgia that crossed the engineer's face. He'd seen it on the faces of every member of his crew from time to time. Thoughts of home and his past life would occasionally drift across his mind, too, tickling and teasing and trying to turn his attention away from the mighty task he'd sworn an oath to achieve. *Oh, the places I have yet to be*, he thought, imagining future adventures. The world had unfolded before Bill this past year and a half, leaving him eager for more. But first, there was a mission he had accepted: Fight the enemy. And win.

Eighteen

HUNGARIAN STEW

Somewhere Over Budapest,
Hungary, September 1944

ON 1 SEPTEMBER, Bill and Joe were tapped to fly their third mission. They'd be working with a different crew for the first time: eight men they didn't know, but at least they'd be working together. They knew each other's techniques well enough by now that they could assist one another if need be.

"Captain Harris is flying second in the first box, which puts you as deputy lead bombardier again, Gemmill," the head of the squadron told Bill at mission briefing. "He's flown some tough runs, the toughest being his most recent over Ploesti. Did you see that 24 with its tail blown off sitting on the tarmac? Harris brought that plane in with every man aboard intact. A damn miracle, I'd say."

"I saw that bomber and wondered about the story behind it. Apparently, we're in very capable hands," replied Bill.

"You are. Harris is well-seasoned and one of the best fliers in the entire bomb group," the squadron commander assured them.

With three mission briefings under his belt, Bill was accustomed to the routine. After the exchange with the squadron commander, Bill and Joe hung back to attend their specialized briefing. When the B&N briefing concluded, they gathered their flight bags filled with maps, pencils, and slide rules and walked back up the steps to the outside. Bill was aware how the light had changed since they had entered the briefing bunker: it was brighter, and the deep orange, lavender, and pinks that brought the dawn had gone pastel.

Joe remarked that the day was a debut for them in a way. "First time we go up without our Pappy," he said.

"Yes, let's make him proud," replied Bill while glancing at the changing sky.

Captain Harris, their pilot for this mission, was waiting for them just outside the entrance to the bunker. Bill thought he seemed old, nearly thirty, with a craggy face that looked like it had seen the worst of this war and lived to tell about it. Seeing the silver bars on the man's shoulders, and the nametag on the front of his blouse, Bill saluted. Harris wasn't having any of it.

"You Gemmill?" he said as he looked at Bill.

"Yes, Sir," Bill replied.

"Let's dispense with the "sirs" and salutes, Gemmill," Captain Harris said. "They make me uncomfortable. I have our bomber assignment. I believe she's a newer plane. The rest of the crew is already assembled over at the airfield. Let's go join them."

"Lead the way, Captain, we're ready for whatever the Hun can throw at us," Bill said. And he meant it. He looked over at Joe, who was matching strides with the pilot. Bill nodded to Joe, encouraging him to introduce himself as well.

"Captain Harris, I'm Joe Parkin, your navigator of the day," he smiled as the captain reached his hand toward Joe, without breaking his pace.

"Nice to meet you, Parkin," Harris said cordially.

The crew straightened up when they saw their captain approach. Soon, all ten of them were walking out to their bomber. As he approached the aircraft, Bill immediately noted the freshly painted tail art: the famous Vulgar Vulture. The Norden exchange came next. As he climbed up through the crew hatch, the thought crossed his mind that each time up as deputy lead served to hone his skills with the device. Once aboard the bomber, Bill and Joe headed to their office and settled in. Harris had been right; she had to be a recent replacement bomber. She was fairly unscathed. All the parts in her bomb deck glistened with newness. Harris had them airborne in moments, and soon after, Bill and Joe got to work on their calculations. Bill was too focused to notice the time go by as he checked and rechecked his figures. He was confident his bomb load, and that of every bombardier toggling their drops off of his, would be spot on. Three and a half hours later, Joe announced over the intercom that they were approaching the target—the heavily defended Aerodrome at Budapest, Hungary.

Joe's announcement was Bill's cue to assume his bombing position. Stretching out on the bomb deck on his belly, he placed his eye over the sight of the Norden. He imagined an adhesive on the bombsight strong enough to make it impossible for him to pull his eye away. He was nearly ready to take over control of the plane as deputy lead and turn the flying boxcar over the initial point when an experimental German ME-163 jet charged the bomber. A swarm of Luftwaffe Fokkers joined in the fray. The intercom filled with chatter from the crew calling out the location of enemy fighters. Bill felt the plane reverberate when the gunners fired, the sensation causing him to grit his jaw and grind his teeth.

The FLAK started up, rough and loud. Bill thought this must be what being inside a garbage can feels like while someone on the outside beats the can with a baseball bat. Shrapnel from the FLAK cut through the metal skin of the bomber, piercing instruments, engines, and flesh. Bill had been introduced to FLAK on his first mission, but it had been light and ineffective compared to the ground defenses of this Aerodrome. Despite the cannons' accuracy, Harris kept her flying.

The B-24 on their wing at nine o'clock was hit directly in the bomb bay; the concussion rocked Bill's plane as if it had exploded as well, yet somehow his pilot managed to keep their bird under control.

The crosshairs began drifting. Rather than recalculate, Bill made the call, "Bombardier to pilot," he said calmly into the intercom, "I have the plane."

"She's all yours," came Captain Harris's reply.

Bill released the load and, watching through the eyepiece of the bombsight, tracked the trail of bombs descending, hell-bent on destruction. Some of the detonating ammunition in the freight cars below seemed to reach nearly as high as the plane. Clouds of charcoal black smoke swelled and billowed out of the bright orange explosions.

"Let's get the hell outta here!" Bill called into the intercom, and Harris resumed control of the plane, which, between the FLAK above and the exploding munitions below, was taking a beating.

As the bomber slowly banked toward home, Bill continued watching the squadron's bombs descend. Beneath the chunky sounds of the airplane's pistons firing, he heard the whirr of an unfamiliar engine. Bill crouched down and looked out the small bombardier's window, trying to locate where the overtone was coming from. He was rewarded with a clear view of Messerschmitt's experimental bat-like jet; not too many people had seen one. It appeared she was headed straight for him—her trajectory straight on and low. He returned to the Norden. On the next salvo of FLAK, the plane wrenched and shook, and his eye slammed into the eyepiece of the bombsight. He cursed in pain and pulled his face away, cupping his hand over his eye. When he pulled his hand away, his palm came back bloody. At first, he thought the blood beginning to trickle down his cheek was coming from his eye socket, but he quickly traced the source of vital fluid to the nose turret above his head. His thoughts sprang to the nose gunner. He looked up to see a steady stream of blood dripping through a seam in the metal plate that separated the nose turret platform from Bill and Joe.

Then he heard the motorcycle rumble from an enemy fighter's Focke-Wulf BMW-801 engines. It felt like it was coming from inside Bill's plane. The Wulf had circled back for a second attack. He turned to Joe in earnest.

"Your eye!" Joe said, pointing to Bill, his own eyes wide and his mouth open in silent alarm at the rapid discoloring and swelling happening on Bill's face.

"Forget it," Bill said as he tried to stand up in the cramped space. "We have to get to the nose!"

"The run is almost over," Joe protested. "We need to stay here!"

"He can't wait!" Bill indicated above their heads, then started to reach up to the turret. It was stuck. Joe saw the path of running blood and followed. They both tried turning the turret around to no avail.

"Damn! We've lost the hydraulics!" Joe shouted his frustration. "That last hit from the FLAK must have shot them out!"

"Can you reach the hand crank, Joe?" Bill shouted over the noise as he stood next to the turret. Joe stretched for the crank and was just able to grab it. He laid it in Bill's outstretched hand. Bill used all his might to work the hand crank, then asked Joe to add his muscle.

The bulky layers of high-altitude clothing and FLAK jackets slowed their progress. Taking turns, Bill and Joe managed to manually get the turret open and reach the gunner inside. The scene was alarming. Air was rushing in through the bullet holes shot through the Plexiglas nose, which created a whistling noise. The gunner was alive, but barely. He had been hit in the stomach, and everything below his left knee was shredded. It appeared the machine gun bullets had severed his leg. Neither Bill nor Joe had ever seen blood pouring from a body, and they decided to leave the young man in his seat; they believed moving him would only cause him more bleeding, more suffering. Using an empty ammunition strap, Bill and Joe tied a tourniquet above the kid's thigh and took turns applying pressure.

"Let Captain Harris know what we're dealing with," Bill called to Joe. Joe stepped down from the nose turret and got on the intercom to communicate their situation to the pilot.

"Roger that," came the reply from the flight deck. "We'll radio ahead to base. They'll be ready for our gunner when we land. Are you two OK?"

"We're A-OK," Joe replied. Bill heard Joe's response and smiled grimly at his friend. They were, weren't they? A-OK? He knew Captain Harris would drop a signal flare as he approached the landing strip and hoped it was red for "wounded on board." He didn't want to think of any other color at the moment but wasn't very optimistic. Judging from the amount of blood the kid had lost and how far they were from base, he didn't think the gunner would make it back alive. He wasn't certain if the poor guy even had thirty minutes of life left, much less more than three hours.

For those next hours, Bill and Joe took turns speaking to the kid.

"You're going to be all right, Gunner," Bill nearly cooed, remembering how his mother spoke to him when he was sick with a high fever or bruised and limping from a bad tackle. "You have to hang on. We'll be back to base soon."

Joe stepped up to help Bill. "Think of the pretty nurses who will be taking care of you when we get back to Italy," he said to the kid. "Think of home because you know you'll be going home after this."

"You'll be up for a medal or two for sure. Something you can show all your friends and folks back home," Bill added. Who didn't like a little glory to come their way?

The flight back to Cerignola was smooth and devoid of further enemy attacks. The kid hadn't regained consciousness, which Bill felt was a bonus. It seemed that everything—the wind, the airspeed, the pilot, and the 24 herself—was conspiring to hurry them back to safety and much-needed medical attention. Bill stared through the nose, reminiscing about his carefree days of riding above camels and farmers and the Tyrrhenian Sea. Those days seemed so long ago.

The thought that he or Joe might be next to be injured, or worse, was sobering, yet it didn't deter either of them from remaining with the young airman for the long ride home. Neither of them knew the kid, where he was from or how long he had been a nose gunner. Bill put himself in the kid's place and knew that if their roles were reversed, if he was bleeding, possibly to death, he'd want someone to be by his side.

When the bomber at last touched down in Italy, she taxied through the smoke from the flare—the red casting a scarlet hue inside the nose. The gunner groaned and tried to open his eyes, to focus them on Bill.

"The ambulance is pulling up," Bill said to the gunner while he watched the vehicle approach. "You're going to be taken off the plane before anyone else." He hoped the medics would knock the kid out with something strong before attempting to move him because it was going to hurt like hell.

Bill let go of the tourniquet, his hands and fingers cramped and numb from holding the strap tight for so long. Then he and Joe moved up and over to the catwalk to make room for the medics. After assessing the damage to the gunner, the medics shot him up with morphine before attempting to remove him from his seat. Once they had him out, they handed the kid down to some of the ground crew gathered at the hatch. Throughout the whole ordeal of getting him out of his seat and into the ambulance, the kid remained mercifully unconscious.

Joe and Bill eased themselves down to the tarmac after the gunner had been put on a stretcher. One of the medics not holding the stretcher turned to them and said, "You two did a great job at stemming the bleeding. He's lost a lot of blood, but he should make it."

Bill nodded to the medic, unable to respond verbally. Joe did the same. They were both moved by the experience. While they watched the ambulance drive away, Bill found his voice.

"Are you shaking?" he asked Joe.

"Like a leaf," Joe replied.

"That could have been either one of us," Bill responded.

"Yeah, but it wasn't," Joe said.

"No, it wasn't," Bill agreed before climbing back up to retrieve the Norden and his other tools. Joe followed so he could pack up his maps and sextant. When they returned to the tarmac, Captain Harris and the rest of the crew were waiting for them.

"Good work, you two," Captain Harris said, complimenting them on their quick thinking and stamina.

"Thank you," Bill and Joe said simultaneously.

"I felt vulnerable up there on my first two missions," Bill said, "but this one really got my attention."

"Likewise," Joe added.

"This probably won't be the worst you have to endure," the pilot explained. "The enemy is getting desperate. He knows he's losing, and that's when he is most dangerous. We can't afford to underestimate him now."

"There's no chance of that," Bill replied, as he and Joe headed to the truck waiting to take them to debriefing. Bill had no intention of underestimating the enemy. At twenty years of age, a city boy new to war, the realization of the carnage of conflict had hit him full force.

Nineteen

TENT BOYS

"Officer Country," Cerignola,
Italy, September 1944

THE RADIO WAS JUMPING with the swinging sounds of Armed Forces Radio: Dizzy Gillespie working his trumpet like the great craftsman he was. The weather on this mid-September day was magnificent: breezy, sunny, and warm with no sign of the persistent rain. Bill had earned a day off. He found both the respite from war and the sunshine much to his liking, except, perhaps, the lack of anyone to play ball or cards with. Most of his crew had been parceled out to fill in crews with a missing pilot, navigator, or gunner for today's mission. He turned to his radio for company—the one encased in brown Bakelite he kept on his scarred and battered desk. It felt like years since his father had sent that radio to him in Texas.

He propped open the door to the olive drab tent, hoping to air out the musty scent held in the canvas, and dragged a folding chair outside. Bill was taking in the sun, the music, and the scene in officer country when a scrawny boy with thick unkempt hair caught his eye—a local lad picking his way through the city of tents. The kid all but danced to the rhythm of the music as he moved along—army disc jockeys played a lot of swing. The boy reminded Bill of Michael Gubitosi, the actor who portrayed Mickey in the *Our Gang* series.

"*Buongiorno!*" Bill waved and smiled.

The kid froze. Deer in the headlights. Bill beckoned him over.

"*Si,* American Capitan, *si,*" the kid complied, saluting Bill. Bill laughed at the sudden promotion.

"*Que se dice,* what do you say? Do you speak English, *parla inglese?*" Bill asked. He figured the boy was about fifteen, but it was hard to tell for certain. Whether from malnutrition or family characteristics, the boy was about five feet tall and rail-thin; his clothes, although clean, were two sizes too big. His dark blue shirt hung off of his shoulders by about two inches. Beneath a few layers of freckles, the boy smiled, his eyes clear and bright.

"I come work. No English." He beamed at Bill, who stood up from his chair, towering over the boy, then crouched down for better eye contact with his newfound pal. The lad kept a hefty distance of about three feet. Bill wondered why the boy was so skittish. Village boys frequently wandered onto the base in search of employment. The practice of hiring these boys to do errands and odd jobs was not exactly allowed by the brass, but a tendency to look the other way prevailed. He was struck with an idea: why not hire this kid to work here at The Manse?

"You want work? *Lavoro?* You want to make money? *Lire?*" Bill asked the kid.

"*Lavoro*, work, *si. Lire si!*" The kid removed his beat-up cap, smoothed his wavy, dark brown hair, and approached a few more inches. He looked past Bill, trying to get a glimpse into the tent—searching for the source of the music.

"What is your name? *Como si nome?*" Bill tapped his chest. "*Mio nome* Bill." After his first couple of weeks in Italy, he'd been able to understand a lot of the Italian he heard from the locals working on base and, most importantly, was able to make himself understood to non-English speakers. He figured he could thank his high school Latin teacher for that.

"*Pasquale!*" The boy turned around, puffing up his chest, tapping it like Bill. Armed Forces Radio kept the hits rocking, beckoning the boy to move closer.

"*Musica!*" shouted Pasquale. "*Americano radio musica!*" He started moving with the rhythm of "Tuxedo Junction," the Hawkins, Johnson, and Dash song Glenn Miller covered so well—and an essential addition to any collection of swing band music, so far as Bill was concerned.

He liked this kid instantly. They already had a feel for music in common. Bill stepped into the tent, walked over to a broom leaning against the center post, and began sweeping the canvas floor. He looked toward Pasquale, who had moved closer to the door so he could see inside, and held up four fingers as he indicated the four cots assembled around the room.

"Four of us live here, *quatro capitans*," said Bill. Pasquale nodded in understanding as he stepped inside the tent.

"Me, I do," Pasquale walked up to Bill, grabbed the broom and began pushing it through the dry dirt as he smoothed the floor, creating a veritable dust devil. He swept with such vigor, Bill laughed out loud. Pasquale stopped his sweeping and looked up at Bill.

"Not so fast, Pasquale," Bill cautioned. "Easy, so the dust doesn't get all over everything else."

Pasquale leaned the broom against the side wall and glanced questioningly at Bill, as if to ask for more chores.

Bill tossed him an empty canvas duffel. A pile of socks, towels, T-shirts, and skivvies had accumulated on Bill's cot, waiting to be washed. "Do you do laundry?"

Pasquale walked over to Bill's bed and began stuffing the dirty clothes into the bag. Looking over his shoulder, he grinned. "*Mama lavare!*" he said enthusiastically. Bill laughed.

"Capitan Bill?"

"*Si*, Pasquale?"

"Who is favorite? What jazz singing you like *il migliore*, most bestest?"

"Best, you say 'best' in English. I like a lot of bands, Pasquale. I like the singer Ella Fitzgerald—" Bill was about to go through his list of top favorites when Pasquale interrupted with a passion almost too strong for his years.

"Ah, *Bella* Ella!" Pasquale clutched his chest, closed his eyes, and swayed back and forth as he conjured up an image of the "First Lady of Song."

"*Si! Bella!* And the big bands you hear on the radio. I play pretty good drums myself," Bill said as he pulled out a set of drumsticks he was in the habit of keeping and beat on the map table Murph had fashioned out of a crate for the officers. "I play standup bass too," he added, miming how a bass would be held and strummed. "Have you heard of Gene Krupa? He is a very famous drummer. I played with him during a high school music camp one summer before the war." *Did the kid get all that?* Bill wondered.

"I do not know Gene Krupa, but everyone in world know Glenn Miller!" Pasquale proclaimed as he continued to sway with the music emanating from the radio. "And standup bass? I have not heard."

Pasquale shrugged his shoulders and raised both arms. Bill chuckled at the kid's comments regarding Krupa, Miller, and the instrument.

Evidently, Bill's approximation of playing the bass had not been enough to explain the instrument to the boy. "Do you know the instrument that looks like a big fiddle, a violin?" Bill outlined the shape and height of a bass in the air. "That is called a standup bass."

"No. Maybe, I think so. Ah, *si*, those cats swing with that, no?" Pasquale mimed, rocking an imaginary bass to the beat of the music streaming from Bill's radio. The kid must have been hanging around the camp a while; Bill could think of no other way he could have learned so much jazz jargon.

"Si, Pasquale, those cats swing," Bill said.

The kid had the job in the bag. Two days later, he appeared at the tent door with Bill's duffel full of clean, folded laundry. The clothes and towels smelled of fresh air. *The scent of the sun.* From then on, Pasquale appeared every day. And Bill wasn't the only one who benefitted from the arrangement. Joe, Wes, and Jug paid the kid to do errands for them as well from time to time. Pasquale quickly became a beloved part of the family. Some days he'd show up unannounced, and on others, at a time determined by one of the officers.

∞

On a rare gloomy late-September day, Pasquale arrived with his friend Giovanni in tow. Giovanni, waif-like and lingering near the black-painted tent door, looked wary and dared not venture any further. It was a drizzly morning, miserable with cold and damp. All missions had been canceled.

"Here is your clothes," Pasquale announced. The duffel bag was full, almost as big as the boy. He unloaded it onto Bill's cot.

"*Are* your clothes," Bill corrected. "Who's your friend?"

Pasquale waved Giovanni inside. "Come in, close the door," he told his friend in English.

Scuffling along on the edges of his pant cuffs, Giovanni entered the tent by inches, unsure what awaited him inside. The knees of the boy's britches were patched, his woolen coat pink from fading. *That coat was probably red at some time*, Bill mused. A moth-chewed woolen cap fell across his dirt-streaked face, and he couldn't keep his eyes from darting about the tent.

"Pasquale," Bill beamed as he opened a tidy bundle of fresh laundry, "your mama always folds the clothes so neatly and they smell as fresh as the outdoors."

"*Si*, the day we had sun, she placed them to dry," Pasquale beamed at Bill.

Joe and Jug strolled in. "Hey Joe!" Pasquale saluted the navigator and copilot, another Mutt-and-Jeff combination of tall and short. Jug shifted a brown paper package wrapped with string he was carrying under his left hand as if it was a football.

"Well, what have we here? The Italian army?" Jug exclaimed, delighted to have someone new to tease.

Joe pretended to be frightened as he approached Giovanni who was, by now, standing in the center of the tent, trying to be as inconspicuous as possible. The boy stared at the funny man whose mouth curled into an impish grin.

"*Americano! Americano!*" Joe fell to his knees before Giovanni, hands held high in surrender. The boy looked at Bill as if he was waiting to be given instructions. Then he reached out and patted Joe on top of his head, relaxing Joe's arms down, and smiled sweetly at the playful man. Joe could disarm even the most reticent of people, young and old.

Jug sat down on his cot and began unwrapping the package he

had carried in. One by one, tins of sweet goodies piled up on Jug's cot.

Giovanni moved closer to the copilot, staring at the bounty.

"Y'all like peaches?" Jug beckoned both boys closer. Giovanni watched wide-eyed as Jug opened one of the tins. When he caught the strong, sweet aroma drifting from the contents, he tilted his head back and took a long, luxurious inhale as if to remember the scent of fresh fruit.

"My mama sent these to me. She puts them up, too, but these are store-bought. They still smell like home," Jug explained to the boys as he dug a spoon into the mass of gold.

To everyone's surprise, "Giovanni the Timid"—Bill had decided this was just the right handle for Pasquale's friend—reached for the spoon. Jug pretended to growl, then smiled and handed the boy the tin. Soon, syrupy slurps and tasty discoveries replaced any attempts at conversation. Giovanni licked his mouth and fingers, sticky from peach juice—a taste of America.

He looked at Jug, pointing to the can, "*Questo?*" he asked.

"Peach. Peaches from my home state of Georgia," Jug guessed at the question and answered in English.

"They have sweet," Giovanni smiled with delight as Pasquale shared a bite.

"Yes, they do. They have sweet, that's just the right description," Jug warmed to the boy. He couldn't argue with his grammar or his taste. He smiled at Giovanni and patted the boy's back.

∞

Giovanni became almost as regular a visitor as Pasquale. Instead of *lire*, which were hard for service men to come by, Bill and the other officers paid the boys in sacks of flour scrounged from the mess cooks, an arrangement their families heartily agreed to. On days when Giovanni accompanied Pasquale, they'd share the work and the flour.

"I wonder what Giovanni does with his share," Bill said to Joe. "That kid looks as hollow-cheeked as ever, like he's not getting enough to eat."

"Yeah, and he's so quiet. Have you ever heard him mention a mama or papa?" Joe was concerned for the boy.

"No," said Bill. "I have not."

∞

"Was it rough hell today?" Pasquale respectfully asked Wes, Bill, and Jug as they straggled back into the tent after a particularly rough mission over Belgrade, Yugoslavia.

"Your English is improving, kid," Jug said, as he collapsed onto his bed. His voice was faint and devoid of his usual macho energy.

"Yes, Pasquale. We took some bad hits," Wes answered for the weary officers. The day's bomb run had been particularly difficult. Wes had flown second seat with a new crew flying their first combat mission.

"The nose gunner in the plane next to us was killed," Joe said as he came in the door and tuned into the topic of conversation. As happened often, the crew had once again been split up: Jug as a stand-in copilot for another crew, Bill to replace a wounded bombardier on yet another. Joe had flown as a replacement navigator for Captain Harris on the same mission and was just getting back himself. He greeted his mates with a look and a nod; that was all that was necessary to communicate how his day had gone.

"*Maledizione!* Damn *Tedeschi!*" Pasquale shouted, shaking his fist as he walked to Bill's cot. The boy was upset and reverted to the Italian slang for any soldier or airman in Hitler's "employ."

"Nazis, Pasquale," Bill corrected the kid, now sitting at the foot of his cot. He sat down next to Pasquale, his rounded shoulders revealing his fatigue. Bill never slumped. "We call them Nazis."

"*Tedeschi*, Nazi, damn them all to hell!" exclaimed Pasquale. Bill tousled the boy's thick hair and tried to smile, but he was so exhausted, even smiling was an effort.

Pasquale looked at his lanky mentor and said, "My mother, she asks that you all come for eating this *Domenica*."

Bill felt himself giving in to the overwhelming tiredness that was quickly enveloping him. He fumbled with the laces on his boots, then gave up. Pasquale knelt down, loosened the laces, and removed the black leather flight boots, setting them neatly at the foot of the bed. He knew Bill preferred them that way, ready for the next mission.

"You are very tired?" asked Pasquale.

"Si, *mio amico*. Very tired," Bill replied, his voice heavy with weariness.

"I sweep outside the tent today! It was a good day, no rain," Pasquale reported, clearly pleased with himself.

"Good work, Pasquale. Your mama must be proud," Bill whispered sincerely. Unable to hold himself upright any longer, Bill closed his eyes and sunk into the mattress. He was asleep before his head hit the pillow.

Pasquale stood looking down at his friend for a moment when Wes spoke up. "Jug and I have to report to a special pilot's briefing at 1600 hours on Sunday," Wes fibbed sleepily, glancing over at Pasquale. He was aware of the food shortages still plaguing the former breadbasket of Italy. He knew that adding four additional mouths to feed at Pasquale's family table would put too much stress on the family's food sources.

Fortunately, Bill's wingman answered for him. "That is a very nice invitation. Tell your mama Bill and I accept," Joe said lazily. He was lying on his cot with his boots and flight suit still on. Halfway to sound sleep and talking dreamily.

"Good night, *mio amicos*," Pasquale whispered as he glanced at the figures lying prone on their cots. Soft snoring filled the tent as Pasquale backed out of the room, ever so quietly.

∞

On a balmy September Sunday, at 1600 hours, Bill and Joe followed Pasquale on foot for twenty-five minutes down a well-worn path toward his home and dinner. The dirt was dry and pebbly, and their boots kicked up fine puffs of light-brown dust as they made their way. The pace slowed as the trio neared a shabby farm building. The roof was partially collapsed in, and a bent and twisted bicycle lay like a wounded soldier in the front yard. A farm truck was parked off the side of the house, its tires flattened, windshield smashed, and doors bashed in. To Bill, it looked like it had been mid-ride when the damage occurred.

"Look at this, Joe; they had a pretty good-sized farm before the Nazis invaded," Bill said as Pasquale ran ahead into the front yard. Fields left to fallow surrounded the path, and a midsize crater was visible in what must have been the garden closest to the house. Bill knew the farm had been bombed. He hoped it had been the Germans, not the Americans, who had sent that shell to destroy Pasquale's home. Walking past the useless bicycle, Bill discovered scraps of red paint on the frame and wondered if that had been Pasquale's mode of transportation. He stooped to ring the bell dangling from one of the handlebars, but it had rusted in place.

"Welcome to my home: The House of Castrignano!" Pasquale bowed graciously and spread his arms wide to take in the dusty court, the decimated acres beyond. A slender woman, her black hair streaked with silver, stepped out into the dusk and stood behind Pasquale, her hands on his shoulders. Bill presented her with a freshly baked apple pie, courtesy of the squadron cook.

"*Grazie. Prego.*" The woman smiled, accepting the pie, and gestured the two officers inside. Bill reckoned she must be Senora Castrignano.

The ceilings were low; Bill had to hunch his shoulders to fit his frame into the room. The few small windows provided scant light and the larger window was papered over. Bill thought it might have been blown out from the bomb blast but decided it was impolite to ask. He might not like the answer. A wondrous aroma wafted from the direction of the kitchen: basil and oregano. After so many months of army cooking, Bill had forgotten about the scent of fresh-cut herbs.

"Sit. Here," Pasquale indicated mismatched stools and chairs gathered around a rustic wooden table.

"*Buon appetito!*" Papa Castrignano said in a deep baritone voice as Senora exited from the kitchen with a steaming bowl of home-made pasta.

"*Fusilli a la olio,*" Senora saw the question in Joe's face.

"I only know spaghetti, you know, the straight kind of noodle. I love the look of this corkscrew pasta. Look Bill, no tomatoes, just as you like and the aroma of that garlic and basil!" Joe was genuinely charmed by his hosts and his environment. Pasquale translated for his mother.

Senora's eyes crinkled with a smile and thanked them for the flour. "You eat it today," she said, pointing to the pasta. "Without Pasquale work, it very hard to eating."

"You speak some English, then?" Bill asked her. The woman beamed at her son, "Pasquale, he teach me."

"Oh, that could be dangerous!" Bill laughed.

"We'll have to watch our language!" warned Joe, teasing.

"Son of a bitch!" Pasquale laughed aloud and his father joined in. Papa laughed often. His wiry, muscular frame looked designed for hard physical labor. Bill recalled how Pasquale had told him his father was working in the village, sweeping and mucking stables at the livery, and that he liked to sing to the horses.

"Ha! *Si, O Solo Mio, e Verdi, e Puccini!*" Papa laughed again.

"Papa is happy man. He make the wheats happy when he grow them. Now, no wheats. He make the horse happy with his songs," Pasquale explained.

"There are many farms not far from where I come from," Bill attempted to start a conversation with Papa. "The state of Illinois is farm country."

"Bill is from Chee-ca-go, Papa," Pasquale explained to his parents. "That is in Il-ee-noy, United States."

"Chee-ca-go bang, bang, si, haha!" Papa nodded his head vigorously and pointed his fingers into a mock gat. Senora joined him, nodding and laughing. It appeared they were no strangers to gangsters.

"Joe is from I-o-wah," continued Pasquale, no doubt showing off for his parents.

"*Donde?*" Papa asked his son.

"I-o-wah, near Chicago. *Multi maize, como so,*" Bill indicated how high the corn grew.

Needing no prompting, he and Joe began singing an old state song: "Oh, we're from I-o-way, I-o-way, that's where the tall corn grows!" At the word "that's" they held their arms up, indicating how high the corn can grow. Mama, Papa, and Pasquale mimicked the two Midwesterners, raising their hands, laughing, and shouting out, "I-o-way!"

"I say wrong? It not I-o-wah? It I-o-way?" The kid was perplexed, but his father interrupted, speaking rapidly, animated, pumping his arms up and down. Pasquale translated.

"Papa remembers when this place had many farms. The *Tedeschi*, I mean, the Nazis, come take everything, then shoot big guns and burn what is left when they leave," Pasquale translated, then added, "They did not have to do that, ruin everything so that many of us cannot come back to the land."

"*Niente.*" Tears danced at the rim of Papa's eyes.

"My brothers protested and they get lock up. We don't see them for two years. When the Americans were coming, they release," Pasquale explained.

"I didn't know you had brothers, Pasquale," Bill said.

"*Si.* Two brothers," the kid responded.

"Where are they now?" asked Bill.

"Ernesto leave to look for work in Naples; Piero is a boatman on Capri. He sings to the people he takes to the cava."

Bill turned to look at Senora. She knew that the topic had turned to her boys—the woman didn't need English to tell her that. Her face softened at the sound of their names, sad with the worry that distance brings. He thought of Frances.

Leave it to Joe to ease the mood. Three plates of *fusilli* later, he couldn't help but comment. "Yum! Now, that's a good meal," he said as he rubbed his belly and pushed his chair back. "Nothing like home cooking."

"Joe, your capacity for food never ceases to amaze me!" Bill laughed.

Then Papa rubbed his belly in dramatic satisfaction and rolled his eyes at Joe. Everyone laughed again.

"Pie of apples?" Pasquale asked his mother in English. Joe's eyes widened at the thought of more food.

"*Si, Pasquale. Camminare?* We walk first, no?" Mama understood the need for a pause in dining.

"*Si, Mama!* Let's walk," Pasquale agreed. "We can show Bill and Joe the farm."

Papa led the small group out to a large, burnt-out field. His eyes scanned the horizon, but this time Papa wasn't laughing.

When American armed forces first arrived, they cleared land, just as the Nazis had done, so they could lay down runways for the airfields. Bill didn't know how many acres of rich farmland had been utilized for the Army Air Corps, or how many the retreating Germans had destroyed, but the scene before him touched him deeply. Thinking it through, Bill deduced it had to have been the Nazi forces that had destroyed this field; it was too far from base to serve as a landing strip for heavy bombers.

"*Ecco ... fuoco*," Papa sighed, "here ... fire." Then his voice trailed off. Bill met Papa's eyes with genuine empathy while simultaneously understanding that war's reach is long.

"The ashes from the fire should enrich the soil," Joe offered, looking to spin something positive out of the devastated land.

"There's hope for the farm," Pasquale translated what Joe had said to his father, then came back with his Papa's response. "First, he has to find the wheat seed and then a way to buy it."

Bill listened to the kid's translation, then asked, "Is seed available anywhere nearby?"

"I will buy my papa seed." Pasquale stood at Bill's side and beamed up at the tall American. "I work!"

They all turned toward the house, gazed at it for a moment, then set out on a somber return past the scorched fields. Realizing the time, Joe and Bill exchanged knowing glances.

"It's time for us to get back to base. Please enjoy the pie; I have no room for a piece myself. *Senora, grazie*," said Bill, turning to address Senora Castrignano.

"I'm pretty full as well," Joe agreed.

"Thank you, Senora, Papa. *Multi grazie* for the meal and the fine walk," Bill and Joe said in unison as their hosts escorted them to the trail.

"*Grazie* to you, for help Pasquale," Senora took Bill's hand.

"You have a good boy there. *Lui e un bravo ragazzo*, Senora. He's part of our family too. Up in the sky we fly and watch out for each other. Pasquale is part of our ground crew. He watches out for us here. Just like family, *si, familia*," Bill hoped his sincerity got through the language barrier.

"*Per favore* to be here again," Senora said and held his hand for a long moment.

"Thank you, *grazie*," said Bill.

Papa could only smile and shake Bill's hand, then Joe's. His tears returned. "*Americano multi buono.*"

Pasquale walked part of the way back to base with Bill and Joe. He was pensive; something significant was weighing on his mind. At last, he stopped in the brush and turned to gaze up at Bill.

"Capitan Bill?" asked the kid.

"Yes, Pasquale?" said Bill.

"Does everyone in America have peaches growing in back of yard?" the kid was eager to know.

∞

Pasquale waited after every mission for the crew to return, placing that act high on his list of priorities. After finishing the cleaning chores and running the laundry to his mother, he'd return to darn socks, or nap in the tent during foul weather, or kick a soccer ball, or pace outside if the day was pleasant. The boy developed an instinct for knowing when the group was returning. With hearing keen as any canine, he detected the hum of the engines long before anyone else at the base.

His pacing would become more agitated—on a dry day he'd wear a shallow trough into the dirt from all his marching—and he'd wring his hands and count until he heard that every plane had landed safely. There were too many days when the count was short, which distressed the lad. He'd wait outside the old wine cellar for his extended family to complete their mission debriefings, then walk back to their tent. When he spied one or more of the officers approaching, he'd stand in salute, honoring them. There were days they'd file in, jolly with energy to spare, but on most, the officers dragged their tired bodies into the tent and collapsed onto their cots.

Pasquale waited for everyone to arrive back at The Manse before heading home to the family farm at the edge of the village. He always brought stories to tell of the American fliers' battles with the *Tedeschi*.

Twenty

GONE MISSING

Grounded in Cerignola, Italy,
September 1944

HALFWAY INTO THE RETURN flight from a mission to Steyr, Austria, Bill began feeling slightly achy all over. It was 10 September, and he was flying lead with a different crew. He figured he was more sore than usual from clenching his jaw and tensing every single muscle in his body for hours on end. The objective of the mission had been to destroy aircraft manufacturing plants, and it had been a rough one. The FLAK had been intense, heavy, and accurate, but the pilots in Bill's box kept flying on; not flinching was one of the things the 15th was known for. Ten enemy ME-109s had swarmed their bomber and the gunners had shot each and every one down. The bomber had taken a real beating though—she lost an engine and the top turret. When they were safely back on the ground, Bill walked around her, assessing the damage. He lost count of the bullet holes in her skin; she looked like Swiss cheese. He couldn't explain how no one had been killed or critically injured. A miracle, perhaps?

When he woke before dawn the next day, in time to gear up for their next mission, Bill found the effort of dressing exhausting. Even his eyeballs hurt and he thought his chest would explode from the force of the cough that ripped through him. He saw Wes watching him, his brows knit together with concern.

Despite what Bill knew in his bones to be a severe upper respiratory infection, he remained hopeful the flight surgeon would let him fly—he had no choice but to see the doctor. He was scheduled as lead with his own crew, something he had looked forward to for weeks. *I really am OK*, he told himself. *I need to fly with my crew.*

Sitting on the exam table, Bill tried to persuade the doctor that he was fit to fly. Having to pause between chest-deep hacks did not help his cause.

"Hey Doc, don't break my good attendance record. I can do this; I'll wear my oxygen mask. It'll be OK." Bill wheezed from the effort of speaking and considered the facts: *Who am I kidding? I'm having trouble getting air into my lungs right here on the ground.* He knew how difficult it is to breathe at twenty-three thousand feet in an unpressurized aircraft and was wise enough to know how impossible it would be to attempt it with this infection. He was aching from a soaring temperature, now impossible to conceal, but he ached worse to go with his crew. The flight surgeon wasn't impressed no matter how much Bill pleaded; he denied the bombardier flight status.

"Go back to your quarters, climb into bed, and stay there," he ordered, handing Bill a packet of pills and a bottle of cough medicine. "Take one of these pills every eight hours. You can use the cough medicine every four. Come see me in two days and we'll hear what your chest has to say. Then maybe you can go back up."

For the first time in his aviation career, Bill was being grounded—temporarily barred from flying. His crew was heading to the oil refineries at Blechhammer, Germany, without him; they'd already been assigned a replacement bombardier. His thoughts were spinning, or maybe the infection had reached his brain. He knew it would be impossible for him to breathe even with the oxygen mask. And the wracking cough would make wearing the mask impossible anyway. Yet, he still was eager to go.

Bill stepped out of the field hospital to find Wes and Joe waiting for him. They had come from the preflight briefing where they had been assigned Silver Beauty, of all planes; however, Wes told him they would be flying tail-end Charlie. Jug had gone to the airfield with the rest of the crew to meet Bill's replacement. "Tough break, Gemmill. We'll miss you up there with us today, but you can make it up to us again right soon," Wes tried to sooth Bill with his Texas drawl. He turned, gave Bill a nod, then headed toward the airfield to join Jug for their preflight check. *News sure travels fast around here*, Bill thought. He was sorely disappointed.

Joe felt so sorry for his pal he hailed a Jeep, went back to the tent with Bill, and tucked him into bed. "Fine way to get out of work, Gemmill," he joked. Then he left to catch a ride back to the airfield and rejoin the others.

It took Bill only six or seven minutes to throw off the covers and take off after Joe. Halfway on his walk out to the airfield, he got lucky—a Jeep making its way through officer country stopped to give him a lift. A slight drizzle had begun, and he turned up the collar of his leather flight jacket to keep most of the rain from sliding down the back of his neck.

Bill arrived on the tarmac just in time to watch each aircraft begin its lineup. It never ceased to amaze him: the powerful engines turning over, loud and eager, smoking and churning. Bill suffered a coughing spell that compounded the rumbling of the machines he felt in his body as he searched the tarmac for the tails of each B-24. His chest was taking a beating.

He found Silver Beauty, but the crew was busy unloading all of their equipment and hauling it over to a standby plane: the "Bucket of Bolts." Wes or Murph must have detected something wrong with "their" plane and requested a replacement. Bill groaned. Whoever had named the aircraft had a wicked sense of humor. He had flown in her before and remembered her troublesome left engine. As the plane started up, Bill could see Wes through the cockpit window and knew it was business as usual up there. Wes and Jug were going through their checklist, too busy to notice the gloomy figure standing at the edge of the tarmac scudding his feet around in the mud, shoulders slouched, hands stuffed into the slash pockets of his jacket.

Joe noticed Bill at the last minute as he pulled himself up into the belly of the bomber. "Put on a hat!" he shouted over the roar of engines revving and the propellers' spin catching the air.

Bill could see Joe's lips moving but couldn't hear much above the roar of the symphony of squadron engines. Then he saw Ritt waving from the nose turret. He caught himself feeling sorry he was being left behind. *Pull yourself out of your socks, Gemmill. Give these guys a good send-off.* Having no breath to speak of, he began waving his arms and grinning like a fool, the effort astoundingly difficult between coughs. Wes brought the plane into takeoff position.

Bill stopped waving, stood at attention, and saluted. As they passed by, he called out weakly, "Hurry back! I have no one to play with!" Bill imagined his words being sucked up into the draft of the propellers, sliced, diced, then dispersed into the atmosphere. He watched as the bombers headed east into the rising dawn, then Bill walked with significant effort back to the tent to wait out his fever and the mission.

∽

A deep, fever-fed dream led Bill through dense smoke and merciless FLAK. He was in a bomber that was on fire. There was no sound to his vision. Each crew member moved *sotto voce*, donning parachutes and leaping one by one from the broken plane. Puffs of white silk dotted a blackened sky. Bill looked around at the nine men dangling in midair at varying distances from him in their noiseless drift to earth. He didn't recognize one face. He didn't remember jumping.

The distinctive drone from approaching B-24 engines shook Bill awake from his codeine-induced sleep. The drugs the flight surgeon had given him had been working while he slept—his chest didn't feel as constricted as when he had drifted off to sleep. He sat up and swung his feet over the edge of the cot, immediately realizing his mistake. His easy breathing had been a hopeful imagining because now his breaths were coming in short strangled gasps. Nevertheless, he shuffled out to the wash basin they had rigged up outside the tent, rinsed his face and hands, then headed to the airstrip to watch the squadron's return. The sky was turning an ominous oily shade, like squid ink.

The bombers began coming in, some limping, some with engines on fire and flares blazing. Bill noticed the red flares first. There were too many critically injured on at least a half dozen planes. Three yellow flares drifted from other planes, indicating dead on board. Two of the aircraft flew low, releasing green flares to indicate they had lost their landing gears and were awaiting instructions on where best to attempt to land. He didn't need anyone to tell him the group had taken a devastating hit. One B-24 landed well enough, yet when it turned away from Bill, he could see a tank-sized hole in its belly. He forced himself to return his watch of the sky, seeking out the Bucket of Bolts.

Another plane approached, its landing gear missing, locked down or shot off; it was hard for Bill to determine. A nerve-wracking moment for the pilot and crew, to be sure. Still, she kept coming on. That pilot had "the touch" because he managed to bring the ship down safely, albeit scraping and screeching along the metal tracks of the runway. Was that Wes? He couldn't see the tail. Everyone watching from the ground let out a collective breath when no fires were seen. Bill wasn't even aware he had been holding his.

Bomber after bomber landed and still there was no sign of Bill's crew. Thirty minutes after most of the squadron had been accounted for, a straggler streaming black smoke from its tail appeared low in the sky. *Ah*, Bill thought, *this will be Wes and the boys making a grand entrance.* But as the plane neared the airfield, he saw the "Stella Blue" design on the nose—one of the few bombers in the 15th that chose nose art over painting the tail. Where was Wes? He knew the crew of the Stella and walked on out to ask about the Bucket of Bolts. The pilot and copilot were going over the aircraft making note of bullet holes, broken stabilizers, and blasted-out turrets. Bill approached them and inquired, through a series of painful coughs, about his crew's bomber. Had anyone seen the Bucket of Bolts?

"We saw her get hit in the far-left engine and the other wasn't engaged at all," the copilot reported. "There was a lot of smoke when we last saw them. The right engine was feathered, and they were losing altitude somewhere over Val Mezirici, Czechoslovakia; they couldn't keep up."

That's all the Bucket of Bolts needed, Bill considered as he stood listening to more firsthand accounts from some of the Stella's crew members: a hit in the left engine. Damn *Tedeschi,* he cursed under his meager breath, using Pasquale's term for the enemy for the first time.

The tail gunner walked up in the midst of the copilot's report and concurred. "I've flown on that bomber. Yeah, she got hit. FLAK was awful. Some of it was the size of a tank."

The bombardier of the Stella Blue had also heard Bill's plea for information. "We saw her take the hit. She shuddered then righted herself, so we thought she was going to be OK. But when we turned for home, we could see the Bucket rapidly losing altitude before she entered an undercast, obscuring it from view."

"As you can see, we were pretty shot up ourselves. We were busy staying airborne," added the copilot.

"Did you see any 'chutes?" Bill asked. A sinking feeling was coming over him, and he feared the answer.

"Come to think of it, no … although I don't know for sure. It was pretty dark up there with all the smoke. I'm sorry, Gemmill, I was so caught up with keeping us airborne, I couldn't … maybe they got out all right."

Bill's throat tightened. An angry despair enveloped him like an anxious mist. Out there amidst the bustle on the tarmac, he felt terribly alone.

Well after dark, after waiting in the chilling drizzle far longer than was prudent for someone who had been grounded for a chest infection, Bill returned to the tent. Pasquale and Giovanni were waiting. When they saw the look on Bill's face, the boys hung their heads, bearing yet another burden of the nightmare of war. By now, they had seen this scene played out in other officers' quarters after someone failed to reappear after a mission. They were keenly aware of the unspoken rule about the dispensing of an absent crew member's belongings. A missing-in-action crewman had five days to return and claim his gear, or it was up for grabs.

"Pasquale, help me pile their things over here in Wes's corner," Bill asked the kid. Bill needed to move, to be busy. And he wanted to safeguard the few items that had made the tent so comfortable.

"Si, Capitan Bill," Pasquale answered solemnly. His head was bowed, and he transferred Wes and Jug's personal favorites with reverence.

∽

Convinced that his crew would return, the usually personable bombardier resented the three replacement officers who showed up five days later. He viewed them as intruders, and although he was feeling a lot better, he spoke to them as little as possible. His conversations were internal and one-sided: *That is Jug's cot, what right do you have to put your lucky pillow on it? Hey, Joe likes his head at the other end of the cot. Boy, will he be hot when he sees how you've turned it around.* Sitting on his own cot, Bill observed that the replacements were respectful yet wary of his lack of enthusiasm. He let his silence speak for him—his face implied that he was not up for conversation.

The change in Bill's otherwise outgoing personality did not escape the squadron commander's attention. And the flight surgeon recommended that, due to the persistent head and chest infection and Bill's current state of mental health, he keep Bill grounded a while longer. The squadron leader agreed.

Bill, on the other hand, was itching to get back up in the air so he would have something else to think about or feel beside the huge hole where his heart had been. He no longer told jokes or impersonated Mussolini with Pasquale. He no longer participated in anything. He felt as if a part of him was drowning.

Ten days into this personal isolation, and feeling the last remnants of the chest infection, the replacement pilot came into the tent to tell

Bill he was to report to the squadron commander on the double. Bill hiked over to the commander's quarters and was stunned to see Jug, Joe, Mike, Bob, Murph, and George huddled together laughing. Bill felt as if his grin would break his face as he gazed admiringly at his mates. The lucky half dozen of the Bucket's crew appeared somewhat cocky and full of adventure stories about Yugoslavia as they talked through their debriefing and the tremendous help they received from the group of Partisans they had encountered. No one knew the whereabouts of Wes, Hill, or Ritt, so plenty of cause for concern remained. Still, Bill could barely contain his joy that most of his family was home. The replacement officers would be reassigned another tent; Bill's world was righting itself.

Apparently, Bill's joy was contagious; the commander ordered all officers and enlisted men of the crew to the Isle of Capri for three days of R&R, Bill included. In a large way, the ordeal had been just as difficult for Bill as it had been on the boys trying to make it back to base. The sunshine and sea air would be healing on many levels.

Bill felt conflicted. He wanted to go to Capri with the others, but he had missed a week of flying while grounded, and three of his friends were still unaccounted for; how could he take a vacation? It helped that Ritt made it back two days later, none the worse for wear after spending quality time with a group of Partisans in Yugoslavia, but that still left Wes and Hill. *Where are they?* Bill wondered.

"They're alive, Gemmill, that's for sure," Joe reassured Bill as he rearranged his bed the way he liked it.

"Seven of us fell to the Partisans in Yugoslavia. I figure Wes and Hill were either picked up by the Germans or Chetniks. Your replacement too. They'll be given pretty good treatment in either case."

"Did you speak to the intelligence officers at your debriefing?" Bill inquired. "Could they shed any light on where Wes could possibly be?"

Joe understood and shared Bill's concern, but he didn't want to add any more to his friend's anxiety for Wes's well-being. "I know that Wes was the last man to jump. A search party found his 'chute. He was nowhere around, but that's proof in itself he's in shape to travel—and pretty fast too, 'cause the search party wasted little time in reaching the spot where his 'chute was found."

"I guess that does give us a clue to his physical state. How 'bout Hill? Did anyone have eyes on him?" Bill asked.

"Not to my knowledge, but for all we know, he could be in just as good a shape as Wes," Joe responded. "The seven of us got away without severe injury. Well, Murph, Ritt, and Jug were bruised up in landing, but not badly."

"Is that why Jug is still in medical?" Bill wanted as many details, on as many members of his crew, his family, as he could find.

"Yeah, I figure they'll release him in the morning," Joe answered, then winked and said, "Big baby." He wanted to relieve the tension he saw in Bill's face and knew humor was just the ticket.

"I have to admit," Bill said, loosening up a bit, "that boy will go to the infirmary for a stubbed toe. So then, whaddya say to a few days in Capri?"

Twenty-One

HERE ONE HEALS

Rest & Relaxation, Isle of Capri, Italy, October 1944

JOSTLING ALONG in a six-by-six truck, Bill focused on the positives: the majority of his crew had returned after having been shot down, it was a fine sunny October day, he was on his way to the Isle of Capri, and he didn't have to drop bombs on anyone or anything. Not for a few days at least.

On the drive west, he spotted town names on hand-carved wooden signposts, including Candela, Vallesaccarda, and Saviano. Brutal battles had been waged here. Acre upon acre of once-fertile volcano-fed land had been destroyed. Periodically, washerwomen appeared at the road's edge, waving handkerchiefs and bright aprons, cheering, "*Americano, Americano, grazie, grazie!*" Bill and Joe smiled and waved back, moved by their warm appreciation.

As they entered Naples, Bill was momentarily taken aback. Between the German occupation and the Allies' heavy bombing, the buildings of the once-diverse cosmopolitan city lay in rubble. Bombed and wrecked gantry cranes lay on their sides, partially submerged in the harbor's water, their metal frames twisted and bent like abandoned erector sets.

The six-by-six pulled up to the ferry's dock, and the boys jumped down from the back of the truck. They were immediately inundated by a boisterous group of Neapolitan street kids, malnourished and coated in dirt, asking for candy. Bill and the crew had come prepared for just such a scenario.

Bill noticed a hungry-looking child and gave her all ten of the Butterfingers he'd brought along. A nest of tangled blond curls obscured her face until her head rocked back with joy, and he saw her eyes grow wide at the sight of the bounty she'd been given. Joe handed out Hershey Bars. Murph and Ritt gave out packs of Beeman's chewing gum, and Harvey, Stohlman, and Belding created a stir when they passed out half a dozen Baby Ruths.

Bill purchased a map of Capri and Anacapri at a dock-side kiosk and joined the rest of the crew as they boarded a ferry bound for the island. He pardoned himself through a wide array of passengers as they began to board the ferry: Army Air Corps personnel in their khaki uniforms, Allied doctors and nurses in starched white costumes, and workers carrying various items such as a sausage, basket of oranges, or several yards of light woolen material. Life trying to recapture a sense of normalcy.

Forty-five minutes later, Capri came into full view. A rugged mountain rose from the center, and the town, which began at the coastline, staggered its way up the hill. Bill's map showed that the tallest point on the isle was 1,932 feet. His attention was drawn to the wooded areas between the wharf and village and the whitewashed structures higher up on the mountain. Orange groves grew abundantly. The ferry slowed and glided into Marina Grande, the main harbor on the Isle of Capri.

As soon as his feet hit land, Bill felt ready to explore. But first, they had to locate their hotel. He gathered up Joe and Jug and moved with the flow of people walking down the gangplank onto the dock. Murph was there waiting for them with his boys. Then Bill spotted the ferry captain nearby, lighting up a smoke, and made his approach. The captain's face was permanently etched brown by a lifetime in the sun, his forearms tattooed by the saltwater spray.

"*Donde Hotel Quisisana?*" Bill asked the wizened seaman with the rolled-up shirt sleeves while pointing to his map. The Quisisana served as the designated lodgings for American Army Air Corps officers on R&R.

Tracing the route with his finger, the ferryman drew a path from the dock to the hotel. "*Capisci?*" asked the ferryman.

"*Si, grazie,*" Bill smiled his thanks.

"*Divertiti!*" said the man, as he tipped his frayed white fishing cap and grinned with a wave and a whitewashed smile. "Enjoy yourself!"

The autumn day was mild and perfectly sunny. As Bill stood next to woven baskets filled with the catch of the day, the fresh scent of the sea and its bounty wafted around him. Bill was no fan of fish and eager to leave the docks before the sun could change what was fresh and welcoming into something difficult for him to inhale. He grabbed up his duffel bag, slung it over his shoulder, and headed in the direction of the hotel with the crew tagging along behind him. It only took a few minutes before Murph and his crowd peeled off.

"Have a good time," Bill called after his chief engineer before heading toward the Quisisana. Bill was getting his bearings as he led Jug and Joe through town. They wound their way through a riot of flowers: their reds, purples, and yellows cascading over every balustrade on each steep street and into the main town square. Wisteria-lined walkways cast a lavender glow over pavers worn soft by centuries of foot traffic.

"Ha! Here, Via Tragara, this is it!" Bill said, as he directed his friends to the street he had been searching for.

"You better be right, Gemmill. We've used up half our leave just looking for the place," Jug chided.

"Some navigator," Joe ribbed Bill. "You do know we're here to rest, right?"

"You guys kill me. This place is so tiny, you couldn't get lost if you wanted to," Bill exclaimed.

The hotel stood invitingly at the end of Via Tragara. The hotel doorman perked up when he saw the three Army Air Corps officers approach. The slightly bent man wore his cocoa brown double-breasted hotel livery proudly. Its highly polished brass buttons blinked in the sun, which also caught the sheen of his silver hair that was clipped short. He took all three duffel bags off their hands with ease and said proudly in English, "Welcome to The Quisisana."

"*Grazie*," Bill replied and smiled at the doorman. Joe and Jug handed over their bags, too, grinning at the doorman. Bill checked them in at the front desk. While the hotelier waited for Bill to sign the registry, he explained in English that the hotel was once a health spa—the meaning of the word Quisisana was "here one heals"—as he fastidiously smoothed his thick, slicked-back mane. Bill hoped the name proved appropriate; he needed a break from the tension of bomb runs.

They were assigned two rooms, with Jug grabbing the single. Bill and Joe took the double and walked into a comfortable sunlit room overlooking a well-tended flower garden. They tossed their bags onto the beds—real beds with clean white cotton sheets.

"Let's get cracking," Joe said, turning to Bill.

"Roger that," Bill replied. They unpacked and arranged their civilian clothes and extra uniform shirts and pants, but remained in their gabardine flight uniforms. Bill liked how the short, dark khaki brown jacket paired with the lighter khaki trousers, blouse, and tie. He felt it was a striking ensemble; besides, the jacket made a great canvas for displaying his lieutenant's bars, bombardier wings, and ribbons.

With everything in order, they went across the hall to collect Jug. The Georgia boy was wearing red swim trunks, black rubber slippers, and a white terry cloth pool cover-up. The three officers stopped in for a quick beer at the hotel bar before Jug went down to the water.

"You fellows fill me in when you get back. All I want to do is sit on the sand and drink beer. I don't want to hear the rumble of engines or any blasts of FLAK," Jug announced. "I need some quiet."

Bill and Joe waved as they headed in the opposite direction. "Enjoy your rest," they called to Jug simultaneously.

Bill and Joe explored Capri, absorbing as many details of the island as they could: the turquoise tint of the sea, the salty scent of the fresh catch of the day, the way the sunlight bathed the square. Bill enjoyed listening to the lilt of the townspeople's conversations and envied the ease and gracefulness in which they seemed to live their lives. As if the war was not raging close enough to send airmen and soldiers to such a spot in order to recover their nerves.

All the smells and walking made Bill's stomach grumble. "You hungry?" he asked Joe.

"Are you kidding?" Joe answered. "I've been ready to eat ever since we passed that bakery about half an hour ago."

"Hotel restaurant?"

"Sounds good to me," Joe agreed.

After finding the garlic wafting out of various restaurants and seeing plates of snails, squid, and other seafood he couldn't identify, Bill was all in favor of supper at the hotel; his taste for adventure didn't extend far into the world of cuisine. He was no fan of seafood, and as he was quickly deducing, Capri was a seafood kind of town. He took comfort in the fact that the American chef at the Quisisana knew which foods visiting American boys liked to eat: steak and potatoes. After a filling meal at the hotel, Bill and Joe headed to the bar next door to round out their first day on the isle and reconnect with Jug.

∞

Bill was up with the sun. In his mind, he had overslept. He was accustomed to pre-mission briefings beginning at 0400 hours, when the sun had not yet risen. He looked over at Joe and shook his head at his friend who was still snoring lightly. After a quick shower, he dressed in his clean uniform. "Bombardier to Navigator!" he shouted close to Joe's ear.

"Wha'? Have we been hit? What's going on?!" Joe fumbled awake, tangled in his sheets and blanket.

"No, Joe. There is only so much daylight and we want to see the sights!" Bill explained impatiently.

"OK, Gemmill, I will indulge you this time, but don't get used to it," Joe said as he pretended to groan. "I can be ready in ten."

Bill headed down to the cozy lobby café to wait for Joe. When the waiter arrived, Bill ordered coffee and a pastry.

"American coffee?" asked the waiter. "Or *espresso*? We have the finest *espresso* in all of Italy."

Bill had heard about *espresso*; it was strong. If he couldn't stomach the local *frutti di mare*, perhaps their brand of coffee? He looked up at the waiter and said with a sincere smile, *"Espresso? Si. Per favore."*

When the tiny cup arrived, garnished with a thinly sliced piece of lemon, Bill wondered if he had been gypped out of a full cup. He removed the lemon—he couldn't imagine lemon and coffee together—then noticed a cube of sugar sitting on the saucer. He plunked the sweetener into the rich brown brew and stirred it a few times with the miniature silver spoon that accompanied the drink. He had never tasted anything so strong yet creamy in his brief, coffee-drinking experience, and he loved it.

Ten minutes later, Joe was sitting with him, chugging a cup of hot American-style coffee and going after the pastry basket with vigor. Anacapri awaited them. Bill hurried Joe along so they could get going.

∽

The *funiculare* took sightseers and residents on a five-minute ride up the side of Mount Solaro to Anacapri, the only other town on the mountainous island. Of course, one could always walk up the ancient Phoenician steps built into the side of the mountain—all five hundred of them.

"I figure walking up will take us a couple of hours," Bill said to Joe as they stood near the short line of people waiting to purchase tickets to ride the cable car. He watched as a few young men hoofed it up the steps. He and Joe bought tickets.

As the *funiculare* wound its way up the edge of the mountain, Bill marveled at the view. Windswept pine trees stood like ghostly sentries surrounding the tracks of the cable car. White-roofed buildings in the town below clustered around Marina Piccola and dotted the hillside. Sunbeams shimmered and danced on the crystal blue Gulf of Naples, while out in the offing the Tyrrhenian Sea beckoned. Birdsong surrounded him as a steady breeze played about his head, disturbing the hair he had so carefully combed that morning. He could almost forget there was a war raging to the north and east. *And that*, he reminded himself, *is the point of R&R.*

The tracks of the cable car stopped at a terrace surrounded by early Roman walls, demarking the town center. The honey-colored fortification looked solid; sturdy enough despite the parts that had crumbled away over time. Moved by the antiquity, Bill ran his hands over the worn limestone, feeling for history.

He was especially eager to explore Villa Jovis, the Emperor Tiberius's castle—the first ancient ruins he had ever seen. It sat high on the cliff overlooking Capri and its harbor. As they reached the site, Joe stopped to buy a brochure of the island from the ticket-taker. "Listen to this, Bill," he said as he scanned the map. "It reads here that Tiberius would push people who displeased him off this very spot." Joe waved the pamphlet at Bill.

"Look at those rocks down there," Bill said, leaning over the edge of Salto di Tiberio. "That must be several hundred feet!" Bill watched the waves as they smashed against the cliff far below.

"A most unpleasant end," Joe observed.

"I'd sure say," Bill replied before adding, "What do you say we take the stairs down?"

"I like how you think, Gemmill," Joe agreed, and the two young men set off to find the way back down Solaro.

"Race you to the bottom," Bill challenged Joe.

"You're on!" Joe said and started running. Bill set out after him, counting as he went along. He passed his friend on the forty-eighth step. Both of them were laughing and panting hard when they reached number five hundred.

"That may have been the silliest thing I've done in months," Joe laughed between gulps of air.

"Silly does a man good," Bill proclaimed as he, too, laughed and tried to catch his breath.

∞

Back at the Quisisana, the boys met Jug in the bar for a few beers before heading to their rooms to clean up; they were ready to spend the evening on the town. Drawing a hot bath in the deep iron tub, Joe settled in for a soak. Bill busied himself with smoothing his dress uniform, polishing his shoes and bombardier wings.

"Hey, Joe, this uniform still smells like the inside of a gas tank!" Bill had done his own "dry- cleaning" with aviation fuel the way Joe had taught him. He had never gotten used to the smell. The sound of running water trickled out of the water closet. Wanting a response, Bill draped the uniform on his bed and stuck his head inside the bathroom.

"Holy shit!" he shouted. Water was still flowing from the faucet, the tub was close to overflowing, and Joe was submerged.

"Joe!" Bill cried out. He ran to the tub and in one motion lifted Joe's head out of the water as he shut off the taps. He grabbed the navigator under the arms and pulled him out of the tub. Then he slapped Joe's cheeks and shouted his name again. Joe began fighting back.

"What'd ya do that for?" Joe bellowed when he came to.

"Because I didn't think you wanted to drown on R&R," Bill shouted back. He knew it was the adrenaline coursing through him, yet he found shouting at his good friend unsettling.

"I guess I fell asleep," Joe said, grabbing the towel Bill was holding in his hand and wrapping it around his waist sarong-style.

"Yeah, or passed out is more like it," Bill said more gently.

"Gemmill, you saved my life. Now I'll be indebted to you forever. Do you realize that I'll have to repay you? There'll be no end!" Joe cracked wise with his bombardier.

"You can bet I'll think of something," Bill laughed. His heart was still pounding against his ribs, but he felt a rush of relief that Joe had found his humor again so quickly.

The "near drowning" was the talk at dinner that evening. Jug was full of "what ifs."

"What if Gemmill hadn't come in and found you?" he asked Joe. "What if you hadn't hiked down the mountain and tired yourself out?"

"What if we drop this topic of conversation?" Joe shot back. Bill knew Jug cared, but he also knew Joe. All the navigator wanted was to be out of the spotlight.

∽

Bill was ready to head out early, eager to experience the Blue Grotto. Joe was with him 100 percent, especially having read about the natural phenomenon in Bill's brochure of the island.

Jug advised them over breakfast he would be remaining at the beach. "Fellas," he said, "this may be my last chance to truly relax for a while. I'm still really tired."

Bill noticed the whites of Jug's eyes were more yellow this morning than they had been yesterday. "You take it easy Jug," he said. "We'll tell tales from the grotto that'll make you believe you were there with us."

Jug looked relieved. "Thanks, Gemmill, you be sure to do that," he said. "Come find me after."

"Roger that," Joe answered for Bill.

As they walked away, Bill turned to Joe and asked, "Does that brochure say what makes it blue, Joe?"

"Let's see … says here that the light passing through the water creates the blue cast," Joe read the explanation to Bill.

"That makes sense, I guess; the water out in the marina looks turquoise," Bill said as they approached the dock. They got in line for the excursion boat that took people out to the cave. Bill looked out toward the grotto and watched a flotilla of crafts bobbing in the water. When they reached the front of the line, Bill engaged the ticket-seller.

"*Quanti costo?*" Bill asked the young boy distributing tickets. The kid was wearing a blue-and-white striped T-shirt and dirty shorts that may have been tan after their last washing. His hair was kissed by days in the sun—streaks of red ran through the brown.

"*Trente lire,*" the boy replied, holding his hand out to first Bill and then Joe. Bill dropped the exact change—about a dollar and thirty cents US—into the boy's hand and took a seat in the bow of the boat. Joe did the same.

Outside the cave's entrance, they transferred to a small, flat rowboat painted bright white. All the boats going into and out of the grotto wore the same luminous coat of paint. An extremely tan boatman manned their boat. He grabbed the oars and maneuvered them into position. Bill and Joe had to wait their turn—only a handful of boats were allowed into the grotto at one time.

Not wanting to miss a thing, Bill twisted and turned for a varied view as the boat began to move toward the grotto. When they got close to the mouth of the cave, Bill wondered at the size of the opening; it was quite low.

"Lie down!" the boatman called and waved to Bill, indicating for him to flatten himself in preparation for entry. "The rocks, they can hit you on your head and kill," the man said. He was serious.

Once inside, Bill was awed by the stalactites hanging like chandeliers from the roof of the cave and how the water winked and shifted through shades of blue. *Magic*, Bill thought and smiled at the wonder. The boatman told them the history of the cave, how long-ago shifting tides had carved the arches and crevices and how sunlight passing through an underwater cavity shone through the water, turning it blue. Then he burst into song.

"*O Sole Mio*," the boatman began in earnest. Several other boatmen joined in, and the song grew into a round with Allied airmen heartily participating. Bill and Joe sang loud and proud, always eager for an audience. The fact that they only knew the refrain and didn't speak the language was no deterrent. The tune echoed off the rocky walls of the cave. It sounded like a chorus.

"This will be something to tell the folks back home," Bill said, in awe of the experience.

"Yeah, it's even better than our 'I-o-way' routine," Joe could always find a way to get in a laugh.

Remembering his promise to Pasquale, Bill turned to the boatman as they exited the grotto and asked in a mix of broken Italian, English, and hand gestures, if he knew of another boatman by the name of Piero. "*Si, si!*" the tanned and sinewy man laughed, "*Molti!*" Bill laughed too—of course there were!

Once back at the marina, the boys headed to the beach. They wanted to check on Jug.

"I'm starved," said Joe.

"Yeah, we haven't eaten since breakfast. I could use a little something myself," Bill agreed.

"Let's try some local joint, not the hotel," Joe suggested.

"As long as it isn't fish or tomatoes. Let's make Jug come with us," Bill added.

The boys walked down to *la piccolo marina*, the tan-and-black pebbly beach where Jug would be tanning. They passed individual changing stalls on the beach painted in pastel blue, green, and pink. Curious, they poked their heads in a cabana or two and discovered names like Manfred, Heinz, and Dietz carved into the interior wood walls. Remnants of the recent German occupation of Italy.

"I wonder what these guys were like?"

"I imagine they were just guys like us."

They found Jug sunning himself at the edge of the ocean; his beach chair poised at the water line so he could soak his feet.

"Hey! You're blocking my rays, Gemmill," Jug said as he squinted up at the tall bombardier.

"Sorry, Jug," Bill said as he stepped to the side.

"Hear that you two?" Jug asked.

"Hear what?" Bill and Joe replied simultaneously. They looked at each other and laughed at their timing.

"The sea, the waves?"

"The motor boats?"

"No, the lack of engine noise!" Jug had managed to distance himself from combat. Bill wondered if it would be tough for the copilot to get back into the clamor of war. Heck, he wondered the same thing about himself as Jug stood and walked to a nearby cabana where he changed into his casual khaki uniform.

Walking into town, the trio settled on lunch at one of the cafés on the Piazza Umberto. They were seated at a table with a clear view of the sparkling Tyrrhenian Sea. They ordered beers and tried to make sense of the menu. They settled on spaghetti with red sauce for Jug and Joe and a plain pizza for Bill, safe bets all the way round.

∞

The next morning, Bill and Joe took the *funiculare* up the mountain again. The chapel at Villa San Michele was the draw; they'd heard the lore that keeping a chapel bell in your flight suit brought good luck. Sitting close to the highest spot on the island, the church had a mystical appearance that drew crowds of Army Air Corps men, believers and non-believers alike. Bill stood musing before a tiled pavement depicting the fall of Adam and Eve.

"I'm buying a bell, Joe," Bill announced.

"Yeah, me too," Joe responded.

The boys arrived at the chapel and took their places at the back of a queue—a dozen young airmen were ahead of them. Carved marble corridors echoed the conversations emanating from the line. When Bill got to the entrance, a young nun selling the storied treasure beamed up at Bill from her table of shiny silver domes, her smile both broad and comforting. He dug in his pocket for a few *lire* and dropped the coins into her outstretched palm.

"*Grazie,*" she spoke softly as she dropped the little charm into his outstretched palm. "*Andare con Dio.*" Bill inspected the miniature silver bell. It was engraved with "*La bella Fortuna de San Michele.*" He curled his hand around the cool silver shape and smiled down at the diminutive woman dressed in her habit of white and black. The thought of going back to the chaos and waste of war had moved up in his consciousness here in the peacefulness and relative seclusion of Capri.

"*Grazie,*" Bill said. He held the nun's gaze for a moment and thought: *Anything to get me through to my last mission and back home.*

Twenty-Two

NUMBER THIRTEEN

Cerignola to Blechhammer,
13 October 1944

THERE WAS NO WAITING for the rested. No sooner had Bill and the crew returned from Capri, their entire squadron was assigned missions to Latisana, Trieste, and Bologna, Italy. Targets on 10, 11, and 12 October were a bridge, oil storage, and ground support. The FLAK was light on each run, no enemy fighters were sighted, and none of the bombers sustained any damage.

Bill welcomed the three milk runs in a row—his stress level declined significantly. He had been assigned group lead on the run to Trieste, which meant he was both lead bombardier of Able Box— the center squadron of the first unit of bombers—and lead for every other section of the formation. The deputy lead flew on his left wing.

He was happy to guide everyone to the IP and back without incident.

Winter was coming, and the weather was turning more unpredictable, which made air corps meteorologists uncomfortable. They couldn't send entire squadrons up if they couldn't see the target. General Twining determined every squadron in the 304th Bomb Group needed to take advantage of each day of decent flying weather. Once again, the crew was broken up and sent to replace injured or missing gunners, engineers, radiomen, pilots, bombardiers, and navigators on other crews. Had Wes and Bill Hill been there, they would have been assigned elsewhere as well.

He missed Wes. The whole crew felt his absence. There was a new officer in The Manse now—another pilot. Bill looked over at the new guy's personal effects laid out neatly on Wes's former cot. He appreciated how difficult it must be to move into the space of a beloved crew member, especially their leader. He wanted to introduce himself and make the pilot feel welcome, but they had never occupied the tent at the same time. Bill didn't even know what he looked like, much less his name.

The day after the mission to Bologna, Bill was up early to dress for another mission. He pulled on his white athletic socks—by now, everyone from his crew to the squadron commander knew he never flew a mission without those lucky socks. Wes had known Bill would rather face a dressing down from group command than fly without those white cotton socks. Thinking of Wes, Bill hoped his friend was safe and healthy wherever he was. Before standing up, he tucked his "Bella Fortuna" into the left front pocket of his blouse, buttoned it down for safekeeping, and gave it a reassuring pat. He looked up at Jug who had walked over to Bill's cot while he was securing his pockets. The man with the wisecracks didn't say a word about the socks or the bell.

Jug wore his own non-regulation attire under his uniform: a bulldog-red and arch-black University of Georgia football T-shirt. Bill thought Jug looked worse than he had on Capri; his eyes were noticeably yellow, and he slumped a bit as he sat on the edge of his cot. All Jug carried was a clipboard and a pencil. He reeked of fatigue.

"Are you up to flying today, Jug?" he questioned the copilot.

"I'll be OK, Mother. I'm just a bit tired this morning is all," Jug replied. Bill let the crack at being called "Mother" go. The last thing he wanted was to match barbs with Jug before a mission.

Once Joe was geared up and his sextant packed in his black leather flight bag, he signaled to Bill that it was time to head out. Bill layered up and grabbed his own flight bag. The three friends stepped outside of their tent, checked the wind and the stars, then headed to the briefing bunker. It was the thirteenth day of October, 1944, and Bill's thirteenth mission.

"Feeling lucky today, Gemmill?" Jug asked. As was their custom by now, they took seats near the front of the room.

"As lucky as any other day, Jug," Bill replied with a shrug. He looked around the familiar room with its arched ceiling and plaster walls lined with hundred-year-old cracks. The setup hadn't changed while he had been on Capri—the mission map hung waiting behind the same green drape, the podium stood to the left of center where it always had been, and rows upon rows of chairs were lined up for the officers of every squadron to sit during briefings. He didn't know what he had expected; his mind wandered to the wine casks. *What had they done with all the wine casks?* Jug's voice pierced his thoughts.

"No, I mean, do you feel like you've got Lady Luck in your back pocket?" Jug persisted.

"What in hell are you talking about?" Bill asked, then followed to where Jug's finger was pointing to the calendar visible just to the right of the draped mission board and under a large clock.

"Holy cow," Bill exclaimed after looking at the date on the target board. He had been oblivious to the significance of the day's date until Jug brought it up.

"That's what I was trying to tell you: your thirteenth on the thirteenth. The target isn't a coincidence, that's for sure," Jug said, nodding toward the front of the room again. The squadron leader had dropped the curtain, revealing the mission map. Even through the haze of smoke from a hundred lit cigarettes, the target stood out plainly: the oil refinery at Blechhammer, Germany.

To confuse the enemy, the route to a bomb run was never plotted in a straight line, even though by now, the Germans were pretty good at guessing the most likely path of oncoming Allied aircraft. As he listened to the intelligence officer discuss the approach to the target, Bill began considering the best direction from which to take the oil refinery, and a secondary one if the original proved too heavily defended. This way of second guessing the navigators' and weather men's thinking had become second nature to him. As bombardier, it was prudent for him to have an alternative in mind—over and above what intelligence dictated—should they have to change plans quickly. After hearing all the intel, he favored the route that had the squadron flying across the Adriatic Sea and over Yugoslavia, Hungary, and Czechoslovakia, before heading on to Blechhammer.

The Nazi oil refinery was one of the toughest targets the 15th had in its repertoire. The squadron leader approached the podium, the map behind him. He looked out over the assembled officers with a purposeful gaze. Bill figured he was gearing up to burn the significance of his message into every pair of eyes looking back at him. Then he began issuing orders.

"Gemmill, you'll fly group lead with Harrison's crew. They're short a bombardier."

Bill nodded a communique at Captain Harrison. The two men

knew each other; their tents stood side by side in officer country. Harrison was A-OK in Bill's book, even if he was no youngster at twenty-eight years; he smoked cherry-flavored tobacco in a burled pipe, for Chrissake. The man was about as tall as Bill and had a swagger like Jug. He also had the calm and good humor of Joe. Bill had yet to fly with Harrison and his crew, but he'd heard that the captain was one heck of a pilot.

"You'll be equipped with both a Norden and a Mickey," the squadron leader continued. "We want to see how the H2X radar platform performs on this mission; our meteorologists expect heavy undercover. Radar is still a new tool."

Bill had seen the Mickey, having inspected MIT's answer to "seeing" through dense clouds and fog when General Twining demonstrated the device at a required B&N meeting earlier in the week. Intelligence officers reported that the navy had been having success with the contraption. Bill heard that a pilot from the 8th Air Force said the device looked "Mickey Mouse"— as in amateur, patched together—and, as a result, the platform began to be referred to as a Mickey. Anyone operating it was called a Mickey operator. Adding up his responsibilities, Bill realized he was going to be lead Mickey. He laughed at the idea, then wondered if Captain Harrison had flown with a Mickey-equipped bombardier yet.

After the meteorologist gave an updated weather report around the target, the officers filed out of the tent and made their way to the airstrip. Another "day at the office" was about to commence.

∞

Bill huddled in the nose with Harrison's navigator, both of them busy making ready. Bill's training was such an integral part of him:

calculations were determined, checked, and rechecked; plot points charted; the gears, knobs, and gyros of the Norden set. Having something to do for the duration of the flight kept any anxiety he might feel at arm's length. The skies were clear, but he set up the Mickey anyway so he would be prepared if and when they encountered heavy cloud cover.

"Navigator to radioman," Bill's "office-mate" du jour called into the plane's intercom. Bill liked the little navigator. He looked like the legendary leprechauns of Ireland with his bright red hair and green eyes.

"Radio here," the radioman's reply traveled from flight deck back to bomb deck.

"What's our weather looking like up ahead?"

"Same as it looked thirty minutes ago," the radioman chided.

Nothing to do but wait, Bill thought. Wait out the cold and the boredom and then, when the FLAK starts up, wait out the ever-present fear.

To pass some time, Bill pulled an old letter out of his flight bag, the one from his father he carried like a talisman, from when Senior was in North Africa. In it, his dad spoke about the growing number of POWs overrunning the resources at his camp. Bill returned the letter to his flight bag, shoving the bag under the navigator's desk to keep it out of his way.

Bill heard the navigator request another weather report. "Same as it was an hour ago," came the reply. The radioman then added, "We're nearing radio-silence range so quit your obsession with the weather. It's weather; you'll know exactly what that is when we get there!"

Bill double-checked the control panel on the Norden, and its gauges and dials, for a second time. *Funny to think those are real human hairs*, he marveled, looking at the ever-vital crosshairs lined up beneath the glass, pointing the way to his targets. This mission called for him to "walk" the bombs over the refinery—it called for precision timing. The bombs would be released in successive drops so that they staggered over the designated area.

"It will be good to finish Blechhammer!" the navigator shouted over the drone of the B-24's four big engines.

"The Nazis sure know how to pack a punch. They'll go down fighting to defend their precious refineries," Bill said, recalling his first attack on Budapest.

As they neared the target, the clouds cleared and the FLAK picked up, just as army intelligence had predicted. Bill glanced at the radar, its indicator sweeping steadily and showing nothing, then back at the Norden. Suddenly, dozens of enemy fighters appeared out of the clouds to greet the bomb formation. The Germans had put everything they had up in the air to protect their precious fuel. The FLAK became heavier, more intense, and more accurate.

"What'd I tell ya?" Bill shouted to the navigator. Then he took his *campana di buona fortuna*—bell of good fortune—out of his jacket pocket. He blew on it for luck then tucked it into the shin pocket of his pants. He could feel the small metal dome rubbing against his leg as he laid himself flat on the bomb deck floor, eye on the Norden bombsight. He'd never get over how tight and compact the aircraft's designers had made the bomb and navigation deck.

∞

Just ahead of the target, as Bill was lining up the run with the IP, the bomber was struck by a hefty piece of FLAK. The plane heaved, yet remained steady. This was the most dangerous part of a bomb run, when the bomber had to fly straight and level with bomb bay doors wide open. Enemy fighters knew this was their moment—the right strike and the entire bomber would go up in flames. Any minute now,

Captain Harrison would hand control of the plane to Bill.

"Captain! It's Frank, he's been hit," the left waist gunner called frantically into the intercom.

"Frank? Hold tight, we're in a mess up here," Harrison called to both gunners. The fighters were hitting the bomber with all their guns.

At the same time, large chunks of metal FLAK were grinding holes in the aluminum shell of the plane. The FLAK was intense and very accurate. Bullets pinged off the tail. The din was ear-splitting. Bill couldn't escape the deafening sounds of metal on metal and the gunner shouting into the intercom. He also listened to the quieter voice in his head telling him to stay calm until he could release his salvo.

"We need help back here! There's blood everywhere! Someone has to push Frank out of the way!" the left waist gunner called frantically into the intercom. With Frank down, the left waist gunner was trying to man both the left and right waist guns. The young gunner had gone down quietly.

"Pilot to engineer, get back there and take up that gunner's position!" Captain Harrison's command crackled over the intercom. Just as quickly, he altered his order. "Hey the waist! Wait until we clear this zone, then see to your gunner!" They were too close to the target and had too great a wind advantage to abort the drop; the whole crew knew they'd have to carry on before seeing to their wounded.

Harrison held the plane steady a moment longer before turning the controls over to Bill. The crosshairs aligned, and Bill signaled to Harrison over the intercom, "I've got her." Captain Harrison relinquished control of the bomber to Bill, who dropped the timed load then called into the intercom, "Bombs away!" The plane began to bank.

"Bombardier to pilot," Bill said as he scanned the radar screen. "Looks like we got a good walk." There was too much smoke for him to detect the accuracy of his strike through the Norden, but the Mickey could see through the billowing dense clouds rising from the target. He turned to the new device to watch as radio waves sent from the device to the ground bounced back to the machine. Those radio waves were data; they showed flattened oil tanks. The surrounding buildings were flattened. Once again, Bill was impressed with the ability of the Mickey to detect and confirm the accuracy—or lack thereof—of a bombing mission.

Bill stretched out on his belly again and looked out the bombardier's window to watch the salvos of the bombers toggling off of him. The smoke had thickened and obscured his view so he turned again to the Mickey. There, on the circular screen, he saw bombs hitting the target again and again. Bill was officially impressed.

"Copy that," Captain Harrison's reply was crisp. As he was about to comment further, the call was interrupted by the plane's now-lone waist gunner.

"Captain! I need help back here. It's gotten really slippery, and I'm trying to man both guns." Bill heard the call and started making his way to the waist. He knew what was probably making the deck slippery, and he could do something to help: man a gun, help stop the bleeding, or both.

It was slow going at twenty-four thousand feet on a ten-inch-wide catwalk, which was the only way to get from one end of the B-24 to the other. The full flight gear and oxygen tank were cumbersome and slowed his progress. Before he got to the waist of the plane, Bill had been rocked and knocked down several times by nearby bursts of FLAK. When he reached the waist, Bill saw the injured gunner slumped over on the floor. His body was blocking access to the machine gun mounted at the right waist window. The kid's head was in his hands, as if he was sleeping and didn't want to be disturbed. Bill reached the downed gunner and turned him over. There was a lot of blood.

It covered the boy's hands and ran down the front of his FLAK suit. When he looked at the gunner's head, a large hole gaped at him where the boy's face used to be. Bill didn't know what he had expected when he turned the boy over, but he knew it wasn't this. He kept staring at where the kid's smile should have been, where his green eyes had greeted him just hours before, and couldn't explain to himself where they could possibly be.

"You OK, Lieutenant?" asked the engineer who had come to take up the gunner's position in the waist. "You're white as a ghost."

"He's dead," Bill said numbly. "I remember him. We played basketball together, hell of a free-throw shooter."

"He was just a kid," the engineer reacted, shaking his head. "Lied about his age to join up."

Enemy fighters appeared once more to bedevil them; mourning Young Frank would have to wait. For the rest of the ride home, Bill remained in the waist, first manning a machine gun and then keeping Young Frank and the engineer company once the fighting had subsided.

∞

Nearly eight hours after they had left Italy, Bill's plane limped into Cerignola. The engineer and friend to fallen Frank fired a red flare on the approach, signaling a need for a priority landing: wounded on board.

The ambulance drove alongside the bomber as she taxied in. Once Captain Harrison had the plane parked, corpsmen removed Young Frank's body before the rest of the crew was allowed off the plane.

When he slid through the crew hatch to the tarmac, Bill's knees were shaking. He steadied himself by holding onto the wing while the navigator, nose gunner, and tail gunner eased themselves down. The left waist gunner appeared next, face ashen. The gunner's boots and gear were thick with blood, which prompted Bill to look at the state of his own gear. A wide expanse of thick red matter covered the leather of his FLAK jacket; his gloves and the soles of his boots were sticky with coagulation. He exchanged an empathetic look with the gunner who took off down the tarmac, not bothering to wait for a truck to take him back to his quarters. Bill was shaking all over when Jim Harrison dropped down through the hatch. Seeing Bill and recognizing shock when he saw it, he stayed with the bombardier.

"First death?" he asked Bill softly.

"Yes," Bill replied solemnly. His face tensed at the thought of what had happened. He looked to be in pain.

"Don't get used to it," Harrison advised. "And if you're going to keep flying, don't imagine yourself in the same state as Young Frank. We need bombardiers like you up there with us. You really kept your cool."

Bill didn't feel cool, but listening to Captain Harrison steadied him. The transport truck pulled up, and Bill rode to the debriefing tent with Harrison and the rest of his crew. Those were the stakes, he ruminated. Possibly the highest stakes every young man, on every side, fighting every kind of war, had to make peace with.

∞

Back at The Manse after debriefing, Bill was unusually quiet. He drew into himself, assessing the day. The men around him respected his need for reflection, waiting for the numbness to subside. Joe and Jug put a lid on their usual cheery antics. Pasquale regarded his friend and honored his silence. Bill needed time to recover his good nature. A knock on the door brought him out of his fugue.

"Hey, Gemmill," the familiar voice of Jim Harrison called out.

Joe opened the door of the tent and let the captain in. "Permission to approach?" Harrison asked, looking at Bill.

Bill was sitting on the edge of his cot. He looked up at Harrison and nodded "yes."

"How're you doing?" the pilot asked Bill. He waited as if he had all the time in the world.

Slowly, Bill found his words. "I'm OK, Jim. Just pensive, you know?"

"I do know," Jim Harrison answered. "Are you slated to fly again tomorrow?"

"That's going to depend on the weather," Bill answered.

"Well, I'm not going to tell you to 'shake it off' when you do fly your next mission. That young man's death will be with you a long time. So, get back up there and bomb the hell out of those Nazis. Do it for Frank. Do it for yourself. You'll be amazed at how cathartic it can be." Bill appreciated the pilot's supportive gesture.

"Thank you, Jim," Bill responded respectfully. "I'll be just fine." He just needed to compartmentalize the visual of Frank's face when he had turned him over. Twelve missions and he hadn't seen anyone, not his original crew or any other crew he flew with, killed. Sure, he had seen bad injuries, but no deaths—not until now. He thought about the kid on one of his first missions to Hungary, the nose turret gunner who he and Joe had helped. That kid had been lucky enough to survive. Sure, he had been shot up badly and lost a leg, but he had been sent home alive. He sank back into his cot as Captain Harrison walked out the door.

Death stalks the plane like a ghost every time we go up, he thought. Was he somehow more of a man now that he'd seen it up close? He considered the impact of watching someone perish. Death has that power: to transform and clarify; to put life into perspective and reason, yet it also offers up as many questions as it does answers. Especially for a young man of twenty.

Twenty-Three

BILL'S TURN TO BAIL

Cerignola to Munich to Somewhere Over Yugoslavia, November 1944

THE BLECHHAMMER RUN had shown Bill what Death could look like at twenty-four thousand feet in the air: sudden, freezing, wet. He took Captain Harrison's words to heart and readied himself to fly again the next day, but the weather had other plans for the bombardier. In fact, the entire 15th Air Force was grounded due to the low ceiling brought in by a string of storms. Bill took advantage of the chilly, damp days to read some of the books Wes had accumulated before he'd gone missing. Currently, Bill was caught up in Lloyd Douglas's *The Robe*. If the weather kept grounding the squadron, he'd be through that in a few days and on to John Marquand's spy series, *Mr. Moto*. Wes had three of them on hand, and Bill loved a good mystery. He also caught up on his letter writing home, napped, and learned to lose badly at gin rummy to Jug and Joe. These weather-related lulls were hard on Bill; he wanted to rack up as many missions as possible and go home. He cursed the dark, mid-morning clouds and the pelting rain for standing in his way.

Bill woke early on 20 October and peeked outside, where the stars were splayed across the pre-dawn sky like a dusting of glitter: his signal to make ready for mission briefing at 0400 hours. This would be his fourteenth run, actually his twentieth—counting the six double sorties he'd flown hitting two targets in one run. Sitting in the briefing bunker with Joe and Jug, he watched as the green drape obscuring the target was drawn aside: the oil refineries at Innsbruck, Austria. He took notes on the target, the weather, and any intelligence shared about the defenses. He was assigned to fly lead with a crew new to him. They'd be seven hours in the air. The lengthy missions were arduous and took a toll on his body when he was finally able to stand up: his back was sore from arching during long stretches on his stomach, and his shoulders stiff and achy from propping up on his elbows to peer through the Norden's eyepiece. But he rarely noticed how long the missions were when he was in the thick of calibrating, calculating, or seeing to wounded gunners. He only noticed his discomfort when the tension left him and he was back on the ground. He'd begun to bite his nails; they were chewed down to the nub after six months of steady bombing, and he'd already forgotten his downtime and adventures in Capri.

The mission to Innsbruck was a success. He had the Norden, and his bombs met their target: storage tanks at the refinery. The orange of the flames and the black from burning oil were amplified by the togglers dropping their bombs off his. He watched bursts of black and orange continue to rise from the refinery as salvo after salvo reached the ground. No fighters were sighted, and their bomber sustained minor damage from FLAK.

On 21 October, Bill participated in an attack on the airdrome in Szombathely, Hungary. Again, the FLAK was accurate but not intense. Again, no enemy fighters were sighted; the bomber took very few hits. Bill welcomed these bomb runs; they were a respite from the inevitable rough ones awaiting him. After the Szombathely debriefing, Bill was awarded his first oak leaf cluster signifying he had attained another Air Medal.

"Congratulations, Lieutenant, you've earned it," Major General Twining said as he pinned the small bronze bar on Bill's uniform jacket.

"Thank you, Sir," Bill replied, shaking the major's hand. Back at his tent, he held up his shaving mirror and proudly regarded the bar. He planned on adding some bronze and silver acorns and oak leaves to the ribbon before his tour in Italy was over.

The missions kept adding up between bad weather days, and there were a lot of bad weather days. When a string of storms lifted, Bill flew lead and Mickey on a run to Vienna, Austria. Vienna's oil refineries were heavily defended. He returned to Vienna the very next day as group lead and lead. On his third pass at Vienna a few days later, he repeated serving as lead and Mickey. On all three runs, the FLAK was intense and accurate. As many as twenty enemy fighters appeared each time, ten ME-163s and ME-109s swarmed the formation at any one time. Bill's bomber sustained heavy damage from a group of ME-109s and FW-190s. Every mission to Vienna lasted over six hours, and Bill was certain his number was up at least a half-dozen times. Bill knew the odds: that every time he was up in the air he might die, yet he accepted his mortality like the well-trained man he'd become. Soiling his pants out of fear was a tangible reminder.

After more winter weather kept the bombers and their crews on the ground, Bill went up again. He bombed the rubber works in Zlin, Czechoslovakia, as lead and Mickey, and toggled off the lead on runs on troop concentrations at Sjenica, Yugoslavia, and the marshalling yards at Vicenza, Italy. He felt less responsibility for the entire mission when he toggled, primarily concerned for his own timing, but it was rare for him to toggle. He continued to fly lead or deputy lead the majority of his time in Italy.

On 22 November, his twenty-fourth mission—thirty-first counting seven more sorties—Bill returned to the marshalling yards at Munich, that German railroad hotspot. The 304th Bomb Group had taken heavy beatings over Munich, but disrupting the Nazi supply lines was key to the Allies' plan to cripple the enemy. Bill took note of the sky surrounding him as the bombers formed up. It calmed him to be reminded of the beauty in the world, what with all the destruction of the war. And that natural beauty didn't disappoint: the sky was a clear, bottomless blue, while below, the winter sun's rays danced and glittered off Adriatic waves. Once again, he was flying lead bombardier with a crew of virtual strangers, with the exception of Navigator Bill "Braz" Brazelton. Braz and Bill had met during B&N training in Las Vegas, and they had become fast friends. As luck would have it, they both ended up in the same bomb group in Italy, the 304th, but this was the first time they were flying together.

"Well," Braz said to Bill as they stepped into their office on the bomb deck, "here we are, together again at last."

"Except this is no training mission. It sure feels good to be flying with a friend again, Braz," Bill said as he reached inside his flight bag for his pencils and notebook. "I haven't flown with anyone from my crew since the mission to Casarsa. Were you on that run?"

"That was the bridge, right?" Braz asked Bill.

"No, the tank works," Bill corrected Braz. "Fiat."

"Right. Yes, I was. Flew with a crazy pilot. A real sonofabitch," Braz recalled.

"How so?" Bill asked, waiting to see if Braz's description was close to any pilot he had flown with.

"Besides questioning my navigational skills, he kept yelling into the intercom to keep off the intercom when none of us were on the damn thing. Drove me nuts!" Braz said. The guy didn't sound like any pilot Bill had flown with so far. He hoped he never pulled an assignment with him either.

The engines started up, and the bomber taxied into position for takeoff. Once in the air, their pilot took the lead in the second box as directed, then the group headed north. As they approached the Alps, Bill was contemplative, quietly studying the maps he knew so well or just watching the ground below shift and morph from rolling countryside to foothills. Braz was quiet as well.

While turning for the bomb run, just before they reached the IP, Bill's formation was jumped by a group of enemy fighters: fourteen ME-210s and a German B-24. The Luftwaffe pilots were relentless; they swarmed the sky like bats hunting mosquitoes. A second wave of fighters took on Bill's formation, coming in just behind the first. Gunners in the waist and tail were calling in heavy damage and losses; men manning the turrets were overwhelmed and soon stopped communicating altogether. The bomb runs of both formations were in jeopardy. Despite the chaos, every bomber pilot maintained altitude and speed through the dense, accurate FLAK and the onslaught of enemy fighters. Bill was itching to unload tons of high explosives on representatives of the Third Reich below. *Just another minute,* he encouraged himself, *wait for it.* His eyes were all but glued to the eyesight of the Norden, watching for the crosshairs to align.

A squadron of Tuskegee Airmen in their speedy P-51s—the Red Tails were every bomber's friend—arrived to chase away the enemy attack. Over the intercom, Bill's pilot announced that their hydraulic system had been damaged and that he had to feather one of the propellers on one of the left engines. Still, he kept the plane level, awaiting his bombardier's signal. He didn't have a long wait.

"Bombardier to pilot, I'll take her from here," Bill called into the intercom, advising the pilot they had reached the IP.

"Roger that," the pilot replied, relinquishing the bomber's controls to Bill.

"Fighters at two o'clock high!" The call came from the airman manning the guns in the nose turret. A dozen enemy ME-109s were closing fast on the bomber. Bill was seconds from dropping his payload when the plane took a hit in the nose. The concussion took out the B-24's electrical system and another engine. Worse for Bill, it caused the aircraft to veer, and he watched helplessly as the crosshairs on the Norden drifted off target. Then the tail gunner called into the intercom that they had lost half of the tail. In spite of the maelstrom in which they found themselves, Bill fought to maintain his speed and direction. Relying on his training and experience, he worked quickly to bring the crosshairs back onto the target, only to watch them drift away again, though less dramatically than before. Making the necessary final adjustments to the creeping range hair, Bill made the judgment to release his load and called out "Bombs away!" into the intercom. He was eager to hand the bomber back to the pilot so they could get the hell out of there. He watched his incendiaries descend until an enemy fighter strafed the nose.

"Jesus, my leg!" Shock and pain crackled over the intercom. The nose turret gunner had been hit.

"This must be what the inside of Hell is like!" Bill yelled to Navigator Braz. Braz was shouting, but Bill only saw his mouth moving; it was impossible to hear anything through the din. Enemy bullets tore away the skin of the plane, connecting and destroying everything in their path. The sound of metal on metal was deafening, and Bill was terrified.

The pilot was back in the driver's seat with two engines feathered and both the electrical and hydraulic systems out. The bomber slowly began losing speed and altitude; they were now flying below fifteen thousand feet. Bill watched the escort of P-51s approach. They arrived just in time to keep the enemy fighters from picking off the stricken bomber and bought the crew time to escape. Bill knew the German pilots could see that his bomber had been disabled, that they were helpless.

"Pilot to navigator," the pilot called to Braz.

"Navigator here," Braz shouted into the intercom.

"Hey, we aren't going to make it over those mountains, are we?" the pilot said. Bombers from the 15th Air Force had to clear the Alps—which stood at 15,781 feet—both going out to a bomb run and returning to base. It was the return that was dicey, especially if that bomber was shot to pieces and barely limping.

"Not at this rate," Braz answered, fully aware of the mechanical damage to the plane.

"Plot a course from this morning's intel briefing. See if we can ditch in friendly territory," the pilot ordered.

"Roger that. Partisan activity was reported just ahead. If they're still there, that's our best bet," Braz said optimistically.

"Pilot to crew! You've heard what's going to happen. Make ready to abandon ship," the pilot ordered. Bill made ready, grabbing his parachute and escape kit of money, food, medicine, and silk maps. In a matter of moments, he was geared up and in his harness.

With Braz frantically making last-minute calculations, Bill got the nose wheel emergency escape area ready so that he and Braz could leave in a hurry. Their office was just above this getaway route, and Bill was taking no chances. *So, we're going to bail,* Bill thought as he visualized the scant procedures for bailing out of a plane he'd learned at basic: one morning of going over the parachute itself, one afternoon of jumping off a high tower strapped in a 'chute, and an evening of watching the film *How to Handle a Parachute*. He was about to make his first actual bailout in combat. He felt he had every right to be nervous. Meanwhile, the bomber limped along without her electronics. Bill felt her shudder from time to time, but she was staying up, for now.

"Nose turret to pilot," a voice came over the intercom, loud and clear. "I'm hit and I can't get the turret open. I think it's jammed." Bill forgot his fear and jumped into action.

"Watch your head, Braz! I'm going to help the gunner out of the turret," Bill called out to Braz as he grabbed the hand crank and started working it desperately. *Damn those fighters,* he cursed, *they would have to shoot out the electronics!* With great effort, he manually cranked the nose turret around. When he finally got the hatch opened, he saw that the gunner's pant leg was soaked in blood. He worked quickly to assist him out. With the gunner freed, Bill returned to the bomb deck. Bill looked out the navigator's window and noticed more details on the ground. The bomber was continuing to slowly lose altitude.

Bill was required to disable the top-secret Norden before a bailout. Bill removed his Colt .45 from its holster and took aim at the Norden. For a fraction of a second, he considered the waste of a good machine, then decided it was better than having American technology fall into the hands of the enemy.

"What in Hell are you doing ..." Braz's query hung in the freezing air as a .45 slug tore into the sight. Pieces of Norden ricocheted all over the nose compartment. "... trying to kill us?" Bill left the explanation for later and followed Braz into the escape hatch.

With the wheel up, the three men were cramped in the nose. The gunner's leg continued to bleed steadily. There was no time to see to the damage and no time to bind the wound. The gunner limped around

Braz, crawled up to the flight deck, then headed back to the waist, dragging his shot-up leg behind him and leaving a trail of blood. The guy was going to bail out with his buddies in the waist. Bill and Braz could see the ground from their perch and figured they'd better hear the order to go soon or they wouldn't have enough room to jump safely.

Being active had helped to keep the fear away. Bill had rescued the gunner from the stuck nose turret and destroyed the Norden. Now, waiting for the command to bail, Bill felt the tension spreading throughout his body. Frozen with anticipation, he positioned himself directly above the nose wheel and sat on the nose wheel doors. At the order to jump, he pulled the red emergency handle, and with a *whoosh* the doors flew away and took him with them, headfirst.

Bill dove into the atmosphere and tumbled a bit before righting himself through sheer will. When he pulled the rip cord, the force of the parachute opening took his breath away, and he was jarred to a momentary stop. He hadn't pulled the chute harness tight enough. When the canopy deployed, the webbed straps bit into his groin. He was instantly, and intensely, nauseous. *So this is what Joe was referring to*—Bill imagined his friend's voice—*a right wringing of the balls!* He heard the rush of the wind in his ears replace the rumble of the bomber's engines and felt the peaceful suspension of gravity. The frigid air iced his cheeks and mouth. For a moment, there was no war, only the wind.

As he sailed to earth, he glanced back up at the pilotless bomber as it continued its slow descent. Above him, he counted five parachutes descending. Above them, he watched as a group of Red Tails flew past several times. He figured they were providing cover and protection for the crew; Nazi pilots were prone to shooting at men in parachutes. The men of the Red Tails—The Tuskeegee Airmen—were true heroes to Bill. He looked down at the 'chutes of the crew members who had preceded him out of the crippled plane. Then he noticed the treetops.

They looked so far away yet were coming at him fast. Closing his eyes, he tried to get a feel for the speed of his descent. He opened them just in time to see a wall of rock at the base of a steep slope. Pulling what felt like the appropriate cord, he crossed his legs as he had seen in the training film and hit the top of a pine tree. The tree's rotten top branches absorbed his weight like a sponge, then his 'chute lifted him once again, slamming him into a rocky ledge four or five feet off the floor before landing in a grassy meadow. His mid-back and right ankle took the force of the blow, yet Bill detached from the 'chute and quickly began to gather the cords and silk into a bundle.

His ankle was in bad shape; Bill could barely touch it, much less put weight on it. He wondered if it might be broken and hoped it was merely a bad sprain. He stood surveying the immediate area, then turned to inspect his hand: he was certain he had broken a few fingers. He was in a valley, but which valley? And where? Was he still in Austria, or did the pilot manage to get them over Yugoslavian airspace before he ordered the bailout? Where was Braz? Why hadn't he asked Braz their location before they jumped?

As if in answer, two women emerged from the woods wearing multiple layers of multi-hued scarves and woolen clothing against the cold. They were young, possibly late-twenties. Bill connected the forest with the treetops he had seen on his way down. The women seemed unfazed by his appearance, as if they had seen the likes of him before, and sprang into action, arguing and pulling at the parachute. One was brandishing a sickle and was about to cut into the material when Bill explained there was silk enough for them both. With the women's help, they divided the material. Bill claimed a swatch for himself as a memento of his first bailout, hoping it was his last.

Looking around, Bill saw no signs of the rest of the crew. Communicating with the local ladies through mime and gestures, he learned that other fliers had come down in parachutes further up the valley. The women began walking toward the nearest mountains and indicated for him to join them. He chose to follow them. The going was rough; crossing a meadow thick with tall grasses and low bushes, Bill had to pick his line of advance carefully. The pain in his back grew with each step; he could no longer bend the fingers on his left hand, and the agony in his ankle was nearly unbearable until his entire foot finally, and gratefully, became numb.

Twenty-Four

TREKKING THROUGH YUGO

Somewhere in Yugoslavia,
November 1944

THE AIR WAS DOWNRIGHT FRIGID, and an unrelenting damp drove the chill straight into his bones, especially the fingers on his left hand. One of the women diverted into a thick stand of poplar trees and emerged with a good-sized branch for Bill to use as a crutch. He watched as she stripped it of leaves and side-shoots before she presented it to him.

He grinned when he took the stick from the woman. She was pretty in a fierce, warrior woman way. Copper-headed with freckles spanning the bridge of her nose and sprinkling her cheeks, she kept most of her hair tucked up under a forest green beret.

"Thank you," he said to her as he tried out the crutch. It was easy for him to grab on to and strong enough for him to lean on.

"You welcome," she replied and returned his smile.

The support did take the pressure off his ankle somewhat, but it added more on his back, and gripping the stick with his swollen fingers was not possible, so he let them dangle. Despite the discomfort, he clung to the branch and continued on, eventually crossing a narrow stream and skirting a rutted dirt road. Bill saw a well-carved wooden sign indicating twenty kilometers to Zenica and stopped to adjust his crutch. The women kept moving, so he hobbled as quickly as he could to keep up. He figured he was better off with people than alone, even if he didn't know the people he was walking with.

Twenty-five minutes later, they came into a small village. There was no welcome sign, not even the name of the place carved in wood or stamped in stone. Army intelligence had twice briefed the fliers that German troops were billeted in Zenica, yet the word from men on the ground was these Germans were reluctant to chase downed Allied airmen too far into the hills. There was no sign of Nazi soldiers, so far as Bill could tell as he observed the details of his surroundings. Several buildings might have been people's homes; they had low roofs and firewood stacked along the sides. Everything he could see was built from wood: the houses, the barns, and what Bill guessed were storehouses. Chickens ran loose afoot. One lone, empty clothesline was strung up between two houses, but no sign of Nazis. He followed his escorts to the entrance of a large barn; its wide doors were open and swung back against the building.

"Hey! Lieutenant!" Bill heard his rank called out as he entered the shelter. He recognized two faces from his downed crew: the radioman and the chief engineer. They were reclining on a large stack of hay, beaming at the sight of him. Their clothes were ripped and torn and black with dirt, as if they had fallen through the treetops on their way to the ground.

"Am I glad to see you guys," Bill said, his spirits cheered upon seeing fellow crew members. *At least we avoided going down near the coast.* Bill remembered the briefing: all fliers were instructed to avoid the coast where the Germans were amassed.

Two tall men, wearing even taller sheepskin hats embroidered with skull-and-crossbones insignia, stood to the side watching the reunion. Full bandoliers were draped over both shoulders, American .45 caliber automatics hung in their webbed belts, and they each carried a rifle. Just as Bill was assessing the situation, about ten similarly dressed men stepped into the barn with two more members of the crew. Bill was grateful the locals had seen the plane in flames and spread out to round up survivors.

He soon found out they were in the hands of the Chetniks, always a questionable predicament. The Chetniks were royalists, deeply loyal to their exiled King, Peter II—the last king of Yugoslavia who had fled to London after the annexation of his country by Germany and Italy. Through the last intelligence reports he had heard, Bill knew that the Chetniks favored Germany. However, if they were in a good mood, they could be persuaded to hand the Americans over to the communist Partisans, their staunch enemies. The Partisans favored the Americans and would see that they made it back to Italy. Their hosts could also make their captives' lives miserable by offering the Yanks to the Germans for spite or for barter. *Which will it be?* Bill wondered.

The armed, bearded, flint-eyed fellows in the tall hats herded the crew together and led them out of the barn. A third man joined them, and after hearing him speak authoritatively to the other two, Bill singled him out as the leader of the trio.

"Excuse me, do you speak English?" Bill said as he approached the leader. The man wore a black jacket and had pulled a matching lambswool cap over his ears. His beard was thick and his eyebrows the color of coal. He would easily blend into the night.

"Not speak. Quiet," the man in black placed a finger over his mouth to indicate silence as he led the group in a line on foot out of the village. They waded a wide stream, the cold water temporarily easing the pain in Bill's ankle, then started hiking up a trail through mountainous woods.

The group soon stopped at a second village about the same size as the first. It appeared to Bill that their guides were avoiding larger towns, which made sense. It was probably too risky for the Chetniks to move Allied airmen through more heavily populated areas. The sky was darkening and the temperature had dropped. It was damp and frosty cold, and Bill was grateful it wasn't snowing. He glanced at his watch in the dimming light, then up at the purpling sky. It was 1730 hours, and evening was approaching.

∞

They reached a stopping point, and the downed fliers were turned over to an English-speaking Chetnik. His slightly wavy hair was dark as carbon and tucked behind a set of extraordinarily large ears. He stood well above Bill, who had to look up at the soldier. The guy was doing everything possible to appear menacing, and succeeding. His military-style clothes appeared in need of a wash, but he had fewer weapons on him than his comrades. Languidly pulling on a hand-rolled cigarette, he explained that the copilot and navigator had been injured and were being treated by a doctor in the village. *So, Braz made it!* Bill celebrated, privately. There was no news of the pilot. From what the rest of the crew could tell him, nose gunner Hank and his injured leg were last seen drifting toward the ground.

The Americans were taken in for the night by several villagers. Bill was paired with an elderly man and his wife, who gestured for Bill to follow them. They wore several layers of clothes that bulked them up, causing them to walk like windup dolls; their movements restricted and stiff. He wondered if the couple were simply that cold or prepared to leave home at a moment's notice.

When they reached their home, the white-haired wife led Bill to the hearth and motioned for him to sit. She fetched a pail of water that had been warming by the fire and poured salt into it, pointed to Bill's foot, then to the pail. He removed his boot and sock; his ankle was several shades of purple and the skin surrounding the center of the swelling, a mustard yellow. He dropped his foot into the pail. The warm saltwater felt soothing and eased the soreness. After the soak, and over a dinner of boiled chicken and rice, Bill attempted to converse with his hosts.

"The food tastes delicious, thank you," he said in English as he smiled and rubbed his stomach. The aged couple was hospitable and friendly. He tried to impress them by miming his fateful bomb run and bailout that day.

"Bombs—boom, boom!" The old man laughed and threw up his hands. His wife held her rosy cheeks in her hands and laughed along. Bill laughed too. Then, exhausted and achy, he fell into the soft feather bed, mumbling his thanks for the meal, the bed, and the soak before surrendering to a demanding weariness.

The old man was bent over Bill, shaking him awake. By Bill's watch, it was 0500 hours and still dark out. He got up and limped to the warmest part of the house: the kitchen. A bright wood fire was burning in a cast-iron stove and beckoned Bill over. An altogether different Chetnik soldier, who spoke English quite well, was waiting for him at the table with a cup of coffee. Bill took it gladly.

"We have to leave before light. That is when the Germans make their morning inspection," said the Chetnik in perfect English.

"Otherwise, everyone in this village will be in danger."

Bill observed that the Chetnik's only weapon was the sidearm he wore slung over his waist and deduced they no longer considered him a threat.

The airmen were escorted down a rocky road that led past the common water well and out of the village, paralleling a dense evergreen wood. The downed American fliers, their hosts, and the Chetnik escorts stopped at a crossroads at the edge of the wood to regroup. Bill imagined that under different circumstances, the small crowd could have been mistaken for revelers in a parade. After much handshaking and good wishes from their hosts, the American fliers followed the Chetniks into the woods and deeper into the mountains. As it turned out, Braz had broken his leg in the jump; the villagers had generously provided him with one of their precious mules. He waved to Bill from his high perch as Bill hobbled along on his makeshift crutch; the soreness in his ankle easing some as he worked it.

The climb was long and arduous, especially with a bum ankle. Reaching the top of a ridge, they stopped to rest. Stale bread and a salty, fishy spread satisfied as a snack. Bill ate the bread and skipped the spread. While the group was catching its breath, one of the guards came up from the rear.

"German patrol below." He spoke quietly in English to the leader.

The crew was ushered ahead a few feet, then three of the Chetnik guards swept the area clean of footprints with fallen tree boughs. Bill was impressed. It was obvious they had been doing this a while, probably throughout the war. It appeared to be routine, hiding their presence from the Germans, or anyone else for that matter.

This particular Nazi patrol was not spotted again as they walked on, but by nightfall a cold, continuous drizzle was falling. Flight suits and jackets provided the fliers' only warmth; they couldn't risk a fire when they stopped to rest. Everyone was hungry, but no one was eating.

The band of Americans and Chetniks rallied after the break and pushed on in the dark. They reached the next village in about two hours. Despite the late hour, the entire populace came to cheer the group, not at all concerned their rousing welcome might be heard by enemy patrols. *We've been told to keep quiet this whole time,* Bill wondered. *Could it be we are in friendlier territory now?* Once again, they were taken into individual homes and given a warm meal. Bill was the guest of a friendly farmer and his pink-cheeked wife, who smiled and laughed at his attempts to communicate with them.

"Mmmm, boiled chicken and rice. Momma's favorite," Bill complimented his hostess, adding a wink toward the husband.

"Is nice?" the wife asked in what little English she knew.

"Mmmm, can't get enough of the stuff," Bill said, sincere in his compliment. He was grateful for each freshly cooked hot chicken and rice dish he ate along the way. He could feel his strength seeping back.

"Is good," said the husband, beaming.

"Is good," Bill smiled in agreement. He slept like never before. He reckoned it was a combination of pain—the swelling in his ankle had turned completely purple black—the hot chicken soup, and his utter fatigue.

All too soon, it was morning. He limped to the kitchen and sat in front of the fire, nursing the cup of coffee the pink-cheeked wife had offered him when he sat down.

A loyalist guerrilla stuck his head in the kitchen door. "Come, we go now." Bill sat his half-full cup of watery coffee on the table, thanked the woman, and followed the guerrilla fighter out the door. What he regretted most was having to leave the warmth of the fire. Once he was outside, he joined the rest of the group assembled in the yard.

A local doctor was going over Braz's leg and made a quick adjustment to the original splint. Then he assisted his patient onto the mule and the fliers returned to the road again. Three hours later, they came to a rise in the woods that overlooked the trail as it continued into the valley.

The Chetnik leader walked up to Bill and pointed to a clearing. "You must make it to there," he said, indicating a glade where the mid-morning light was streaming between the trees.

"And then?" Bill asked.

"You must make it to that place on your own. A band of Partisans will be waiting for you," explained the Chetnik leader.

"You're turning us over to them?" Bill wanted details.

"We fight each other, but sometimes we help each other when it serves us to do so," the Chetnik leader smiled, held his hands palms up, and shrugged his shoulders.

"We thank you, Sir," Bill said, genuinely relieved, and took the Chetnik leader's hand for a shake.

"You may keep the donkey," the leader added with a wink.

"Thank you again! Thank you and your men who risked your own safety to help us."

Braz called to his new Serbian friends as he prodded the donkey in the direction of the clearing. "Thank you for everything!" The Serbs raised their hands and rifles in response.

∽

It took an hour and a half to follow the trail, having lost sight of the clearing when they entered the dense woods. Just as they located it again, they were surrounded by a band of men, dressed and armed much like the Chetniks, each soldier pointing a weapon directly at them. American weapons.

"American, American!" The airmen held their hands up in the air.

Bill began guessing at words that he had heard over the past three days, using his hands to indicate the bailout.

"Bomb, bomb. Germany … plane is hit, we jump," he said in English.

"Yes, you were shot down. We know," the speaker stepped forward. "My name is Lieutenant Spaski. I speak English. Very well," Spaski emphasized the *very well*. His eyes were like iolite: dreamy and filled with imagination, with a bit of humor lurking behind his position of authority. Set against the sheen of his blue-black hair, the impact was striking. He allowed a slight smile.

"Welcome to Partisan territory," Spaski said. "Your sidearms please?" Spaski held out his hand as if he expected full compliance with his request.

The Partisans needed the weapons more than the fliers did, and if they encountered German troops, the Partisans would be doing the shooting, not the fliers. Yet the Chetniks had not seen the need to demand their weapons. Bill realized they were in no position to argue.

"Of course. Give them your weapons," Bill instructed Braz and the copilot, the only others in the group with pistols.

"We will take you to your collection point. This is another six to seven days' walk from this spot," Spaski explained. "Do any of you require medical assistance?" He looked at Braz on the donkey and at Bill with his crutch.

"We're good to go, Lieutenant," Bill assured the Partisan.

Spaski turned to his men, signaled silently, and soon they were in the woods once again, where it was rough going in the darkening light of late afternoon. They couldn't risk using torches because of the many German patrols along the way.

Seven hours later, they walked out of the woods and into a village that looked much like those they had seen earlier. Paint-chipped rafters and window trim, a water pump in the middle of the square. Once inside the village confines, they were herded into a large barn, empty of animals.

"Make beds in the hay. Others have slept here before you," Spaski ordered. Soon afterward, a few women entered, bringing rice with some unidentifiable meat mixed in.

"Coffee?" A pretty woman with thick dark curls offered. After his first sip, Bill realized it had been days since he had enjoyed a cup of village java. It tasted vague and earthy, nothing like Chief's heavenly brew. Still, he drank it down and slept until light for the first time since he had bailed out.

The dinner servers were back in the morning with hard-boiled eggs and more coffee. After breakfast, the group reformed. They made their way out of the village and walked alongside an actual road. A dirt road, yet still a road. Bill was happy it wasn't full of rocks and pebbles; the soil was compact, easier to walk on with a sore ankle. With numerous Partisan patrols around, it was deemed safe enough to travel more openly; there would be plenty of warning and time to hide should a German unit be sighted. The going was faster along the road, and as they passed the mountain villages, people turned out and cheered quietly, many flashed "V for victory" signs with their fingers.

Spaski and his party were distant and cool toward the Americans. Bill understood; they had just come from the Chetniks after all, their sworn enemies. His thoughts turned to the possibility that Spaski might not want to get too close to any of the fliers in case he had to defend them or abandon them. Bill's head was full of questions. As they plodded along, Bill wondered if Joe and Jug and the rest of his crew had met up with a bunch similar to this on the day they were shot down. The day he was too sick to fly. He didn't voice his thoughts, and Spaski told him nothing. The Partisan leader eased down the road with long, powerful strides, not once looking back at the group of wayward American fliers.

Bill's ankle was still puffy, discolored, and somewhat sore, yet Braz's fractured leg was healing rapidly. The Chetnik bonesetter had done an expert job, and there was little pain. Having the mule to ride was a blessing and must have been quite a sacrifice for the Serbian villagers.

Two scouts appeared and approached Spaski. The group slowed to a halt. The Americans followed suit. Ever the navigator, Braz took a chance at angering their guides by pulling out a silk map. "I want to know where we are," he whispered to Bill. Just then, Spaski turned and addressed the fliers.

"We will continue through the woods and skirt the next village. We were to rest there for the night, but now a German unit is arrived," the Partisan leader explained, then he switched the topic of conversation. "Those maps are convenient, no; so lightweight?" He didn't miss a thing, even with his back turned, Bill observed. It was the most Spaski had spoken the entire day.

They moved on past the village, picking their way through the woods. After an hour of walking in the dark, they stopped for the night. It was frigid cold, but at least it wasn't raining. The ground was just as hard as it had been the first night out with their original group of Chetniks. Bill asked himself: *When was that?* He realized it had only been three nights ago, but it felt like it could have been weeks. He didn't have a clue how long the journey would last.

∞

Every day of their trek, formations of B-24s or B-17s, on their way to or from their bombing missions, rumbled overhead. Their Partisan escorts could tell by the sound long before the planes came into view what kind of bombers they were.

"Bomber," the guerrilla fighter walking closest to Bill pointed to the sky. "B-24. Big. Ass. Bird," he flashed a cigarette-stained grin Bill's way.

"I used to do that in college," Bill replied. "Guess the make of the plane as soon as I heard the engines." Bill remembered that he and Norrie had been pretty darn good at aircraft identification by the time they signed up for cadets and wondered how his friend was getting on in the war.

"We hear every day and we are happy," the Partisan fighter said thoughtfully.

"Yes, the sound makes me happy too," Bill concurred. He didn't feel so stranded out in unfamiliar territory when he heard American or Allied planes.

Five days into their trek with the Partisans, the group was caught out in the open by a German motorized patrol. The patrol must have cut their engines; they crept up on them without making a sound. It was only when the Partisan fighter who was leading them stopped to scan the field they were crossing that Bill knew something was amiss. Then he saw it, too; tall reeds at the edge of the clearing were swaying but there was no wind. The fighter put his finger to his lips, signaling them to remain silent. Bill froze in place with the others. Braz on his donkey was still on the periphery of the field. When the Partisan indicated they should run, Bill took off as fast as he could despite the pain in his ankle. He had to trust that Braz was being protected because he could do nothing for his friend.

The escort split into two groups: one took up defensive positions and started firing, the other ran with their American charges up into the hills. Bullets pinged and thudded the ground around them and ricocheted off tree trunks. Splintered bark flew out in every direction. The Chetnik mule was amazingly agile and hurried Braz to safety. The pace slowed to a walk after the sound of gunfire and bullets died away.

"The German occupation troops are either very young or very old men," explained Lieutenant Spaski, who had warmed considerably toward his charges. "And they seldom have the courage to follow us into the hills."

"It's lucky for all of us they don't," Bill remarked.

"We'll sleep on the ground again tonight. It is safest," Spaski told Bill, ignoring his comment.

"You're used to this," Bill responded. "This happens to you a lot I guess, but I've never been shot at before."

"Is it hard on your ankle?" Spaski smiled and asked Bill about his injury. "Yes, but resting it is out of the question. I'm thinking of our man on the mule," Bill nodded toward Braz.

"His injury was well cared for by the other side, no?" Spaski seemed curious to know Bill's opinion of the doctor's expertise.

"Yes. I guess that medic knew what he was doing," Bill said, agreeing with the Partisan leader.

As they made camp that night, the Partisan defenders caught up to the group. Two of their members had been killed fighting to keep the Americans out of the hands of the Germans. Two others had been severely wounded and had to stay on in the village. Bill had never before known such deep appreciation for selflessness and courage than he did for these men.

∽⌀

Days of trekking and hiding from Nazi patrols were taking their toll on everyone, mentally and physically. They all could use a pick-me-up, Partisans and Americans alike. The group was approaching the largest town they had seen thus far, and Bill began to mentally prepare for another dinner of chicken and rice, when hundreds of townsfolk started to appear. They waved and cheered. Bill wasn't certain if they were cheering the Americans or the Partisans; either way, he straightened up as best he could on his crutch and limped into the town square with his head held high.

"Hey, our first parade!" Braz shouted from his perch atop the donkey.

"Yeah, look proud like the conquering hero you are," Bill laughed. Just the sight of people welcoming them was enough to restore his vigor.

The mayor was waiting for them in the middle of the square. He wore a top hat and a wide red sash across his chest. "Welcome," he cried out in perfect American English. "Welcome to Ljubuski! Here each one of you is our honored guest. Please, make yourselves at home." With that announcement, the crowd cheered and the Americans beamed their thanks. Even Spaski was smiling.

Once again, various individuals took the aviators in. The homes were simple affairs, furnished with only the necessities for cooking, bathing, and sleeping, much like the homes in their previous stops. Flavorful meals were prepared with food that had been hidden from the Germans: onion soups, minced lamb sausages, and plum brandies for starters. Chicken and rice seemed to be off the menu. After dinner, an impromptu music jam ensued. A man with a lively mustache began strumming an instrument Bill thought closest to a mandolin—a tamburica—and the crowd began clapping along to what he guessed was a favorite national tune. He smiled and clapped with them, enjoying the moment.

After about an hour of singing and dancing, the villagers dispersed and headed back to their homes, American fliers in tow. The couple that was assigned to Bill insisted that he take their bed.

"Please," the husband said.

"Please, be so kind," his wife agreed. Standing in the doorway of their bedroom, the couple gestured toward their bed. It was a beautiful sight: downy feather mattress, downy quilts piled on top. Bill didn't argue very successfully.

It was the best sleep he had had in a week, and he could have kept on sleeping well into the next day, but he was mustered early in the morning. After yet another rousing send-off from the locals, they set out for the woods.

∞

"This is some climb," Bill mentioned to Spaski after the group had trekked for over an hour.

"Yes, it is going to be a very physical day. And long," the Partisan lieutenant warned the bombardier. They pushed on for hours after dark. Spaski had gone out ahead, and when the group caught up to him, they found him arguing with another Partisan leader.

"Looks like we are being challenged," Braz had the best view from atop his mule.

"Well, aren't they all on the same side?" one of the young enlisted airmen asked no one in particular.

"Not necessarily. But it looks like we're in luck today," Bill patted the kid on the back. "See? Everyone is sharing cigarettes and laughing now."

This was it, Bill realized. They had reached the pickup point. The perimeter guards ended their challenge to Spaski and took over his Partisan group, escorting the Americans to a well-disguised lean-to.

We made it, Bill rejoiced with a sigh. *We're going back.* He hadn't realized just how tense he had been for more than a week until this very moment.

Twenty-Five

TRANSPORT IMMINENT

Somewhere in Yugoslavia, Bound for Bari, Italy, November 1944

WHEN BILL'S GROUP ARRIVED at the rendezvous point—a lean-to deep in the woods—they were met by several Allied airmen, including two RAF pilots and a Tuskegee P-51 pilot, also awaiting transport. The structure was constructed of forest green canvas siding and what looked like tent poles to Bill. The shelter was taut and secure, anchored to the sturdy pines of the forest. Bill hobbled up to the refuge, and a trim, compact man stepped forward wearing the green khaki wool uniform of the British army.

"Major Reginald Andre, at your service, my lad," the man said in greeting. "British intelligence. Let's have a chat before you get too comfortable, shall we?" He indicated Bill was to follow him several feet away from the lean-to. "Now, what is your name, rank, and serial number?"

Just as Bill was beginning his report, an American Air Corps intelligence officer arrived, gasping and panting for breath.

"Sorry I'm late," the army captain offered. "I was seeing off another group of airmen at our rendezvous spot about two clicks from here. Captain Andrew Sorenson." The breathless captain held out his hand to Bill as he identified himself.

"Glad to meet you, Captain Sorenson," Bill said, shaking the captain's hand. "Lieutenant Bill Gemmill, bombardier," he added with a nod.

Now that both intelligence officers were on scene, Bill got down to the business of describing events from just before the bailout to once he was on the ground in Yugoslavia: the topography, the numbers of Nazi patrols, Chetniks, and Partisans. When he finished speaking, both intelligence officers thanked him for the details as they made entries into their notebooks.

"Especially of the terrain," Major Andre remarked. "Those specifics will come in handy for our lads on the ground, both the army and the air corps."

"Indeed, they will," Captain Sorenson agreed.

"I'm glad my information has been helpful, Sirs," Bill said respectfully. Pre-mission briefings emphasized the intelligence but didn't delve too much into how they got a lot of their information: through details gathered from debriefings just like this, on the ground and straight from the horse's mouth. He never really considered how important the post-mission briefings were until that moment.

With that thought in his head, he followed his nose to the mess-in-the-forest where everyone, including all the Partisans who had escorted them to this point, shared a hearty meal of whatever K rations their rescuers had amassed: The breakfast pack with canned eggs and ham, a bar of fruit paste, fighting biscuits, a bag of coffee, chewing gum, three pieces of sugar, and water purification tablets. Or the supper pack with minced corned beef or pork-carrots-apples, fighting biscuits, two bars of chocolate, three pieces of sugar, toilet paper, chewing gum, and a pack of four cigarettes. Or, of course, the dinner pack with concentrated bouillon and canned pork, ham, or cheese, along with fighting biscuits, five caramels, a pack of four cigarettes, matches, and fifteen bags of milk powder. Every K ration pack came equipped with a key to open the can.

"Spam! My favorite," Bill said in all sincerity as he peeled back the lid of a can from the brown cardboard box he had been handed. "This came out of the breakfast pack," he added, laughing. "I may just go back for seconds, see if they're holding out on the supper box."

"K rations. Man, I never thought I'd miss this stuff," Braz joked. He was perched on the trunk of a large felled tree, a mound of loose dried grass plumped under his healing leg. Bill dipped under a low-hanging branch and handed him a blue cardboard box. "Wow, Gemmill, the dinner box. You sure know how to treat a guy," Braz laughed as he tore open the box in his lap. He ate the caramels first.

One of the RAF pilots sitting near Braz asked him about their bailout. "Did you break your leg after landing?"

Braz looked over at Bill and winked, inviting him into the conversation. "Well, this guy here and I were on the same bomber," Braz began, raising his thumb in Bill's direction.

"We dropped our payload and were critically hit for our troubles," added Bill.

"I bailed and the wind caught me, drifted me several hundred yards from where I was aiming," Braz said. "I should have sat where Gemmill here was sitting."

"Where was that?" the RAF flier asked.

"On the nose wheel doors," Bill said. "Best idea I've had this whole war." He mimed the moment: the nose wheel doors opening and him being pulled into the sky.

"And then we were picked up by different bands of Chetniks, my leg was treated by a Chetnik doctor, and Gemmill and I reunited in a Chetnik village," Braz explained.

Bill turned to the African American pilot sitting next to him.

"You an escort pilot? Tuskegee?" Bill asked with genuine interest.

"Sure am. Best job in the world," the pilot replied. "Unless, of course, you get shot down!" His laugh rang out like a song.

"Well, I want to thank you and this may be my only chance," Bill said. "One of your outfit saved my bacon a few weeks back ... saved the whole damn ship. And this time, when we had to bail, your group shielded us as we floated to the ground. I've never seen such nerve. You kept those Germans from picking us off one by one. Mighty impressive," Bill held out his hand to shake the pilot's hand.

"Then, I will say 'you're welcome' from the bunch of us!" the fighter pilot beamed and shook Bill's hand heartily in appreciation at the recognition.

"By the way, my name is Bill. William Billings Gemmill Jr.," Bill introduced himself to the Red Tail pilot.

"And I am Charles Dryden, aka 'A-Train,'" said the pilot. Bill couldn't put his finger on why, but A-Train's smile and demeanor put him more at ease than he had felt since being shot down. He could actually feel himself relaxing, like he didn't have to be super diligent, aware of every sound at all times anymore.

Tuskegee Airmen was the name of African American pilots who trained in Tuskegee, Alabama, and formed the 332nd Fighter Group and the 477th Bombardment Group of the United States Army Air Corp. Bill often saw them escorting his bomb runs and was grateful each and every time. Until his own experience, he had heard tales of their marvelous daring-do as well as their sacrifice. He truly had never seen such courage in all his twenty years.

"Say, do you know where you ditched? How long did it take you guys to make it this far?" Bill asked, genuinely curious.

A-Train made a stab at pinpointing the location where he went down; he thought he had been over Austria when his plane took a fatal hit. Bill grabbed their one kerosene lamp; the flame was turned as low as it could be without forcing it to die out. He walked over to Braz and borrowed his white silk map, turned, and handed it to A-Train. The Red Tail pilot remembered hiking for two weeks as he peered at the map.

In low voices, men began sharing their escape stories. Their tales got longer and more colorful as the night wore on. It was interesting, hearing the accounts of the other men, and it gave Bill something with which to compare his own experience. His thoughts returned to Joe and Murph: how they had told him about their bailout and journey back. He considered everyone but Wes and Hill fortunate: they each had at least one story of bailing out while seeing their plane execute a flaming nosedive into the earth, or the ocean, or head-on into the side of a mountain. Bill looked up through the overstory and wondered, *Where are you, Wes? What's your story?*

Slowly, the fliers' voices died off in the dark. Bill's eyelids grew heavier and heavier as sleep impressed itself upon him. They slept on the ground, in sleeping bags, for six glorious hours of shut-eye.

∞

"Up you blokes! You've got thirty minutes to roust yourselves and be ready to move," Major Andre called out as he loomed over each slumbering lump on the ground. The British intelligence officer was in a jovial mood. Likely because he was about to be relieved of this group of fliers and ready to receive the next. Or perhaps he was just happy for all the men heading back.

At the sound of sturdy aircraft engines, Lieutenant Spaski appeared out of the shadows of the woods. He stood straight, hands crossed behind his back, observing. He might have been there awhile. He blended in too well in his dark green field jacket and camouflage pants. He was one with the forest and its darkness. He smiled briefly when he saw Bill respond to the engines and Major Andre. Bill jumped up and gathered his flight jacket, but he left the crutch behind. He shook Spaski's hand, and the two men exchanged a look of understanding. They were fighting the same fight, in the only way they knew how, and for all the right reasons.

Flares lit up along a grassy runway, piercing the predawn sky. Bill hadn't detected the runway in the daylight yesterday, which was probably a good thing. If he couldn't see it, neither could the Germans. As the transport plane approached, the pilot cut the engines and the RAF C47 Dakota drifted in for a landing.

"Make ready, lads!" cried Major Andre as all the young men stood and lined themselves up, more or less. The crew on the transport opened the side panels of the fuselage and waved the aviators aboard.

"Go! Go! Go!" both the British and American intelligence officers waved the men toward the plane.

The bulk of the group sprinted to the open midsection of the aircraft and climbed aboard. Bill and A-Train braced Braz between them and lifted him off the ground as they half-ran, half-limped to the rescue plane. Bill was doing the limping, but even so, he carried his fair share of Braz's weight. When they reached the midsection, they shoved Braz through the door where a crewmember pulled him in the rest of the way. The pilot started up the plane's engines and began taxiing before his crew could close the door. He took off into a deep lavender sky, the fading glow from the flares his only guide.

∽∾

The rescue transport was based at Gioia del Colle Air Base in Bari, Italy, on the Adriatic coast—a five-hour flight. Bill slept the entire way. When the plane touched down and taxied to a stop, Bill waited for Braz to be carried out, then stepped onto the tarmac; he reckoned Italy had never looked so good. A tinge of salt and ocean bounty swept through the breeze, *a bit like Capri only different*, thought Bill. They were deloused, shaved, and showered at the army hospital. The last time he saw his uniform it was lying in a pile on the shower room floor. Bill thought it looked like it had once been a living thing, now frayed, torn, and streaked with the grime from his adventure. His flight boots were pretty chewed up too. Somehow, his flight jacket looked better for the wear and tear. Surprisingly, that thick combination of lambswool and leather had kept him warm enough while on the move and come through with nary a scratch in the end. After the shower, he donned the pajamas and robe the hospital had lent him for a trip to the infirmary.

Army nurses soaked and wrapped his ankle and sent him on his way with instructions to remain on crutches—the proper wooden kind—and keep off the foot for another week. Braz was another story. After he was cleaned up, his orders were to report to the head nurse and remain in the hospital for evaluation. Bill stood up from the exam table he had been leaning on and rewrapped his white terry cloth bathrobe. Anyone returning from a bailout went through the same delousing process and was given the same pale blue cotton pajamas and hospital bathrobes to wear until they could get to the supply sergeant or quartermaster for new uniforms. He looked at Braz who also was leaning against an exam table. He stood with the foot of his broken leg resting on the top of the unbroken leg and his arms were crossed.

"See you around, kid," Braz said to Bill as he nodded toward an orderly heading his way. The kid was pushing a wheelchair and had a determined look in his eye.

"See you soon, no doubt, Braz," Bill replied as he watched Braz roll out the door. He was certain he'd meet up with his friend in no time. He hadn't seen where A-Train had gone after the delousing, but the fighter pilot had been in excellent shape. He may have been sent straight back to his unit. Bill knew firsthand how badly they needed men like Lieutenant Dryden back up in the air. Reflecting on A-Train, Bill realized how much he wanted to return to Cerignola, to get back in the air, back to The Manse. He crutched his way to the supply room.

"Welcome home. Sign this chit," the quartermaster at the hospital said gruffly before changing his tune and chuckling. *How many men has he seen return from being shot down only to fight again?* Bill wondered. *Must be plenty since he finds the giving out of uniforms so comedic.*

"You officers have it rough, Lieutenant. Having your pay docked for uniforms," said the quartermaster half-jokingly.

"So much for our harrowing experience, right?" Bill responded with a quick laugh.

Next stop was the Red Cross office where he happily endured a wait in line. He had to wire his mother; there was no telling if she had received a telegram from Major General Twining or what worry she was putting herself through. With his telegram on its way to Chicago, Bill went in search of a ride to the 740th. At transport, he was told there were no more trucks heading to Cerignola that day, and he darned-sight wasn't walking ninety kilometers back to base. He'd had enough of walking for the time being. An overnight stay at the swank, transient officers' quarters in Bari would do him just fine. The place had been a hotel for European elite before the war.

In the morning, he boarded a truck loaded with a few other returning fliers headed for Cerignola. He proudly carried his Red Cross toilet kit representing the very best in American toiletries: Bucky Beaver's Ipana toothpaste, natural bristle toothbrush, Gillette US service razor, and a can of Barbasol "overseas special" shaving cream. He found it odd that he was the only one from his group on the ten-day trek through Yugo on a truck east. They reached Cerignola after dark, but the driver refused to drop everyone off at their individual camps. Bill finally hitched a ride to Major General Twining's office in the back of an MP Jeep.

"Whoa, look what the cat dragged in," Twining's aide joked when he saw Bill walk into the squadron commander's office.

"Didn't anyone in Bari mention that the major general sent a truck to pick you up yesterday?"

"No," Bill answered. "No one mentioned a thing about it to me."

That explained why he was the only one he knew from the 740th on the transport. "Crossed wires? Miscommunication?" Bill offered, shrugging his shoulders.

"It is the army, after all," laughed the aide. "What can you expect?"

The debriefing with Major General Twining took less time than it had with the CO in Bari. Twining was more interested in their treatment by the Chetniks than anything else. "The war is turning," he explained. "The Chetniks aren't so lovey-dovey with the Germans these days. Dissension in the ranks," the major general added.

"They treated us alright, and their doctor did better than alright with Braz's leg," Bill replied. The change in the war might just well explain how cooperative the Chetniks had been, getting them to a Partisan unit.

"That's good to hear, Lieutenant. This war's not over yet, and we may need to keep them friendly a while longer. You're dismissed. I am certain your mates will be wanting to see you."

"Yes, Sir, thank you, Sir." Bill saluted the major general and hobbled out of headquarters. He flagged down another Jeep and asked the driver to take him to officer country. Being lame and on sticks—that's what he was calling his crutches now—was a real benefit when looking for a ride.

∞

The Jeep dropped Bill off in front of The Manse. Bill stood looking at the tent for a moment, suddenly flooded with relief. Then he pushed open the door and met a rush of bodies.

Major General Twining hadn't been exaggerating—his mates did want a piece of him. Joe threw himself at Bill in a friendly hug followed by Murph, Mike, Ritt, George, and Bob, who crowded around to pound him on the back. Bill wobbled on his crutches before anyone noticed he was using sticks. Jug stood to the side waiting for the hubbub to die down before claiming his moment.

"I knew you'd be back, Gemmill," Jug said. "Never had a doubt." He couldn't say any more than that, the Georgia Bulldog was on the verge of tears and clamped his mouth shut. He held onto Bill's shoulder with a tight grip and blinked rapidly to disperse the waterworks forming.

Pasquale stepped through the scrum wrapping his arms around Bill's waist and burying his face in Bill's abdomen. The gesture melted Bill's heart. They hugged and laughed and hugged some more. Now he knew what it was like to come back after having been missing. Now he understood every one of these men—young, old, boy, man. He knew without a doubt what it felt to be a part of something far greater than himself.

After the handshaking, the hugging, and the back-pounding, the boys wanted to hear Bill's tale. He agreed and they all sat around the officers' tent, spread out on the floor and lounging on the four cots. They listened respectfully as Bill told his tale. At least eight or nine times. Tired of repeating himself, he looked around for the first time since entering the tent.

Unfamiliar calendars of Betty Grable and Ginger Rogers, photos of Vivien Leigh and Dorothy Lamour, were tacked on the canvas walls. Only Jug and Joe's spots looked familiar. They had moved their cots closer together and rearranged Bill's desk and lamp. Jug explained that two new officers had moved into the tent in his absence. Bill's things were gone.

"They packed your personal effects and sent them to await shipment back home," Joe explained, reading his friend's face.

"That would not have pleased my mother," Bill said. *In fact*, he mused, *receiving that box without word he was OK would have devastated her*. But he was back and he had the same cot he had left more than eleven days ago. His pals had saved his desk and the beat-up brass lamp from being poached. And in a week, he'd be back on his feet and up in the air again.

"When we heard you were in Bari, we told the supply sergeant," Joe informed Bill. "He said you can claim what's left in the morning. But that was yesterday."

"I'll do that," Bill said comically, sticking his chest and jaw out to convey his conviction. "At dawn."

Bill was at the quartermaster's first thing the next day. He went through his stuff, making an inventory of everything missing.

"Where's my air mattress? My chest of drawers?" he inquired.

"Look kid, I just store this stuff, ship it home when the unlucky ones don't come back for it, and open it up for grabs even if they do eventually return, like you did," the sergeant said through an enormous wad of gum stuffed into his right cheek. Bill was close enough to smell the sweet cinnamon scent of Dentyne. To him, the sergeant looked like he had one of the biggest abscesses in the world. Guinness World Record big.

"Yeah, OK thanks, but no thanks. You let them take my best stuff!" Bill made sure the sergeant knew he had noticed. He also knew not to complain for too long; he might need this sergeant's help yet. Hell, he was back in one piece, his ankle had all but healed, and he was in great shape. A nine-day trek through rugged Yugoslavian countryside will do that to a body. That and a diet of boiled chicken and rice.

Twenty-Six

HOMECOMING

December 1944 to March 1945

ON THE RAINY EVENING of December 17, 1944, Bill was lounging on his cot in The Manse reading one of Wes's novels. Joe and Jug were sitting at the desk engaged in a hot game of gin rummy. All three of them were relaxing after a rough mission to bomb the oil refinery at Odertal, Germany, earlier that day. Between the lethal FLAK and twenty ME-109s, his squadron lost eleven B-24s and their crews.

The makeshift door of the tent creaked open partway. Bill looked up from his book, thinking it might be Murph or maybe Harrison come for a visit. He wasn't expecting to see the face that greeted him.

"Wes!" Bill shouted, bringing the card game to an abrupt halt. He got to the missing pilot first and threw his arms around his captain. "When? How?" was all he managed to say.

Before Wes could answer or move fully inside the tent, Joe darted over, knocking down the chair he had been sitting in. Then Jug scuttled to the scene, absolutely beaming. Wes began to weep.

"It is so good to see you fellas, I can hardly speak," the pilot said to his friends. "My tale of the last three months is long, but I'll give you the highlights. But first, I have to get off my feet."

"Of course," Bill said, ushering Wes to the overturned chair. Bill righted the seat, then helped Wes sit down. The returned aviator looked thin but otherwise hearty to Bill.

"Can I get you anything?" Joe asked.

"No thanks, Joe. The general offered me some ham sandwiches when I went to report," Wes answered. "I've just come from his office."

Jug went to his bunk, reached under, and retrieved one of his last cans of peaches. "Here you go, Pappy. You need these more than I do," he said, handing Wes a can of the sweet, syrupy fruit.

"That's generous of you, Jug," Wes replied, leaving the peaches untouched. "Last time I saw you, we were preparing to bail. It's good to see you made it back OK."

"It's been a while, old man," Jug said, nodding in agreement.

"I know y'all are curious. The short story is: After we bailed, I ended up in the countryside, hiding in caves, on my own for about a week. I was discovered by a group of sympathetic and generous villagers who handed me over to some Chetniks. Bill Hill was already with this group, so we met up then. He can tell his own damn story."

"So, Hill is back too?" Joe asked.

"Yes, he's over with Murph and the boys at the moment. I stopped in there with him to see the boys after my debriefing with Twining," Wes answered before continuing the short version of his tale. "Eventually, the Chetniks handed us over to a Partisan group who got us to the Adriatic, where a British cruiser took us to Vis. From Vis, we were flown to Bari and interrogated before being allowed to come back here."

"Will they allow you to stay?" Bill asked. He wanted the answer to be yes. He liked the idea of finishing out the war with the crew intact.

"I'm afraid not, Bill," Wes said. "I leave for Naples tomorrow." Bill knew that meant Wes would be shipping out from the port of Naples. He also knew he had four more months of flying with different crews. He was OK with that fact; actually, he had become accustomed to it. And there were plenty of opportunities for him to fly with at least one member of the crew before he met his mission quota.

Wes smiled at Bill, then turned to Joe and Jug. "Say, can I bunk here tonight? Twining offered me a room in the temporary officers' quarters, but if it's alright with you three, I'd like to spend my last night in Italy in The Manse."

All three officers agreed wholeheartedly—they were back to being the only three in the tent and had a cot to spare. The rest of the evening was spent catching Wes up on everything he had missed: the rest of the crew's return ahead of him, Bill's bailout and return, the rough missions, the easy ones, and their R&R on Capri. All four officers fell asleep before they could finish their last sentences.

The weather the next day was miserable: cold and wet with a low cloud ceiling. All missions were canceled. Bill and the other officers headed to the mess for breakfast and a last goodbye with Wes.

"You be sure to write to us," Joe said as he shook Wes's hand in farewell.

"Yeah," Jug drawled. "We want to hear about your exploits back home."

"So long, Pappy," Bill spoke to Wes last. He shook his captain's hand and patted him on the shoulder. "Safe home and see you stateside. Remember, we'll keep in touch, yes?"

Wes's eyes teared up as he pulled Bill to him in a friendly hug. "That's a promise, Bill. We'll all stay in touch."

The four officers and friends walked to the motor pool together, where Wes caught a Jeep to Naples. As their captain and pilot drove away, the three remaining officers waved to him until the Jeep was out of sight. Bill felt he had come full circle. His family was back. They would still be parted for a while, but that would end once he got home. Meanwhile, he had missions to fly.

∞

The weather didn't let up until Christmas Eve, and even then, it wasn't ideal. The next day—Christmas Day, 1944—Bill flew seven-plus hours as group lead to bomb the marshalling yards at Wels, Austria. Joe and Jug and the rest of the crew flew the same mission on different bombers. Due to the weather, only four B-24s made it to the target area, and Bill's was one of them. The FLAK was light, no one got hurt, and there was no damage to the plane. They encountered ten enemy JU-52s, and between the four bombers, all ten fighters were shot down. Due to the socked-in weather, the 15th lost several planes that day. Some collided with each other and others hit the sides of mountains. Even though he had flown under worse stress, he was most scared of dying on that day and kissed the ground after returning safely to Italy.

Between Christmas Day and 20 February, 1945, Bill flew eight more missions—fourteen counting the double sorties. The most intense and damaging one was a repeat to Moosbierbaum, Austria, to take out the oil refinery there once and for all. He flew as group lead and had a Mickey alongside—the 455th wasn't taking any chances. If he needed to see through clouds to shorten the war, he was happy to have a Mickey at his disposal. They encountered extremely intense and accurate FLAK and the bomber had severe damage—one entire side of the plane had a hole in it large enough for a German Panzer to fit through—but they made it back to base all the same. His last mission was his third trip back to Trieste, this time to disrupt harbor shipping from the port. The FLAK was heavy and precise, but there was little harm done to the B-24. No enemy fighters appeared.

∞

Bill often found himself thinking he'd drawn the lucky straw in one sense by being based out of Italy. Despite living in the incessant wintertime rain and mud, despite having to cross not one, but two different mountain ranges—both going and returning from missions and often with shot-up aircraft and jammed payloads—he counted his tour of duty fortunate. The way he saw it, the lucky part was that he had seen a portion of the world he'd never dreamed of visiting before, learned the country's language and history, and lived to reflect on it all.

Four months after having gone down over Yugoslavia, and with fifty-six missions under his belt, Bill and the rest of the crew were going home. Twenty of his missions had been double sorties—which meant bombing two different targets on the same bomb run. He felt the passing of time more keenly now that his part in the war was coming to an end. He felt a great sense of accomplishment and pride in the job he had done. And he felt grown-up.

Bill and Joe packed up their gear. He'd miss the old tent but not the cot, he considered as he took one last look at the space. There was his map table, where he'd studied maps of targets and the surrounding areas, or post-mission aerial photos, the gooseneck lamp bent low. The table was empty now but for that lamp. He guessed the next officer to inhabit his space would find the table useful. He felt a bit wistful at the thought, which surprised him. He was ready to go home. He'd left his headshot of Ella Fitzgerald and his pinups of Carole Lombard

and Betty Grable—*man, can she dance*—pinned up for the next officer who would inherit this side of the tent. It was his gesture of good
luck, although he wondered if they would need it—the war was surely
turning to the Allies' favor.

Jug and Joe rousted their bombardier. "Time to get going,
Gemmill," Jug said.

"Roger that."

When the three officers stepped out of the tent, the entire crew was
standing in the rain waiting for them. They walked to the motor pool
and caught a six-by-six to Bari, where they checked in with the CO and
signed the beginning of their discharge paperwork; they'd finish the
rest when they got stateside. After another day of waiting for orders
to ship out, Bill and Joe were called to board the troop ship, the *Queen
Mary*, to New York. Jug and the rest of the crew were scheduled to
leave on a different ship bound for North Carolina later that same day.

On board the converted ocean liner, with its guns and artillery
replacing shuffleboard courts and deck chairs, Bill had time to unwind,
swap stories, and discover old and new friends who had also survived
their time in the Mediterranean Theater. He and Joe held court at a
portside railing on the deck, pushing their way through the throngs
of airmen looking to soak in the sun's rays. After months in the Italian
rain, the warmth of the sun was more appreciated than ever before.
Bill reminisced about recent events still so very clear in his mind. Joe
shared stories of the times they flew on separate missions with different
crews. Bill learned a few details he hadn't heard before and shared feelings he'd never voiced before. Had anyone else considered the magni-
tude of what they'd done? Not only in bringing a brutal war closer to
its end, but the damage and destruction they'd left in their wake to the
lives of ordinary people. Did it cross anyone else's mind? He had been
eighteen when this journey began, like so many other airmen. Now he

was twenty-one and feeling he had lived a lifetime already. Was that something any of them had reflected upon? Bill let the subject drop as if it was the final bomb he would release; apparently, no one wanted a soul-searching discussion. They were going home. Joe was an empathetic listener; he and Bill had grown close through their ordeals, yet he, too, was more eager to discuss the future and steered Bill in that direction best he could. He would give his own deep thoughts on the war some time to settle before he visited them.

∞

The *Queen Mary* was the fastest ship on the high seas in 1945, and her speed was her greatest defensive weapon; she crossed the Atlantic with no trouble from Nazi submarines, although the thought had occurred to Bill once or twice during the crossing. She slid through New York Harbor and pulled into the Port of New York as the sun was beginning its descent. The evening light slanted lavender and golden pink onto the buildings; the colors deepening rapidly. Bill enjoyed the light show and found it a homecoming to remember. He and Joe had changed into their last clean uniforms before shouldering their way to the ship's railing, wanting to make a good impression on the good folks of New York. Also, Joe's fiancé was waiting to sweep him away as soon as his feet touched down on the city's pavement.

The roar of hundreds of cheering men, women, and children grew as the ship drew closer to the Port of New York, the collective voices amplifying the low sheen of the sun's rays. People from every borough of the city, as well as families of the men returning, stood on their tiptoes, waving hands, hats, and the Stars and Stripes. As the ship pulled into the port, among the hundreds of men on this particular ship, Bill was about to have one more unique, needle-in-the-haystack experience: bumping into a good and longtime friend.

As he and Joe walked down the gangplank and were about to disperse into the cheering crowd below, Bill heard someone behind him shout his name. He turned and came face to face with Bill Etheridge, a boyhood pal from Chicago. Incredulous, Etheridge and Bill laughed at the chances of their meeting like this. What were the odds? That they had traveled home on the same ship was an enormous surprise of a gift. What was even more mind-boggling was that they hadn't seen or run into each other during the crossing. Bill steered Joe over to where his pal from school was standing, and introduced them. While the three airmen were meeting each other, Joe's fiancé bounded out of the crowd, nearly tackling Joe with her embrace. Joe introduced the two Bills to Julie, his bride-to-be, before the crowd pushed in.

"Contact me when you get settled," Joe yelled over the backs and shoulders of several joyful people.

"Will do!" Bill shouted back. Then he and Etheridge maneuvered their way through the crowd of well-wishers, hailed a taxi, and told the cabbie to take them to *his* favorite bar. The cabbie with the thick New York accent refused payment, honored to have two airmen in his charge. Once seated at the bar, the two friends learned they had both been bombardiers: Etheridge had flown out of England. Etheridge had caught a transport to Bari so he could see a bit of Italy before heading home. They shared their experiences over a brew and beer nuts, celebrating their having survived the war. The bartender refused to let them pay for their drinks. In fact, several of the bar's patrons bought them round after round of beers until Gemmill had to start refusing the generosity of strangers. Etheridge stopped drinking too.

The two friends hailed another taxi, this time to Union Station. Again, the cabbie refused payment to any boys in uniform. Bill saw Etheridge off on a train to Chicago with a promise to keep in touch, then walked to the southbound tracks to find his train to Washington, DC. He was feeling good after the beers and the respect he had been shown in the city. Now it was time to see his parents. William Sr. and Frances were waiting for him in their new home, and he was eager to show them, and the world, the man he had become.

REUNION
An Epilogue

MY FATHER BEGAN opening up to me about his wartime experience soon after my son turned twenty, about the time I realized just how young that age truly is and how difficult it was for me to visualize either of them making irrevocable decisions about life and death. Twenty is such a tender moment in the arc of a life. Yet, there was my father, beaming at me from the framed photo on my shelf—he had just graduated from advanced bombardier training. In the image, he is nineteen and frozen in time. His familiar smile caught by the camera: his hope and certainty impressing themselves through the lens and upon the film.

Dad was one of forty thousand men who trained and fought as bombardiers in World War II. They were bankers' sons and the sons and grandsons of dock workers, ironworkers, attorneys at law, college professors, bakers, optometrists, roofers, and policemen. Most of them were young, in their early twenties, yet some ancient men in their late twenties made it through training. Each had a photo like my father's sent home to a friend or loved one, taking the place of honor on the family mantel piece.

Dad and his high school best friend, Norrie, who had served as a fighter pilot, reconnected soon after the war's end. Just as Dad had relocated to Bethesda, Maryland, Norrie chose to put down roots in sunny southern California. Theirs was a lifelong friendship of mutual respect. To my father's dismay, he learned that Danny Shea, his high school friend who he'd studied with in Santa Ana and introduced to Dorothy Lamour, had perished when his plane was shot down somewhere over Germany.

Dad never did see Mike ride a bull, or attend a Georgia State football game where Jug ended up coaching after the war, but sometime in the early 1980s, he began attending WWII reunions of various air force organizations. It was at these reunions where he made contact with men he'd served with, and they, in turn, knew the whereabouts of others. Dad took those leads and made it his mission to track down his former crewmates.

He first went looking for Joe, who put him in touch with Wes, who thought he had a way of finding Jug. Once all four officers had reconnected, Dad went searching for Murph. He didn't have to look hard. The former chief engineer had kept in touch with both Wes and Bill Hill, who just happened to know where Mike and George were. Dad found Ritt through the Canadian Air Force group he had worked with in the 1960s. It seems my father wanted to get his family back together.

Eventually, Dad told me about the regularly scheduled get-togethers of the 455th and reunions of the entire 304th Bomb Group, but it wasn't until after his death in 2011 that I learned he'd also attended reunions of former WWII bombardiers around the country, as well as the aviation cadet class reunions at Kirtland Air Force Base and his squadron, the 740th. In my mind, Dad—and probably most of the men who gathered at these events—was looking for the thread of that extraordinary camaraderie they had forged in the mighty Liberator, those nearly indestructible B-24s, while under unthinkable stress.

Once found, my father not only remained friends with his crew-mates for the remainder of their lives, he kept in touch with Mario Capacafalo, another tent boy and friend of Pasquale's, even making a point to visit Cerignola, Italy, looking for Pasquale. I can see him now, reacquainting himself with a place on a map and a time in his life that forged him into the man he became. He had a strong desire to reconnect with that time in his life. Sadly, Pasquale and his family had disappeared after the war. Dad admitted he had waited a long while before attempting to find him, so he was disappointed but not surprised that Pasquale's post-war trail had grown cold.

It turns out, thousands of men from every branch of service who had ever served in WWII engaged in reunions. Although their numbers are rapidly dwindling, some still do. These brave men, who had dropped what they were doing and laid everything they had on the line for the greater good, gathered in friendship to be reminded of who they had been and what they had done. These men of the air had fashioned a unique Band of Brothers: their perspectives came from the view *above* the mayhem rather than on the ground. But it was as loud and smelly, bloody and deadly, as the battlefield, and in the air, there was nowhere to hide.

This might be why my father stood in front of the Parliament Building in Vienna, fifteen years after the war's end, and wept. My mother turned away from watching her three children romp around the famous fountain of Athena, surprised to see tears rolling down her husband's face. He had helped bring Vienna to its knees and the war closer to an end, but he hadn't expected to see the results of his work still evident. He hadn't been prepared for the bombed-out look of such an important building so many years later. What was he thinking?

Late in the eighties, Dad and I rendezvoused in Seabrook, Texas, home to Wes "Cappy" Powell and his wife, "Call me Julie" Juliette, for a crew reunion. Their rambling ranch-style house was painted a pleasing pale yellow on the outside. The trim was rich-earth brown. As we were ushered into their home, I was made to feel immediately welcome, an addition to the day. A special member of the family—this family of men who had been boys together in an air war of mighty consequence.

More cars pulled up to the house. At every arrival, the men seated in the living room—its walls lined with art from far-flung places like Japan and Argentina—stood and walked over to the front door, joking and shouting with joy at seeing another old familiar face.

After everyone had arrived, it was my turn to be mobbed. There they were in the flesh, these men I had heard so much about, at least the ones who were still among the living: Mike and Jug, George and Bill Hill. Wes. Joe dispensed with a handshake and gave me a big hug, telling me he felt he had known me all along, what with how much Dad had told him about me.

Reunions like this one were going on all over the country at any given time—the more intimate meetups coinciding with much larger, official gatherings. Like the crew of The Manse. In preparation of attending them as often as possible, Dad would consult with Wes or Joe, or Jug, and they'd determine the where and when of the next reunion so they could synchronize their schedules with the national bomb group and Fifteenth. Once agreed and decided, Dad would compose an email laying out the details. He titled these (as well as his correspondence to his children) "Bombardier to Crew." I remembered the first time I received one of his typewritten letters addressed this way—how the onionskin paper felt in my hands, light in weight, rippled, almost sticky. I remembered, too, the realization rising as I read and reread the salutation that we, my brothers and I, had been our father's crew; a special team no one else knew about. A secret club.

Standing in Wes and Julie's living room, I was that young girl again, on the verge of womanhood sitting on my parents' bed for one last time, watching as Dad dressed his uniform, curious about the actions he had taken to deserve all that hardware, and wondering what he felt when he reminisced about the war—his war. A realization began to form for me: that he was feeling joy. The joy of having had a family to face his darkest fears and moments with, the joy of having had a great adventure, and the ultimate joy of having lived to be able to share the tales.

I videotaped these men, each of whom had trained hard to fight for their country, to restore democracy to millions of persecuted. Every young man in my father's crew had made it safely home. Nearly every scene in the video replay is one of laughter, a lot of laughter. The camera caught what I was sensing, that as a group they preferred to set a jovial and lighthearted tone for their gathering. They told jokes and reminisced about the ridiculous moments of their war with ease. They teased and nudged ribs as one of them stood to refresh his drink, my dad throwing his head back as if to take in all the air his lungs could possibly hold before letting out a mighty guffaw, as was his way. His interpretation of "gusto." As I watched and filmed, I could see him as a young lad of nineteen or twenty, laughing at a joke or memory, possibly as a method of discharging the strain he had been under for eight hours on a recent mission. That kind of tension demanded release, and humor was Dad's modus operandi. It held his flying family together.

At the time of the Powell reunion, the crew was already missing two of their fellow mates, Lawrence ("Ritt") Rittenhouse and Bob Belding, their gunner who had enlisted on his eighteenth birthday and, to hear the stories, was fearless when he took up his gun in the waist, screaming profanities at the German pilots who aimed their guns back at him. He had RSVP'd to Dad's email and been planning on attending the reunion but passed away a few months ahead of it.

George Harvey had reunited with the gunner through a mutual, post-war hobby, shortwave radio, and shared years together over the radio. To everyone's great delight, Bob's widow, Maurtan, arrived at Wes and Julie's with George.

When Ritt had decided to enlist, Canada had yet to enter the war on the side of the British. Ritt didn't have the money to get to England, so he crossed the border into the US and found himself eagerly accepted by the air corps, who sent him all the way to Texas to train to fight. Ritt had manned the ball turret—a favorite target of Nazi fighters—and was the first of the crew to have an obituary written about him.

The living room hushed quiet as Wes, his eyes glistening with tears, mentioned Ritt's bravado in the ball turret. I could tell by the transported look on the faces in the room that they were elsewhere. I looked over at my father and found his familiar face loaded with unspoken emotion: jaws clenching and unclenching, forehead scrunched, and brows knit. He had liked Ritt. "How could you not?" he had once told me. Ritt had been one of the friendliest people Dad had ever known—a true Canadian full of fairness and lightheartedness. Soon enough though, Jug broke the silence with the story of how Ritt bailed out on that practice mission and ended up in Mexico. Now tears were really flowing from just about everyone, but those tears were awash in laughter. As men, they had resorted to survival mode.

With the light outside dimming to dusk, the party wound down until only Dad and I remained to help Wes and Julie tidy up. As if choreographed, we moved smoothly between rooms, dodging each other as we carried dirty dishes to the kitchen for washing, lining up the drinkware at the pass-through.

In the living room, I helped Wes push the coffee table back into place, noting how all four legs slid easily into well-worn divots in the wall-to-wall. Looking up, I was drawn to a painting hanging over the sofa—one that Wes had done of a Western canyon. It reminded me of a story Dad told me about his time in Albuquerque studying advanced bombardier tactics. How, at the end of one air-combat training mission, the pilot of the bomber they were flying made a detour before heading back to base and took the plane straight through the Grand Canyon while the Colorado River flowed below them. He recalled how all the trainees whooped and hollered with the thrill of the deed, a pure release of boyish exuberance. Of course, such a thing was against regulations. Dad loved to replay that scene.

For the longest time, these were the stories he was comfortable sharing. These and other accounts of the rigorous training he had gone through, equal in time to his actual air combat time, were the ones he could touch without flinching. It was a surprise when, unbidden, he began to speak to me of the fears he felt, the blood he helped staunch, and the onboard deaths he witnessed. His words are woven throughout this book.

The Powells's home was neat and tidy again. It was apparent that the men had enjoyed another successful crew reunion and, for me, it had been one for the books. Dad had been arranging these for a long time now, but this reunion had been my first. I remember being honored that my father had asked me, rather than one of my brothers, if I was interested in attending, and I jumped at the chance to see him from this perspective.

After this reunion, I was made an honorary member of the crew, invited and included in the email chain for subsequent gatherings. It wasn't long before I began to notice, with great sadness, attendance growing lighter due to declining health, or final missions, so to speak. When Dad grew too ill to attend 304th Bomb Group reunions, I went in his stead. The tales told at these diminishing gatherings could have come straight out of that West Texas living room. The sentiments too.

Like Dad and the men of the crew he flew with, these men believed they'd done the job they were trained to do, just like any other job. They did not perceive themselves having done any more than that. Dad felt it was an honor to have to swear an oath to protect the Norden with his life. My respect knew no bounds for all of them. They had lived and sacrificed as my father had done, as all the men-who-once-were-boys had trained and joined the air war against an unfathomable tyranny.

Air worthy B-24s were flown in for these events, and I climbed all over the bomber, imagining myself in my father's heavy leather flight boots—inching my way over a ten-inch-wide beam at twenty-four thousand feet and kicking out an armed bomb that had hung up in the rack, fingers frozen, and sucking wind from an oxygen tank about to run out of air. Dad's story became all too real after we had taxied down the runway and lifted off into the wild blue. The air was crisp-growing-to-cold and the din from the engines deafening. My imagination multiplied as we gained elevation until we reached "mission altitude." This had been Dad's element, his perspective, for two years.

By the time of his retirement from the Air Force in 1972, Dad had amassed more medals and ribbons to attach to that jacket. It wasn't until his funeral that I learned the entirety of what my father had earned: The Distinguished Flying Cross, Defense Meritorious Service Medal, Meritorious Service Medal, The Air Medal with seven oak leaf clusters, Joint Services Commendation Medal, Air Force Commendation Medal with one oak leaf cluster, Army Good Conduct Medal (1942), American Campaign Medal, European-African-Middle East Campaign Medal with seven battle stars, World War II Victory Medal, National Defense Medal, Armed Forces Expeditionary Medal. Medal for Humane Action, Armed Forces Reserve Medal, Presidential Unit Citation (1944), Air Force Outstanding Unit Award, and the Fifteenth Air Force's Certification of Valor in recognition of courageous service in Aerial Combat. Dad was one of those men who served in WWII who didn't decorate their uniforms with the entirety of what they'd earned, partly out of humility and partly out of a sense of something greater: knowing the costs involved with having earned those medals.

War changes everyone, and my father was no exception. Like all the men who trained and fought and made it home to resume their lives, he integrated who he had been before with who he had become and then continued on from there. He wasn't perfect, but man, did he have integrity.

Watching them interact, it occurred to me that the men of this crew had come together as boys for a cause, disbanded, and sought their own paths when that cause was remedied. Then they came together again later, where they honored one another, their effort, and their friendship with ties that ever bound them. They were unique, this crew. They were part of a cohort forty thousand strong. What they accomplished was unique and remains so, yet they saw themselves as nothing and no one special. To me, they exemplify honor and integrity and all that is good about standing *up* for what is right and standing *for* something greater than oneself.

This pivotal moment in my father's story became a mission of my own. And now, that mission has ended. It has owned me for so long, it is time to lay it down, to let someone else pick it up and discover something similar to what I found in the making of it: There are ideals worth striving for; we need only do the reaching.

Bill's skill at placekicking got him noticed.

The B-24, aka "Liberator"

Cadet flight school

Letters home began in earnest during basic training.

Standard work attire for the B-24
bombardier, minus the Norden

The device that
helped the
Allies win the
air war. This
particular one
is missing the
stabilizer.

The bombardier-navigator "office" below the nose gunner

Meet Bill's original crew. Back row, left to right: Charles "Murph" Oltarzewski, George Harvey, Bob Belding, Mike Stohlman, Loren Rittenhouse, and Bill Hill. Front row, left to right: Bill Gemmill, Wesley Powell, Jug Kell, and Joe Parkin.

Bill flew
35 missions
with the
distinguished
Vulgar
Vultures.

Bill kept a
meticulous
account of
his activity
while in
Italy ...

	TARGET	DATE	TIME	RATING	TO PLANE	AIRCRAFT
1.	BUCHAREST, RUM.	26-AUG-44	7:10		12	(2) ME 109 (2) FW-190
2.	DIOSZEG, ITALY	28-AUG-44	6:25		0	(3) FW-190
3.	BUDAPEST, HUNG.	1-SEPT-44	7:30		11	(1) ME-109
4.	NIS, JUGO.	2-SEPT-44	9:20		6	0
5.	CASARSA, ITALY	4-SEPT-44	5:00		0	0
6.	SZCNOK, HUNG.	5-SEPT-44	5:55		3	(20) FW-190
7.	BELGRADE, JUGO.	8-SEPT-44	5:10			(10) ME-109
8.	STYER, AUSTRIA	10-SEPT-44			50+	(5) ME-109
9.	MUNICH, GER.	4-OCT-44	6:25		0	0
10.	LATISANA, ITALY	13-OCT-44	5:55		0	0
11.	TRIESTE, ITALY	11-OCT-44	5:10		0	0
12.	BOLOGNA, ITALY	12-OCT-44	5:55		15	(604) ME-109 FW-190
13.	BLECHHAMMER, GER.	13-OCT-44	7:55		3	0
14.	INNSBRUCK, AUST.	20-OCT-44	7:00		0	0
15.	SZOMBATHELY, HUN.	21-OCT-44	6:15		12	(10) { FW-109 FW-190
16.	LINZ, AUSTRIA	7-NOV-44	7:25		10	(10) { ME-109 FW-190
17.	VIENNA, AUSTRIA	5-NOV-44	6:25		12	(20) { ME-109 FW-190
18.	VIENNA, AUSTRIA	6-NOV-44	6:40		0	0
19.	BRNICA, JUGO.	7-NOV-44	6:10		4	(4) FW-190
20.	LINZ, AUSTRIA	11-NOV-44	6:35		0	0
21.	VICENZA, ITALY	13-NOV-44			7	0
22.	VIENNA, AUSTRIA	17-NOV-44	6:40		0	(11) ME-109
23.	ILIN, CZECHO.	20-NOV-44	7:00		55	GERMAN B-25 (14) ME-210
24.	MUNICH, GERMANY	22-NOV-44	6:20		6	JET ME-109
25.	LINZ, AUSTRIA	15-DEC-44	7:45		6	ME-109
26.	ODERTAL, GERM.	17-DEC-44	7:55		0	10 JU-52
27.	WELS, AUSTRIA	25-DEC-44	7:10		0	0
28.	GRAZ, AUSTRIA	27-DEC-44	6:25		8	30-40 ME FW-109
29.	VERONA, ITALY	4-JAN-45	6:15		8	(6) FW-190
30.	VIENNA, AUSTRIA	15-JAN-45	7:40		20	

MISSION NUMBER	TO: CITY COUNTRY TARGET	DATE DAY-MO-YR.	HOURS FLYING TIME	FLAK RATING	DAMAGE TO PLANE	ENEMY AIRCRAFT
■ 31.	MOOSBIERBAUM, AUST. ⊠ OIL REFINERY	31-JAN-45	7:45	🌀🌀	0	0
✳ 32.	MOOSBIERBAUM, AUST. OIL REFINERY	7-FEB-45	7:25	🌀🌀🌀🌀	25	2↓ GERMAN B-24 (10) ME-109
✳ 33.	KORNEUBURG, AUST. MILITARY STORAGE ⊠	15-FEB-45	7:00	🌀🌀🌀	10	2↓ (6) ME-109
34.	POLA, ITALY HARBOR SHIPPING	19-FEB-45	5:00	🌀🌀🌀	8	0
✳ 35.	TRIESTE, ITALY	20-FEB-45	6:10	🌀🌀	2	0

✳ = DOUBLE SORTY

56 SORTIES

STARTED FLYING AS LEAD BOMBARDIER ON 8TH MISSION.

⊠ = GROUP LEAD

■ = RADAR (MICKEY) MISSION

🌀 = LITTLE OR NO FLAK

🌀+ = FLAK, BUT INACCURATE

🌀🌀 = INTENSE AND ACCURATE

🌀🌀+ = HEAVY VERY INTENSE AND ACCURATE

✳ MISSION #26 - GROUP AHEAD AND BEHIND HIT VERY BADLY — ONE LOST 11 B-24

✳ MISSION #27 ONLY 4 B-24s GOT TO TARGET AREA DUE TO WEATHER OVER ITALY —— THE 4 OF US SHOT DOWN ALL 11 JU-525. (TRI-MTR TRANSPORTS)

... and created a helpful key for deciphering his log.

A NOTE FROM
THE AUTHOR

DAD WAS A MILITARY MAN, very well-suited to the regimentation and discipline of a life in service to his country. He took orders well, and as he climbed up the ranks during his long career, he gave orders in consideration of the men who served under him. He was a devoted senior officer, even taking shifts for his junior officers at Christmas so that they could be home with their young children as they delighted in the magic of the season. He figured his three children were old enough to understand, and we did.

When I first had the notion to write this book, my father was alive and quite willing to tell me his stories of serving in WWII. As we worked on the chapters together, me fleshing out the stories and Dad editing them, the book took on a military tone. These were, after all, his first military experiences, told from his perspective. It made sense that initially the writing was skewed to a certain flavor of book. Then, my father passed away … into the wild blue yonder, so to speak.

Dad's death rocked me, and I put the book away. While it was composting in the third drawer from the bottom of my desk, it morphed. Perhaps it was the long pause between when I shelved the pages and when I resurrected them that gave the book the space to change and grow. Perhaps, that space allowed me the freedom to take all twenty-three chapters we had written together and present them from my perspective because I began to see the book as a coming-of-age story. One in which my father was the lead character, representing all the other young men who served as bombardiers in "The Good War." He, and they, came of age through their military experience with the air war as the backdrop.

Although Dad shared with me about his loves and near-misses in romance during his years training and fighting, I had scant information to work with and chose to leave out most of those stories. Believe me when I tell you, throughout my life, women of every age loved my father. Even my girlfriends swooned when he'd drop me off at school, vying for a position to be noticed. Who cared if he was, well, old enough to be their father! He was a "ladies' man" in the best sense of the word: considerate, gallant, and respectful; a musician and gorgeous on a dance floor. No wonder my mother, and the world, fell in love with him.

Since I was born years after the war's end, I had to imagine the conversations and dialogue that appear in *Blue Yonder*. I also researched the weather and locations to represent days and times to the best of my ability. Most of the names herein were once real people, long gone. With my father on his next adventure, I couldn't ask him for other names that might be important to him. Those, I had to make up.

It was never my intention to put words into my father's mouth, but I have a sense that he struggled the rest of his life to hold in the experiences that were too hard for him to talk about. The effort took its toll on his psyche (although he did his darndest to hide it behind the laughter and goofy antics), but there were times in his later years when he opened up to me, acknowledging how hard it was for him to reconcile what he had done to end the war with the devastation those actions had caused on the ground so far below him. He concluded these conversations by conceding this was the cost of war. And, indeed, it was. There is always a price to pay, and Dad came to understand that well. His story serves as a reminder that coming of age is never easy—whether in actuality or in perception, there are always perils to navigate. When we find a way through, we have the chance to thrive and soar. My father did—and he did it well.

ACKNOWLEDGMENTS

IN THE BEGINNING, *Blue Yonder* wanted to be many things at once: a memoir, a novel, a biography. It took time to listen to the book and for the theme to reveal itself. It also took a bevy of marvelous people to see it through. Never was there a book, especially one's first, where it didn't take a village. In the case of *Blue Yonder*, it took a town and more than one crew: my father's and mine.

From concept to completion, my gratitude goes out to my son, Jon Behler. His faith in me never wavered and neither did his encouragement. Jon was tight with his grandfather; they shared a love of everything airborne. My father, too, believed in me enough to help shape most of the stories before his death, and after, he remained with me every step of the way. Those members of his crew who were still with us as I began writing corroborated Dad's tales. For each of them, and especially my father, I am eternally grateful.

The making of this book had the privilege of encouragement from many early mentors, like Tom Peek, Lee Gutkind, and fellow Air Force brat Phillip Bellury, whose guidance was invaluable and whose friendship is enduring.

For her brilliant assistance in making sense of the mountains of material I'd collected, many, many thanks to Diane Tate. Not only did she organize the papers and letters and my father's scrapbook, she encouraged me to keep going; the stories had intrigued her too.

Early readers like Bing and Teri Lee, Dianne Bernez, and Donna Freidberg provided valuable feedback from a "never-been-exposed-to-the-military" perspective. The last time the book morphed was when, after reading their comments, I realized the story was more coming of age than the art of war.

When I felt like tossing in the towel, I had the great good fortune of having my own squad of cheerleaders: Diane Tate, Randy Hardy, Dianne Bernez, Jill Indyck, Phillip Bellury, Patric Owen, Jean Yanni, Marcia Rose, Tracy Tutag, and my mother, Jean Matus, the Grandma Moses of children's books. As my granddaughters became old enough to understand that their grandmother was writing a book, Rose and Daphne Behler became the strongest cheerleaders of them all. Their mother, my daughter-in-law, Nicole Gragnano Behler, who has a gift for such things, jumped in to help me with many of the myriad details of book marketing, and I couldn't have been happier or more appreciative.

When it came to providing material without which I wouldn't have had much to go on after my father's death, his widow, Carole Gemmill, came to assist by producing the scrapbook my grandmother Frances had kept during Dad's training and while he was overseas. It proved to be a veritable treasure trove.

To my brothers and fellow crew members, thank you for confirming and clarifying family history or sharing yet another one of Dad's tales, even though they did not make it to the final edit.

Blue Yonder took shape under the expert hands of my editor, Donna Mazzitelli. She pushed a bit, just hard enough, when she knew an edit would make the book a better read, and I'm grateful for her tenacity. It is a better read because of Donna, and for that, I'll be forever grateful.

And then, there is Paula Friedland. What can I say about the best coach on the planet? Not enough. Not only did she walk this entire journey with me, she helped me unpeel all the layers under which the stories were buried. She shone a light on the path I was following, making it easier for me to see the way and encouraging me to take one step at a time. Thank you seems too small a thing for the likes of her.

MEET THE AUTHOR

SUSAN L. GEMMILL is a deep-think-ing rebel (born breech in the Year of the Tiger!) and a lover of all things that grow, including people, most especially her son and grandchildren. She currently lives in Colorado with her sixth betta fish named Voldemort.

Having declared she would be a novelist at the age of nine, Susan lived a full and well-traveled life of adven-ture, and misadventure, as the only girl-child in an Air Force family. After nearly five years abroad, she landed back in the city of her birth, Washington, DC, for high school, where she took on the mantle of advertising editor for her high school's yearbook.

Whether it was rifling through her mother's scarf drawer for that perfect accessory—the one she needed, along with her chunky pencil, to add a bon vivant flair to her third-grade class photo—or blazing a trail writing at the US Attorney's Office, where she began the first para-legal program for the Justice Department, Susan saw herself as a writer.

Life led her onward, away from her role in government and back to the path that brought her closer to her youthful declaration. She wrote and researched several coffee table books for The Storyline Group, including the history of such gripping industries as surface preparation, water infrastructure, and an esteemed private school for boys, while at the same time profiling the most interesting of people for magazines, until Susan at long last segued into novel writing. *Blue Yonder* is her first book. Her next one is being outlined at this very moment.

ABOUT THE PRESS

MERRY DISSONANCE PRESS is a hybrid indie publisher/book producer of works of transformation, inspiration, exploration, and illumination. MDP takes a holistic approach to bringing books into the world that make a little noise and create dissonance within the whole in order that ALL can be resolved to produce beautiful harmonies.

Merry Dissonance Press works with its authors every step of the way to craft the finest books and help promote them. Dedicated to publishing award-winning books, we strive to support talented writers and assist them to discover, claim, and refine their own distinct voice. Merry Dissonance Press is the place where collaboration and facilitation of our shared human experiences join together to make a difference in our world.

For more information, visit https://merrydissonancepress.com/.

INVITE SUSAN
TO YOUR BOOK CLUB!

∞

As a special gift to readers of *Blue Yonder*,
Susan would love to visit your book club,
either via video conferencing or in person.

Please contact Susan directly to schedule
her appearance at your next book club meeting.
susan@susangemmill.com

∞

CPSIA information can be obtained
at www.ICGtesting.com
Printed in the USA
BVHW072233041021
618025BV00001B/8